Ego Analysis
IN THE HELPING
PROFESSIONS

Ego Analysis IN THE HELPING PROFESSIONS

---

by Frances Upham

Family Service Association of America

NEW YORK

International Standard Book Number: 0–87304–105–4
Library of Congress Catalog Card Number: 73–78897

Printed in the United States of America

Designed by Herbert Johnson

C 574

To my students from whom I have learned so much

Contents

Ego Analysis
IN THE HELPING PROFESSIONS

Introduction

This text systematically relates ego theory to the use of that theory in the helping process. It distinguishes life motivations from motivations for resistance to taking and to using help. It explores the functions of the ego that provide matching diagnostic and treatment categories for assessing and for increasing ego capacities.

THIS book is written in the belief that the helping professions can advantageously share their understanding about ways of giving help to troubled people because much of what one group has found of value can be used by practitioners in allied groups. Casework practitioners have developed a model of the casework process, and it is used as a beginning point for discussion of method. The social work profession has identified the components of professional practice as including purpose, values, and method. We draw upon this distillation of experience to indicate some of the ways in which purpose and values should become integrated into a method of helping. The values proposed are those that the social work profession has tested over the years. We believe, however, that all the helping professions implicitly use many, or most, of these same values and can benefit from having them made explicit. The illustrative case material used in the book, although drawn, for the most part, from professional social work journals and from the author's experience as a caseworker, should strike a familiar note with practitioners from allied groups. In this book, the term *prac-*

titioner is used generically to indicate the person giving help in any of the helping professions: doctors, nurses, psychologists, social workers, and vocational, rehabilitation, and marriage counselors. Similarly, the term *client* refers to the person receiving help and includes a broad range of designations including patient and consumer. It is hoped that the sharing of ideas about a method of helping can promote rapprochement between practitioners who work together to achieve similar goals in helping.

The method of ego analysis here described assumes that the functions of the ego and the patterning of each function provide the practitioner with a systematic approach to analyzing the client's capacities and limitations in capacity. This method offers a model of health and turns the attention of the practitioner to possibilities for providing the client with opportunities for new learning or relearning. Assessment based on analysis of ego functioning furnishes logical connections between diagnosis and treatment because the diagnostic categories clearly indicate related treatment measures. This book offers a practical approach, based on ego theory, to assessing and dealing with resistance and proposes matching diagnostic and treatment categories. The method of ego analysis identifies systematic linkages between behavioral and practice theory.

The author's experience as practitioner, as casework supervisor, as a teacher of human behavior in the social environment, of casework, and of field work practice has provided convincing evidence of the gap between knowledge about personality theory and its use in the helping professions. The links between an understanding of human behavior and the utilization of that understanding remain relatively weak except in some areas of clinical diagnoses. For this reason, integration between behavioral and practice theories remains problematical. This book attempts to identify significant and relevant aspects of ego psychology and to relate them in a consistent frame of reference to the helping process. It develops systematic linkages between ego psychology and helping, on the assumption that only when the helping process is based on theories about personality and society and when the connections between helping and these theories are made clear do we have a helping method. Ego psychology accounts for stability of the personality, for change over time in the personality, and for individual differences and thus provides systematic linkages between that theory and helping. We show how these links assist in analyzing where change is needed, what changes are needed, and how to effect change—both in the client's functioning and in his social situation.

One reason that the practice supervisor, the field work instructor, and the practitioner find their tasks difficult is that there is a lack of clear formulations for identifying aspects of theory that will illuminate practice problems. How to understand and how to do need to be more clearly integrated. This book attempts to relate ego psychology more clearly to its application in the helping method and to do so in ways that facilitate the assessing of social functioning. At present, we lack a frame of reference for analyzing aspects of capacity; notions about behavior tend to be global, especially in reference to healthy functioning. In the terms of ego psychology, social functioning is ego functioning in the social environment and the carrying of social roles in relation to the social situation. Because the practitioner aims to improve ego functioning in relation to the given situation, it becomes imperative to analyze capacity and limitations in capacity, so as to select treatment measures to improve capacity, and to analyze the situation in ways that indicate how treatment can be made less limiting and more supporting.

This text offers a systematic approach to analyzing ego functioning and using that analysis in related treatment measures. The proposed groupings of ego functions in themselves contain implications for treatment. The groupings of ego functions grow out of analysis of the content of casework literature, where these categories appear implicit in the way the practitioner understands and deals with behavior. When implicit formulations become explicit, the practitioner can use them consciously and more purposefully. In addition, an understanding of appropriate active and passive patterning in each ego function offers still more refined bases for analysis of capacity. The patterning of functions of the ego furnishes related diagnostic and treatment categories; the practitioner's assessment can be more logically and selectively tied to appropriate helping measures to lessen limitations and to improve capacity. An assessment of the client's socially learned patterns helps the practitioner to individualize the client more clearly and leads to the possibility of diagnostic evaluations that particularize the client, thus avoiding the present tendency toward diagnoses that overgeneralize.

At present, some theoretical formulations see assessment of capacity and of motivation as two separate components of diagnosis. Clarity about functions of the ego designates the management of needs and feelings as one of the functions of the ego, suggests ways of strengthening the ego and social motivational forces in the personality, and points up the fact that the practitioner helps the client to select more suitable and more rewarding aims and objects. Thus the practitioner is enabled to help the client to direct and channel his energies toward more appropriate and satisfying goals. Motivations in the life situation can be distinguished from motivations toward taking and using help and the antithesis of such motivation—resistance to help.

Resistance is client behavior motivated by discomfort aroused by lack of congruence between the expectations of the practitioner and those of the client regarding help and their reciprocal roles. It consists, in the frame of reference proposed here, of two types: resistance to taking help or assuming the client role and resistance to using help or carrying the client role. An assessment of this resistance and of the motivations causing it makes possible an analysis of where the client is in relation to taking help and therefore furnishes a way of operationalizing the principle of beginning where the client is. Similarly, an assessment of the motivations causing resistance to using help operationalizes the principle of moving at the client's pace.

Finally, the helping method based on analysis of ego functioning emphasizes capacity and does so in a model of health. It furnishes a systematic approach to improving healthful coping patterns and a way of talking with the client about ways for changing these patterns. Practitioner and client can examine the patterning to see whether it serves an adaptive purpose that enables the client to deal with his problem(s). Their goal can be the development by the client of more effective and satisfying patterns. This approach partializes the client's tasks and differentiates between immediate and long-term goals. This method has particular applicability to clients whose pathology has resulted in damage to the ego. In these cases, the practitioner can use this approach to identify the remaining healthy aspects of the ego that may be supported. With all clients, the practitioner considers the goal of situational changes that enable, enhance, and support improved client functioning.

Although this book does not employ any of the newer psychologies as a basis for method, it does offer a new approach to a widely accepted theory of behavior and the use of that theory by the helping professions. Assuming that the reader is familiar with ego psychology, it focuses on providing rationales from ego theory to enable the practitioner to use the helping process to illuminate practice and to organize it more clearly. Rationales for analyzing ego functioning and for relating that analysis to treatment measures offer new and more explicit connections between assessment and treatment. The new concept of motivation as an aspect of ego functioning emphasizes ways in which the practitioner can help the client to channel energy into more effective coping. Analysis of motivations for resistance lead directly to measures to forestall or lessen this troublesome problem. Finally, because the new consideration of client capacities focuses the practitioner's and the client's attention on healthful coping patterns, it should strengthen hope in both client and practitioner.

The tables in the Appendix outline the related categories for assessing and for forestalling or handling resistance and the related categories for assessing capacity and limitations in capacity and treatment measures to lessen limitations and to increase capacity.

ONE

The Helping Process

The helping process is a process of change. The components of the process are: purpose, study, diagnosis, treatment, and formation and use of a helping relationship, with its values and principles. This chapter reviews these components as a basis for demonstrating the way in which the method of ego analysis develops them.

IN discussing the nature of helping, the distinction will be made between the helping process and the helping method, using the casework model. In this model, the casework process can be distinguished from other processes by its purpose, the component processes of study, diagnosis, treatment, relationship formation and use, and the values and principles that indicate the directions and goals of the process. The view is maintained, however, that the term *helping method* can be used appropriately only when an internal logic and rationale have been instilled into the process by utilizing theory to provide a systematic way of carrying out the study and the diagnostic, treatment, and relationship processes. In this framework, techniques are an outgrowth of method and of the theory base that they help to operationalize. The helping method also requires a defined and planned use of purpose in order for each step in the method to contribute to orderly change toward both proximate and ultimate goal or goals. In addition, the giving of help is guided by values, expressed in relation to principles or other guides to action, so that the use of method is consonant with professional values.

COMPONENTS OF THE HELPING PROCESS

Webster defines process as "a natural phenomenon marked by gradual changes that lead toward a particular result."[1] Helping is a special example of the process of social and personal change. The helping professions specify the locus of change as the person or group with a problem relative to the social situation; they thus distinguish helping from other change processes. The casework model also indicates that improvement in the social functioning of the individual or group of individuals is the purpose toward which change is directed. The orderly series of events in the process can be categorized and conceptualized as development and use of the professional relationship, study, diagnosis (assessment), and treatment (planning and effecting of change). The practitioner uses values and principles to guide the helping process. All the events in the helping process can be subsumed under these integral components of the process.

The development and use of the professional relationship is the process of developing an emotionally based tie with the client through the meaningful exchange of feelings. The practitioner encourages the client to express feelings about taking and using help. He responsively and feelingly expresses empathy and acceptance that enable the client to feel understood and undefensive about his problem-situation. The professional relationship serves to bridge the emotional and social distance between client and practitioner so as to make it possible for the client to take and to use help. Since the professional relationship has been considered so essential a part of helping, it will be dealt with in the later discussion of the method of ego analysis.

In effect, the planning and carrying through of change depends upon having adequate information about what is to be changed or not (social study), upon evaluative judgments as to changes needed and possible (diagnosis or assessment), upon decisions about how to effect changes, and upon activities designed to bring about these changes (planning and carrying through of treatment). Each aspect of the helping process as well as the interrelationships between them can be described with reasonable clarity. Study, diagnosis, and treatment form interdependent parts of an integral whole. Study is basic to diagnosis, which, in its turn, guides treatment. The results of treatment change assessment and indicate the need for further study or for changes in treatment measures, and so on throughout the giving of service. The pattern of these relationships is thus a circular one. Furthermore, study, diagnosis, and treatment processes seldom occur in isolation, although in a given interview one or another may dominate. The practitioner must listen, understand, and attempt to deal with what the client is currently communicating.

Purpose of the Helping Process

Helping has as its purpose improvement of the social functioning of individuals or groups particularly in relation to problems that bring them to the practitioner's attention or for which they are asking help. The person in a situation and the problem clearly have a close relationship. Because the person needs help, the relationship is one of insufficiency in problem-solving. It is generally assumed that all behavior and all social functioning is purposive. Every day and everywhere, individuals solve a multitude of daily problems in living. Behavior is a way of solving problems, and social functioning has as its purpose the handling and working out of problems relating to one's social situation. The aim of helping is the attempt to change the relationship of the person to his problem from one of insufficiency to one of more sufficiency or adequacy. Helping tries to effect those changes that alter the balance of forces by enabling and empowering the client to cope better, to manage life's stresses more successfully, and to achieve, if possible, greater satisfaction with less pain. To achieve this result, theories which explain adequacy in social functioning are required as well as theories about the nature of the social situation which affects social functioning. Such constructs must explain in ways which indicate how proposed changes for the better may be achieved.

Social Study Process

The social study consists of relevant information about the client, about the given social situation, and about the problems which the client has been unable to solve and which bring him to the agency. The social study individualizes the client and informs the practitioner of key aspects of his identity. Social study secures and orders objective facts, not subjective inferences, presumptions, or judgment of the practitioner. The client is the primary informational source about himself, and, in fact, the study includes his views, ideas, feelings, memories, and reports which may be lacking in objective reality. These items, however, possess subjective reality—that is, the client's psychological reality—and so constitute essential data for the study. The study should not only include information about such environmental and external conditions as income, debts, rent, work, housing, schooling, and the family, but also information which deals with the person's unique feelings and perceptions which explain how things seem to him. These facts may be referred to as outer facts and inner facts; both kinds must be adequate to support diagnostic thinking. They furnish the evidence from which valid diagnostic conclusions or assumptions may be drawn. The degree of specificity and the extent and nature of information sought depend upon what the practitioner deems relevant and essential for the evaluative judgments that he must make. These judgments are influenced by the nature of the problems selected for work and the nature of help requested.

During the entire helping process, the practitioner continues to gather and integrate information, as each new contact reveals new facets. Change in the problem focus also necessitates additional study facts relating to the new tasks at hand. Characteristically, each succeeding problem tends to become more internal in nature as the client becomes more able to tolerate anxiety about his own functioning and the changes toward which he needs to work. Therefore, the study facts deal increasingly with needs, feelings, and patterns of functioning. Whatever the problem, the study process should not deal in generalities but should work toward obtaining concrete information. The practitioner always distinguishes information that can be furnished only by authoritative sources, such as schools, medical institutions, courts, and agencies, from that which the client is able to give. No problem relating to such areas as school, legal issues, health, or certain social conditions can be understood without authoritative data. Obtaining appropriate information from these sources usually requires consent of the client. Collaterals, which include relatives and friends, may, if the client is willing, provide additional insights. The study process is a shared one. The client should always understand why the information is needed. He must see the study process as an opportunity to tell his story, to present the pertinent facts so that he can examine them, and to gather together in some comprehensive way the information basic to problem-solving. Usually, social study entails helping the client to identify relevant information that he may have overlooked or failed to consider. The study process becomes effective only when the practitioner has a theory as a basis for the study as well as values to guide the study.

Diagnostic Process

The process of diagnosis identifies the problem or problems to be solved and clarifies what needs to be changed in the client and the situation in order to improve problem-solving capacity. This process includes diagnostic thinking and the more formal type of psychosocial and clinical diagnosis. The practitioner engages in diagnostic thinking throughout the interview; he does not wait until he is alone in his office to think about what has been going on in the interaction between himself and the client. He observes and listens to the client as he notes the client's responses to his communication. He not only remembers the information that he is receiving, but his grasp of theory enables him to put it into a meaningful frame of reference, to sort it out perceptually, and to relate it to those aspects of the client's functioning or situation that it illuminates. Since the practitioner attempts, always, to correct his own perceptual distortions, he may test the accuracy of his understanding by such feedback mechanisms as techniques of resonating or questions concerning the client's intentions, or he may respond to perceived content and note whether the client's response indicates that the practitioner has perceived correctly. This aspect of the diagnostic process is part of the total helping process. It takes place in the interview wherever conducted. It is a process in which the practitioner shares to some extent with the client the perceived meaning of the client's story. On the other hand, the practitioner may ask what the client thinks is the meaning of what he is saying. Such meanings include relationships and connections that relate the study facts in some kind of Gestalt. Not all aspects of the diagnostic process are shared because the practitioner uses his expertise to understand with greater depth, breadth, and clarity than he expects of the client. The practitioner usually asks for the client's reactions to his own diagnostic inferences.

Part of the practitioner's diagnostic thinking that goes on during the entire interview and afterward is the practitioner's thoughtful review of the course of events. In the early stages, such thinking takes the form of diagnostic inferences and assumptions that the practitioner tests out in succeeding contacts with the client. The practitioner frequently records these inferences successively as impressions at the end of a given interview. The meanings that the practitioner assigns to the study facts are meanings indicative of the need for and the possibilities of change that can serve as a guide to help the client see what he must do to bring about change and the help that he needs for this accomplishment. One of the difficulties in making such clear judgments lies in the difference between the practitioner's and the client's cognitive and perceptual frames of reference. The client uses words that either clearly convey his meaning or fail to do so, because the connotation that he gives to a word arises from his individual experience. Some disadvantaged clients may lack verbal ability; other clients have distorted perceptions of their situations. For these reasons, planned visits that give the practitioner a chance to see the client in action in his family or in other circumstances are usually essential for an adequate social study. Feelings—especially anxiety—and needs, both conscious and unconscious, as well as all of the past affect perception. The practitioner, therefore, has the dual job of understanding as correctly as possible the client's meanings and of placing them in a more objective, orderly, and theoretical framework of meaning.

Diagnostic assessment consists of two steps: diagnostic thinking and the more formal relating what has been learned in some systematic way. When, for example, the client says that he wants to fix up his marriage but acts in ways that indicate his desires only to have the practitioner protect him, relieve him of responsibility, and meet his needs, the practitioner, using diagnostic thinking, understands that he is hearing the client's conscious and unconscious expectations of help. This beginning understanding usually precedes the step of putting together a number of study facts to make a diagnostic assessment. The practitioner usually records the more formal psychosocial diagnosis that includes an evaluation of the client's capacity and limitations in capacity and of the ways in which the situation is limiting or supporting in relation to the problem. The formal psychosocial diagnosis also includes the practitioner's judgment about changes that are needed and possible in order to utilize strengths and to lessen limitations.

Only the use of theory will provide a method of diagnosis and provide a systematic way of arriving at an understanding of the client in relation to his situation. Theory provides an organized framework for logical thinking and, thus, a method of developing diagnostic assessments or judgments. Because the diagnostic process is a shared one, the client must understand what needs to be changed in the way that he is functioning or in his situation in order to work toward the changes. The level of his understanding depends upon capacity as does, to some extent, the degree to which he can accept the kinds of changes needed. When the client's pathology indicates it, the practitioner supplements the psychosocial diagnosis with a clinical diagnosis. The clinical diagnosis proves particularly useful when it identifies the nature and extent of the regressive process and the resulting damage to the various functions of the ego.

Social Treatment Process

Social treatment tends to mobilize and to strengthen the client's capacity to handle his problems by working to lessen limitations in capacity and increase strengths as well as to lessen limiting environmental factors and increase environmental support. Treatment measures characteristically aim at relieving pressures, providing new opportunities and new sources of strength and support. Because the problem belongs to the client and can never belong to the practitioner, the practitioner strives to have the client focus on what is getting in the way of his coping abilities, on resources that he can utilize, and on the beginning steps he can take to improve problem-solving. Continuously in the interview, the practitioner lends his own ego strengths to the client, helping him to think, to understand, to feel, and to do. The literature terms this support the professional use of self. The practitioner helps to keep the client related to his social situation and to develop with family members and other persons more reciprocal relationships and more useful ways for problem-solving. The treatment process is an enabling one, with the exception of the fact that when the client is immobilized or incapable, the practitioner may have to act for him to a varying extent. The practitioner carries on the treatment continuously in the interview as he helps the client to deal with material that the client brings out, including his feelings, and as he helps to move the client forward in problem-solving. He also assists the client in planning next steps and, when appropriate, in deciding on any long-range plan on which he can work with support.

In any plan for dealing with aspects of the problem, it should be made clear what the client and others can do and what help will be needed from the practitioner. At first, the practitioner may take more responsibility while the client takes only a minimal share. In time, the client should be able to manage with a lessening amount of help. The treatment process always includes both immediate goals that can be achieved quickly and with a reasonable chance of success and more long-range goals that represent the client's hopes of achievement in relation to the problem. The practitioner and client together decide on these objectives and revise them continually in the light of the client's progress or lack of it, of his changing motivation or situation. Since treatment aims to strengthen the progressive process within the person both directly and indirectly through situational changes and to lessen the regressive process, the treatment process is considered a form of intervention. Intervention constitutes the use of the treatment process to affect other processes, to strengthen progressive growth processes within the person, to lessen regressive or pathological processes, and to affect for the better the social interaction processes between the individual and his social situation. Only the addition of theories of personality and of society, however, produces a treatment method and techniques that provide a rationale for change and for ways of bringing about change that, together with values, indicate the goals of change.

The Core Values

Social work values define the kind of changes toward which the helping process is directed. Muriel W. Pumphrey points out that social workers in performing their special tasks express a "hope that some specific changes can come about in society as a result of their effort" and that this hope for change implies desired goals. She continues, "Values are what an individual or group would like to see happen; what their conception of an ideal world may be; what they would preserve and the changes they would make if given the power to do so."[2] No consensus yet exists about the core values of the helping professions—those values indicating the directions of change and the goals of change in the helping process. However, three core values can be proposed: the value of the worth and dignity of the human being, the value of social relationships, and the value of equal access to social provisions and opportunities, with the value of social relationships and social relatedness taking precedence over the other two that, in a sense, derive from it. These professional values help to define the helping process, because practice values must agree with those of the helping professions.

In the past, giving first place to valuing the worth and dignity of the individual posed problems in situations in which this value appeared in opposition to the common good or to the good of other individuals. The area of practitioner competence and interest lies in the interrelatedness of man with his environment; in reality, the practitioner never deals with the individual in isolation from his social relationships and his situational nexus. Throughout all of the professional literature appears the almost universally implied goal of strengthening the relatedness of the individual to his society. In mental hospitals, prisons, medical hospitals, and in work with families and children, the helping process attempts to knit severed ties between the individual and his community or his primary group. Furthermore, because the purpose of the helping process is the improvement of social functioning, it appears that the prime value of the helping professions should accord with this purpose. Generally accepted basic assumptions hold that personal health, well-being, self-realization, and self-direction cannot be achieved except in the context of social relationships. Professional consensus exists regarding the assumption that social health and well-being require social concern and provisions that foster constructive relationships between society and the individuals of which it is composed. Social good and individual good come together in the value of social relationships, of mutuality, and shared responsibility. The well-being of the individual and of the society cannot be separated. Change goals, therefore, should keep the interrelatedness of the individual and his social setting in the forefront. Mary E. Bergen, discussing an article by Werner Gottlieb and Joe H. Stanley, implies this value when she describes as a fundamental human goal the finding of ways of mastery that do not bring conflict with the environment and that achieve satisfaction for self and others.[3]

The value of social relationships or of social relatedness derives from the reciprocal model discussed by Catherine P. Papell and Beulah Rothman, which delineates a helping process designed to serve both the individual and society. This model

> presupposes an organic, systemic relationship between the individual and society. . . . This interdependence is the "focus" for social work. . . . The range of social work function can include prevention, provision, as well as restoration. Breakdown in the interdependence between systems may occur at any point on the continuum between health and pathology.[4]

The relationship between the reciprocal model and ego psychology, which is the theoretical orientation used in this book, is pointed out by Heinz Hartmann, who states that the functions of the ego are concerned with the task of reality mastery and adaptation and that the concept of "fit" of the organism into the environment underlies the theoretical approach of ego psychology. The concept of fit assumes that a reciprocal relationship exists between the organism and the environment. Processes that change either the organism or the environment may bring about a state of adaptation and increased capacity for self-direction.[5]

Practitioners always see the worth and the dignity of the individual as a core value. This value subsumes related values: respect for individual difference and concern with developing the individual's feelings of self-worth and his capacity for self-direction.[6] Thus, the helping process must be effected in ways that respect individual difference and preserve and enhance human dignity and that aim toward the achievement of the individual's maximum potential.

The valuing of individuals and of social relationships comes full circle when the valuing of equal access is added to social provisions and opportunities. This value affirms that civil liberties and citizen rights are the concern of the helping professions, which must improve service delivery so as to lower the barriers of distance, red tape, and inequalities that interfere with accessibility of services. This value also affirms that the institutionalizing of social services and social programs is essential to the equilibrium of an industrial society and thus the opportunities afforded by society for its citizens should be available to all on equal terms.

Values not only describe what is preferred and to be striven for but, also, furnish a means of evaluating to what extent goals have been achieved. If we assign primacy to the value of social relationships, then goals relative to supporting and enhancing individual worth, self-direction, and self-realization must be evaluated in relation to their ability to promote constructive, equitable, and reciprocal relationships among the individual, family, and community. The various social services and social provisions must meet the test of how well they contribute to the well-being not only of the individual but also of the family and of the community. In evaluating his services to the client, the practitioner may well question himself about how well he has helped the client to find a place of worth and dignity in his society and how well he has helped the family function as an effective unit both within itself and in its community relationships.

Value-based Principles

The practitioner's exercise of value-guided judgments and decisions depends upon the development, from abstract professional values, of principles and other guides to action that sustain him in weighing competing claims and in deciding between conflicting courses of action. The practitioner needs such patterns in order to systematize and operationalize values in all helping methods. The social work profession has identified for each of the values that aid in giving direction to the helping process some derivative principles that can help to pattern the practitioner's use of any helping method. The value of the worth and the dignity of the individual, which includes respect for individual difference, gives rise to the principles of individualizing the client, of acceptance of the client and his individual differences, of confidentiality, of responsibility to evaluate but not judge the client's behavior, and of the responsibility to support and enhance human dignity and worth in the way in which social services are offered. The value of social relationships and relatedness or of man as a social being provides the principle of client participation in the helping process, of self-direction (self-determination), and of support of individual and family strengths. From the value of equal access to social opportunities and social provisions derive the principles of working for both social and societal change. The goals of societal change require the practitioner to support civil rights and liberties and to assign preeminence to the well-being of the client over the interests of organizations or agencies.

Although the foregoing and other principles have been formulated as guides for the use of method in the helping professions, the professions have not explicated the essential nature of many value judgments in conflict situations nor the possible value decisions available to the practitioner. A few value conflicts have been identified, but many others can be discovered only in relation to specialized practice in agencies and in different fields of service—for example, adoptions, work in medical settings, child welfare, and corrections. Some of the value conflicts or problems that practitioners have recognized include conflict between the interests and well-being of the individual and that of society or other individuals; between needs and available resources; between a client or clients and the worker; between the interests of the client and the agency; between the interests of the agency and the community; or between the profession and the agency, to mention only a few.[7] These value conflicts become apparent in practice. Here, they assume the explicit nature and reality that make it possible to fill in the outlines that define the nature of the conflict and make more explicit the characteristic value judgments and principles required to guide the practitioner in solving these problems.

The alternative behaviors open to the practitioner include reconciliation of value positions as well as choice between value positions. Pumphrey has stated that the worker must often choose between "two approved values" or must assign value priorities.[8] Frequently, however, instead of choosing between two values, the practitioner may attempt to balance two values and to develop a workable equilibrium between them. This point of view has been suggested by Mary J. McCormick.[9] Questions that need to be settled by developing much more exact guides for practitioner action include, for example, such decisions as when it is appropriate to change the client's value orientation with the goal of acculturation. Such a goal is suggested in the idea that the client moves from lower-class identification to working-class identification and value orientations but usually cannot jump from lower to middle-class. However, Hyman Rodman's idea that lower-class clients hold many value orientations similar to those of the core culture but cannot achieve them and so develop a "value stretch" in order to handle their realities[10] leads to the notion that clients may need not only to have their value orientations changed but also their life situations changed so that they can achieve the core culture values. Principles might provide helpful guides to professional efforts in such situations as these.

In family conflicts between generations or between a husband and a wife with differing value orientations, the practitioner needs to clarify the nature of the conflict and should also have some principles that point toward reconciliation or toward choice between the competing values. Particularly in secondary settings, the practitioner has to understand both the values that are held by members of allied professions and the values of the given social system. He also needs to know when to strive for reconciliation and when to choose between the competing values. The practitioner must be able to interpret professional values and use principles to guide treatment decisions. The client of the hospital or social agency has his own value orientations, which may add another variable to the situation and to the difficulties of making a value judgment or decision. The practitioner must understand how the value orientations of clients, organizations, colleagues, and others differ from those of the helping professions. He must understand how to weigh these values and to decide on appropriate measures for dealing with the conflict or problem.

Notes

1. *Webster's Seventh New Collegiate Dictionary,* s.v. "process."

2. Muriel W. Pumphrey, "Transmitting Values and Ethics Through Social Work Practice," *Social Work,* 6:68–75 (July 1961).

3. Mary E. Bergen, "Discussion" (of the article by Werner Gottlieb and Joe H. Stanley, "Mutual Goals and Goal-setting in Casework"), *Social Casework,* 48:477–79 (October 1967).

4. Catherine P. Papell and Beulah Rothman, "Social Group Work Models: Possession and Heritage," *Education for Social Work,* 2:-66–77 (Fall 1966).

5. Heinz Hartmann, *Ego Psychology and the Problem of Adaptation* (New York: International Universities Press, 1958), chap. 2.

6. Florence Hollis, *Casework: A Psychosocial Therapy* (New York: Random House, 1964), pp. 12–13.

7. The Ad Hoc Committee on Advocacy, "The Social Worker as Advocate: Champion of Social Victims," *Social Work,* 14:16–22 (April 1969).

8. Pumphrey, "Transmitting Values and Ethics."

9. Mary J. McCormick, "Professional Responsibility and the Professional Image," *Social Casework,* 47:635–42 (December 1966).

10. Hyman Rodman, "On Understanding Lower-Class Behavior," in *Sourcebook in Marriage and the Family,* ed. Marvin B. Sussman, 3rd ed. (Boston: Houghton Mifflin Co., 1968), pp. 172–80.

TWO

The Ego Analysis Method

Only the addition of a theory base provides a helping method. The characteristics of ego theory furnish a rationale for the helping method: The functions of the ego and ego identity provide a basis for assessing where change is needed to increase capacity and to lessen limitations; the patterning of ego functions leads logically to the assessment of what kinds of changes are needed. The functions of the ego and ego identity also provide matching categories of treatment designed to increase capacity and to lessen limitations. In the ego analysis method, purpose is translated into focus, and values become value-guided judgments and decisions.

THE development of a helping method requires the systematizing of what the practitioner does in the helping process. Use of a theory base makes it possible to organize, in a dynamically related manner, study, assessment, treatment or intervention, and development and use of the helping relationship. In addition, the general statement of purpose for the helping process must become an integral part of method by explications of ways to achieve purpose through focus on an orderly progression toward recognized goals. Values have no meaning until they are put into practice. The values of the professions must be applied to the principles that guide the practitioner's value judgments and treatment decisions. When they are integrated into the helping process, theory, purposeful focus, and principles based on values, together with the professional relationship, provide the possibilities of a method. Because an effective helping process must always have a change purpose, the practitioner should always focus method in ways that aim at promoting that change. It is suggested here that problem selection, the planned use of the components of method, guided by value-based principles, serve to focus the practitioner's helping efforts with the client toward achievement of agreed-upon change.

THE METHOD OF EGO ANALYSIS

Use of ego theory to bring about change in personal functioning through helping may be termed the method of ego analysis. Helping methods differ considerably according to the theoretical orientation used. Orientations affect the kinds of study facts gathered, when and how they are gathered, the content of the diagnosis, how the diagnosis is shared with the client and how used by the practitioner, the treatment measures the practitioner employs, and the degree of client participation in the treatment process. Theory also indicates the kind of changes that the practitioner intends to achieve with the client. The practitioner concerns himself with both the personal system and such social systems as the family, small groups, complex organizations, and the community. He can use psychoanalytic ego theory to understand the personal system and use social system and role theories to understand social systems. Since the ego and the entire personal system did not develop in a vacuum but in a sociocultural environment and since the ego functions serve the purpose of adaptation, theories about the personal system and about the social systems can be considered as complementary. According to Heinz Hartmann, the idea of adaptation includes the idea of the organism's "fit" into the environment and of a reciprocal relationship between the two.[1] The client must be understood in relation to his life setting. If the personal system is viewed as open-ended—continually taking in energy from the environment and putting out energy to affect the environment—the personal system can be seen as both influenced by experiences and influencing experience.

The concept of personal system indicates a structural-functional frame of reference. The id, ego, and superego together constitute the structure of the personality or the personal system. Each may be described as a group of functions; understanding the functions explains the system. The id, the source of psychic energy, provides a motivational force in the personality that urges the ego to activity. The superego is conceptualized as a group of functions that warn, guide, punish, and reward and that represent the internalized cultural value systems within the personality. The concept of the ego contains the idea that the ego consists of a dynamically interrelated group of functions whose purpose is to handle pressures from within and from without in order to make adaptation possible. The ego is considered to be the part of the personality that solves problems, copes and uses adaptive and defensive patterns to carry life roles, and thus effects the business of living. In this theoretical framework, social functioning is ego functioning in a social situation. Improvement of social functioning entails the development and strengthening of the ego functions as well as situational change to support ego functioning. Like all systems, the personal system has boundaries that can be described in terms of ego identity—the sense of individuality which sets the person apart from others and defines for him the kind of person he is and his place in society.

Any theories selected as a basis for the helping method must meet the test of usefulness for achieving change. One way of determining usefulness is through identifying the systematic linkages between that theory and the means of bringing about change through helping. These systematic linkages enable the practitioner to identify where change is needed in order to bring about improved functioning (functions of the ego or the social environment); to identify the changes needed (patterning and integration of ego functions or increased environment support); and to understand how to effect these changes (new learning, correction, or support of previous learning). These linkages should be explicit in any theory-based method. In addition, the ego functions provide logically related diagnostic and treatment categories for the helping method that make possible logical connections between diagnosis and treatment. The practitioner may attempt to help the client achieve changes in one, or several, or all ego functions.

In this regard, Ernest Greenwood has said that the systematizing of helping and its progress toward a practice theory depend largely on developing typologies of diagnosis and of treatment that can be used together; that is, each diagnostic type "contains implications for a certain type or types of treatment."[2] He sees the development of such typologies as "a prime need" of the social work profession. In this writer's view, it is a prime need of all the helping professions. Such categories prove economical both for the practitioner and the client. The client can see the relevance of the information he is supplying because his increased understanding leads directly both to what he needs to change and to the method by which he can do so. As has been suggested, theory-based method makes possible the placing of a particular instance of behavior in a class of instances or generalizations about aspects of behavior or of the environment. Such generalizations free the practitioner from the impossible task of dealing with each event *de novo* and lead to thinking of specific kinds of help for specific needs. It becomes apparent that the purpose of diagnosis is to guide treatment and to indicate treatment possibilities. The more explicit the diagnostic categories of the changes needed and possible, the better related can be the treatment plan. Use of the concept of the ego functions enables the practitioner to identify what is limiting the client in his functioning and hindering his problem-solving and to determine what capacities can be utilized to improve the problem-solving. Regardless of the type of client, the practitioner always treats the client—not the problem.

Ego theory accounts for stability over time in the normal personality by the idea that the functions of the ego operate in an organized way and that they become patterned in ways characteristic of developmental periods. These formulations provide a basis for evaluative judgments about where the client is in his development and about the kind of changes needed to correct developmental lags and developmental distortions. Explanations in ego theory about how, in the normal personality, change takes place over time emphasize learning as basic to developmental change. Postulates about the way the individual learns open the door for diagnostically based decisions by the practitioner on how to bring about such desirable changes as new learning, relearning, or the strengthening of old learning and how to do so in the light of the epigenetic theory that identifies the crucial and sequential steps in learning. Furthermore, ego psychology tends to regard individual personality differences (unless the individual is born, or becomes, damaged) as stemming from differences in psychosocial learning experiences and the individual's reaction to these experiences and so provides a rationale for needed situational changes to support or promote learning.[3]

The concept of the "average expectable environment" that is needed to furnish desirable learning experiences utilizes insights from a wide range of psychological and social sciences. Because ego psychology postulates that the ego develops and functions in the sociocultural environment, differences in the sociocultural learning experiences are associated with differences in personality development. This theory furnishes a way of relating an understanding of personality and of environment in an integrated frame of reference.

Where Is Change Needed?

The problem of locating needed changes in client functioning can be solved to a considerable extent by using an understanding of ego functions to analyze behavior. Although authorities agree in general on the functions of the ego, they tend to group them differently. The grouping proposed here is based on analysis of the content of the casework literature and on some rearrangement of Leopold Bellak's categorization.[4] Interestingly enough, although practitioners feel little hesitation in making a clinical diagnosis by explicitly identifying the client's pathology, they tend to be relatively implicit regarding the functioning of the ego or the client's coping ability. This writer believes that making explicit what has been implicit will serve to clarify the practitioner's diagnostic thinking and will do so in a model of health. In this model, assessment and treatment focus on the client's coping abilities and on changes needed to strengthen the progressive forces in the personality and to support ego functioning. As a basis for this thinking, the following grouping of ego functions is used.

The functions of perception assign culturally learned, psychologically oriented meanings to all sensory data from within and from without.[5] Perception includes inner perception, outer perception, and reality testing. Reality testing is concerned with distinguishing thoughts, ideas, and feelings that originate from within from those that originate from outside self. Reality testing serves to prevent ascribing to the environment what should be ascribed to self. Inner perception turns attention inward and the observing ego takes note of its own thoughts, motivations, and acts. Outer perception selectively pays attention to and interprets auditory, visual, and other cues from outside of self.

The cognitive functions comprised in thinking include remembering and the ability to associate, to differentiate, and to select behaviors on the basis of anticipated outcome. The acquiring and use of words in communication, logical thinking, abstract or conceptual thinking, and judgment are other cognitive functions.

The management of needs and feelings includes the capacity to cathect needs which increasingly become ego and social needs and to utilize adaptive and defensive patterns to obtain satisfaction as well as to handle the related feelings. These patterns enable the individual to function in accord with the reality or the modified-pleasure principle.

The executive function controls motor activity and its use in goal-directed behavior in carrying social role responsibilities.

The integrative function affects all other ego functions, comprising as it does the capacity to learn and to integrate new learning into the functioning of the ego.

What Changes Are Needed?

The problem of assessing what needs to be changed in the person's functioning to improve his coping abilities can be answered to a considcrablc extent by an analysis of stable characteristics of the given ego. Ego theory accounts for the stability of the personality over time as a derivative of the characteristic tendencies of the ego toward organization and toward patterning. This theory rests on the basic assumption that in any piece of behavior can be seen all of the functions of the ego operating in an interrelated way and, in conditions of health, in an organized way. Through feedback processes, each function supports and interdigitates with every other function. Postulating that the ego becomes reorganized on progressively higher levels of integration around crucial learning tasks in each development period provides a way of assessing the level of the client's integration. These ideas, together with the notion that each of the functions of the ego becomes patterned in ways characteristic of the given stage of development, serve as a basis for assessing areas of fixation or of failure to progress. Ego theory holds that in normal development the individual progressively learns more active and effective patterns of mastery.[6] René Spitz states that Freud observed the common human tendency to turn passivity into activity, and later authorities have emphasized this tendency as one of the major ways in which the individual learns from a person with whom he identifies. He actively practices what he has passively experienced.[7] The healthy ego constitutes a group of functions developed to safeguard the individual from helplessness. In ego theory, anxiety is the discomfort aroused by the threat or actuality of helplessness and is a signal of ego inadequacy or possible inadequacy. The healthy development of the functions of the ego results from learning active coping patterns, both defensive and adaptive, and the healthy ego uses them, together with passive patterns, to handle self and environment.

During infancy, the child first uses passive mastery to induce the environment to meet his needs with his cries of helplessness and discomfort. He develops a passive patterning and learns to acquire what is given through all of his senses. Such patterns as getting and taking learned at this stage are used throughout life.

The tendency to "patterned motor movement" is, according to Paul R. Miller, the only identifiable "human instinct" or innate behavior.[8] At first, one observes the patterns of organ functioning, crying, smiling, sucking, and head movements. Later, one can observe the learned patterns of ego functioning that make it possible to deal with a great many aspects of living without conscious attention or without having to deal with each experience *de novo.* As Erik H. Erikson theorizes, some ego patterns, particularly those of drive management, develop from organ patterns: oral incorporation, anal retention and elimination, and genital intrusion or inclusion. Patterns continually change in response to new learning about ways to meet new situations. Understanding that the healthy person has learned and is capable of learning patterns of active mastery and of using them appropriately with passive patterns for coping enables the practitioner to understand what needs to be changed in order to promote coping abilities.[9]

The culmination of ego tendencies toward differentiation and organization results in a sense of ego identity that represents the individual's ability to acknowledge his past without having to repress conflictual aspects and his ability, on this basis, to deal with the present and to look forward to the future. Hope for the future depends on the ability to rely on the acquired effective ego-coping patterns for dealing with self and environment and on patterns of social role functioning that harmonize with the culture.

How to Bring About Changes

Formulations concerning the maturation process and the developmental process and their interaction describe the changes that take place in the personality over time as well as the way in which they take place and suggest methods of bringing about change through helping. In Hartmann's account of the change in personality as a result of these processes and their interrelationship, maturation constitutes the built-in biological timetable of growth and represents change in physical capacity.[10] In this timetable, drive expressions center successively in oral sensory, in anal muscular, and in genital zones; the bodily frame grows and becomes capable of locomotion. The individual also acquires capacity for more and more complex muscular coordination and can use his distance receptors in increasingly selective intake from the environment. The brain matures and the ability for thinking enlarges. Thus, through maturation, occur the changes in physical and intellectual potential that interact with the developmental process and set the stage for what the child is capable of learning and what he can be expected to learn because the learning timetable should not progress too far ahead of, nor lag too far behind, the maturational timetable. Learning sets in motion the developmental process, the innate tendency toward differentiation of innate ego functions and integration of functions on higher and higher levels as a result of interaction between maturation and development. Many theorists in ego psychology accept Hartmann's concept of the autonomous ego. He postulates that the ego and the id both develop from an undifferentiated matrix. He believes that the child is born with an innate potential for adaptedness provided he meets an "average expectable environment." These ideas depart from those of Freud, who believed that the ego developed from the id and from conflict between the id and the environment. Hartmann considers that the ego functions of perception, intention, object comprehension, thinking, language, recall, productivity, motor development, and learning are functions of primary autonomy, which develop outside conflict, although they may later become involved in conflict. The other ego functions he regards as functions of secondary autonomy.[11] Hartmann emphasizes the role of learning in ego development. As the child identifies with the mother and internalizes her teaching, he learns and, as a result, develops his own capacities. This view accords with that of Freud, who believed that most of human learning comes through learning from other persons. These formulations account for some of the ways in which external experiences are taken over by the individual, internalized, become part of himself, and change him. The resulting change in human capacity can be described as the developmental process. Hartmann and Rudolph M. Lowenstein state: "We would speak of internalization when regulations that have taken place in interaction with the outside world are replaced by inner regulations."[12] In his chapter dealing with developmental deviations found in the children described in *The Drifters,* Charles A. Malone states that the children from lower-class disorganized families do not appear to form "reasonably lasting identifications; they do not seem to take over the characteristics of others in the integrated fashion usually observed in the identification of preschool children." He states that the children show a "lag in developing stable internalization." Instead of learning, these children use imitation and try to pick up cues from the adult as to what they should do at any given time.[13]

From the foregoing discussion, it becomes evident that ego theory may be viewed as a theory of learning. Hartmann states that the mother puts the premium on learning.[14] To keep her love, the child strives to learn to meet her expectations. It has been said that love makes the child educable. Use of the ego analysis model for treatment points to new learning as a means for developing or strengthening coping abilities, to relearning as a way of lessening the debilitating power of the past over the present, and to support of previous learning as the path to greater health. Ego analysis emphasizes that understanding the effect of pathology on the functions of the given ego is as important as identifying the pathology because a range of pathologies may show similar damage to or distortion of the ego.[15]

The practitioner can then focus diagnosis and treatment on the remaining intact ego functioning, emphasizing support of the capacity for new learning and engaging with the client in a search for health or what can become healthy in his way of operating. In accord with this thinking, Lawrence S. Kubie distinguishes the healthy from the neurotic personality on the basis of the individual's ability to modify old patterns in response to the realistic demands of the new situation. He considers that healthy patterns are "flexible, modifiable, satiable, and under voluntary control."[16] In this framework, helping the client consciously to learn new, more adaptive, more realistic patterns of coping strengthens the progressive forces and the ego-integrative function and lessens regressive forces. Ego theory assumes that, unless proved otherwise, the individual has the capacity to learn and to change as long as he lives, although this capacity varies with the intactness of the integrative function of the ego and with other factors. To the extent that responses are dictated by predominantly unconscious mechanisms, behavior cannot be consciously controlled and changed.

Relationships Between the Individual and the Environment

In summary, the developmental process describes how the individual learns, postulates the crucial learning tasks of each developmental stage, suggests that failure to learn at the appropriate time of maturational readiness results in less adequate learning, proposes for each stage what the average expectable environment should furnish to promote optimal learning, and describes outcomes of development in terms of identifiable steps in the development of the functions of the ego. The ideas relative to the learning experiences that the environment should furnish lead inevitably to the next characteristic of ego theory—the explanations that it furnishes to account for individual differences in personality development. These explanations contribute to understanding the where, what, and how of desirable environmental changes to support ego functioning. The question of individual difference relates to the nature-nurture controversy, a controversy that debates the question of how much difference can be attributed to innate variations in capacity and how much to environmental experience. Research suggests genetic equalitarianism that includes "the full range of human abilities" although it recognizes genetic differences in ability to be influenced by the environment.[17] Ego theory emphasizes early learning experiences as does, for example, Malone's chapter in *The Drifters.* Discussing the developmental lags seen in these children, Malone states that several authorities, in their articles on identification and internalization, "imply, although they do not specifically state, that stable internal models arise under the influence of an 'average-expectable' environment" which has "consistency and reliability." Malone quotes additional sources to the effect that "when a child's early experience with his mother is predominantly discomforting and frustrating, the identification with her is defensive in nature, internalization is incomplete, and the child does not show the gains in adaptive activities and functions which normally accrue from identification." These authors believe that when the child experiences pain and discomfort in relation to the parent, the parent becomes at least partially dangerous. Malone believes that, as a result of this kind of experience, the child tends to ward off the parent and in similar situations, both in childhood and adulthood, tends to form transitory, superficial relationships with other persons and to avoid and fear close relationships. A predominance of discomfort in the relationship with the mother interferes with the ability to identify with and to take over from her and, hence, to learn.[18]

Benjamin S. Bloom has suggested some useful ideas about factors that contribute to individual difference. He believes that the environment produces the greatest effect on the development of human characteristics in the early, most rapid periods of marked change. As an example, he states that as much of the development of general intelligence takes place in the first four years of life as in the next thirteen years: That is, 50 percent of the development at age seventeen takes place by age four. If Bloom's ideas have validity, one might assume that the same percentage of development holds true for other characteristics of the personality. Little has been done to measure the environmental influence, but Bloom suggests that in the case of intelligence the following factors may be related to its development: the learning of language and the use of language, general knowledge about the world around us, the encouragement given the child to learn problem-solving and individual thinking, and the family expectations and motivations for intellectual development.[19] Benson E. Ginsburg and Sibylle K. Escalona believe it is necessary also to measure the effects of these experiences on children with different reaction patterns.[20]

Moreover, ego theory provides some guides for the evaluation of present, past, or future environments. These guides derive from the concept of needs that are characteristic of each developmental period and some general notions that describe optimal ways of meeting needs. Need, therefore, serves as a bridging concept that relates psychological and social science theories. The concept of role provides a similar theoretical bridge which makes possible evaluation of the environmental provisions in relation to the degree to which they support and enhance social-role functioning or fail to do so. These concepts require an understanding of the various cultures, the way in which they socialize the child, and the ways in which they teach different patterns of social-role functioning. Because *social role* describes behavior in a social context, the manner in which the person carries his role in reciprocal role relationships affects others in his role network. In dealing with problems of individual differences, the practitioner is, in essence, dealing with the interaction process in which input from each of the individuals concerned affects the outcome. Ego psychology suggests that interaction characterized by patterns of mutual regulation and of complementarity in role functioning promotes personality development and adaptive social functioning.[21]

This approach to an understanding of individual differences calls attention to early formative years and to the need for greater emphasis on social intervention to prevent early damage that can interfere with the realization of the individual's potential. It also emphasizes that later remedial measures are more costly and less effective. The idea that maturation and development interact also calls attention to the necessity for social provisions that support the maturation process. Research suggests that irreversible intellectual damage may result from malnutrition during early childhood years.[22] Similarly, congenital blindness, deafness, or other physical handicaps may seriously interfere with learning unless the environment affords special provisions to make learning possible. Spitz quotes D. Rapaport and M. Gill who say that "the adaptive point of view demands that the psychoanalytic explanation of any psychological phenomena include propositions concerning its relationship to the environment."[23] This approach emphasizes the necessity for adequate instrumental provisions to support role functioning.

Focus in Method

Because helping is a method of change, it must be focused purposefully in ways that are designed to bring about desired results. Focus, therefore, carries out in concrete ways the purpose of helping. The practitioner has ultimate responsibility for selection of focus, although the client should understand the purposes to the greatest extent possible and should participate in selecting and using a focused approach toward improved functioning and problem-solving. From the two pivotal purposes of ego analysis—problem and method—stem other related purposes and foci. It is in order to examine first the problem focus. The problem on which practitioner and client agree as the one with which to begin work furnishes a stable reference point for the helping method because the desired changes relate to this problem as do also the short-term and long-term goals. The practitioner assesses with the client his capacity and limitations in capacity in relation to the problem that he wants and needs to handle better. Similarly, he assesses the situation in relation to factors that limit or support the client's problem-solving efforts. The client's movement toward improvement in functioning, or the reverse, can be evaluated in relation to changes in capacity to handle the problem. Proximal goals represent steps toward achieving some more final goal of change relative to the problem. If helping efforts are not focused in this way it will be impossible for the practitioner to understand the total person, to survey his total functioning and all aspects of his situation; change efforts will become diffuse and, often, unrelated to clearly defined goals.

The problem focus provides a logical purpose for the focusing of method. The need to secure facts regarding capacity in problem-solving guides study. The necessity to identify what needs to be changed in order to improve problem-solving guides assessment. In a similar vein, treatment takes as its goal changes that will improve the relationship among capacity, situation, and problem. And, finally, the ultimate goal of helping is to accomplish some change in regard to problem-solving. If practitioner and client do not agree on the long-range purpose of their work together and what they hope eventually to accomplish, they may work at cross-purposes rather than take clearly defined steps toward change.[24]

Frequently, the client wants to engage in endless discussion of all his troubles and his feelings about self or family members. The client should understand that the purpose of the clear problem focus is to tell the practitioner and himself why he is seeking help and why they are working together. He should see that selection of a problem enables him to think about why he has been unable to handle it and what can be changed in order to bring different results. This process selects a piece of his difficulty and channels his efforts fruitfully in working on that difficulty. When the client comes to the office "on a trial visit," "on probation," or because the child has "trouble in school," the practitioner must, at some point, move the client from these meaningless generalizations to the selection of a problem as a place to start. The manner and the time of this selection depend partly on the client's resistance to assuming the client role.

The client must solve not only problems in social functioning that concern his life situation but also problems that arise from the helping process itself. These problems may be categorized as related to taking help or assuming the client role, and to using help or carrying the client role. When the practitioner understands the client's problem in taking help, he has a focus for assessing what needs to be changed and a method for bringing about change to increase motivation to accept help. The practitioner must deal with the client's problems of resistance to taking help before he and the client can get to the life problems that bring the client to the attention of the agency. In a similar way, although he has become an agency client, he may not be a user of help but may resist working toward change. Through use of the helping relationship, the practitioner must understand and lessen the client's defensiveness that blocks his perceiving, feeling, and acting in relation to the limiting factors in capacity or situation. The practitioner must handle resistance before he can engage the client in bringing about changes. Problems that constitute resistance to help will be discussed later.

Focusing Through Goals Related to Problem

The practitioner focuses and helps the client focus on the life problem on which they will both be working because the goal of dealing better with the difficulty guides the method and prevents wandering into irrelevant and useless areas. The problem focus circumscribes the area for study, assessment, and treatment; it channels the efforts of both the client and the practitioner in a fruitful way.

The development of a focus on some problem in social functioning on which client and practitioner can begin requires a fuller explanation. The presenting problem brings the practitioner into the case and furnishes an entrée to the client in his situation. The practitioner must do some thinking with the client about this problem before they can select the problem on which they will be engaged. He should first locate the presenting problem in some aspect of the client's social-role functioning. Second, the practitioner should define and describe the nature of the presenting problem, including possible relationships between the presenting and other problems. As a third and final step, the practitioner and the client should select the problem or aspect of the problem on which they will be engaged. The development of the problem focus represents one of the first explicit aims in work with the client, although, in some instances, this development may take some time to achieve if the client is unready to take help. Practitioner and client develop immediate and long-term goals in relation to the problem focus.

Selection of Problem Focus

Use of role theory places the problem in one of the client's major life roles and provides a dynamic connection with his social functioning. A request for a stove or rent money becomes significant when it is connected with the total difficulty in carrying the work role, such as part-time work, low-paid work, difficulty in holding a job, and so forth. The practitioner clarifies with the client the fact that the presenting problem is concerned with carrying his role as citizen; spouse; parent; worker; child in the family, school, or community; or as a patient. Identifying the area of concern in a given role provides boundaries and improves the problem focus because the boundaries are neither too wide nor too narrow. Within these boundaries lie the information, understanding, and activities relevant to the focus. Since the practitioner has designated an area of concern, however, he has some elbow room. The focus is not so narrow as to exclude relevant and significant aspects of the problem situation. The practitioner can also move from one problem in the area to a related problem and is able to consider this possibility with the client early in the relationship. The practitioner may find that locating the problem on a time continuum in the role adds significantly to its meaning. Werner W. Boehm has suggested the possibility of conceptualizing role problems as difficulties in assuming a social role, in carrying the role, or in giving up the role. Each time-grouping has different characteristics.[25]

Not only does role theory locate the problem in a useful way, it also calls attention to the fact that problems tend to cluster around given roles and to be connected in a chain-reaction relationship. This fact adds meaning to the problems. Almost never does the practitioner find an isolated problem. Similar characteristic clusterings tend to appear, making it possible for the practitioner to place the presenting problem not only in a given role but also in some of the expected relationships to other difficulties. Professional literature deals extensively and intensively with these related difficulties, and the practitioner should familiarize himself with what other practitioners usually encounter. This understanding helps his listening as he glimpses the half-mentioned concerns, as he notes the concerns the client significantly leaves unmentioned and those he repetitively emphasizes. This understanding also helps the practitioner to know what the client may need to talk about so that he can guide and stimulate the client's communication in ways that reveal the extent and nature of his difficulties.

If the practitioner has some breadth and depth of understanding, this fact communicates itself to the client, and interaction between them tends to become more responsive. The practitioner is then able to delineate the presenting problem more clearly, facilitating the client's fuller revelation of his difficulties and leading to a more relevant selection of focus. The use of problem network generalizations organizes the practitioner's thinking and helps to organize the client's thinking, without in any way negating the individual and unique aspects of the problems. Recognizing the fact that two teenage boys are having trouble accepting their mother's remarriage following her first husband's death only identifies the difficulty these boys are having in defining their roles and relationships vis-à-vis the stepfather. The contribution of each family member to this situation remains to be explored. The content of the problem is always unique as is its meaning to the individual; both derive from the given life situation. However, generalizations alert the practitioner about what to look for and how to help the client explain his particular burdens.

For a clear example of an interrelated set of role problems, the reader may refer to Catherine M. Bittermann's discussion of the multimarriage family.[26] However, although it has been suggested that the practitioner should familiarize himself with some of the characteristic groupings of problems, he will find considerable confusion in the literature in this respect. Journal articles frequently fail to distinguish the problem with which the client must deal from what, in his functioning, is problematical and interferes with his ability to achieve a satisfactory solution. When a person asks help because he has discovered that he must take a family member home from the hospital, this initial request is clearly one with which he needs help. It may be related to some situational difficulties, such as lack of equipment or plans for medical supervision. These problems, however, must be differentiated from those that, in the client's functioning, need changing so that he can cope with his difficulty. Limitations in coping may be lack of understanding about the medical condition and medical care, ignorance about financial or other resources, ambivalent feelings about the family member, anxiety about his own adequacy to give home care, or poor patterns of household management. The efforts of practitioner and client will focus on attempts to bring about changes in the client's ability to cope with his difficulties. In dealing with the family who cannot get along in the community and are constantly moving, the practitioner must select the problem that they want and need to solve. For example, do the parents want to see what can be done about the father's speech defect that causes him to be made fun of on his job or do they want to work on the problem of constant quarreling with neighbors? The parents may need help in dealing with self-image and image of each other, with problematical feelings, defenses, distorted perceptions, poor role patterns, or other related aspects of functioning that limit problem-solving. They also need support for use of their capacities.

Often, the practitioner can only hypothesize about relationships between problems that he and the client are beginning to glimpse in the problem complex. Sometimes chain-reaction relationships seem apparent: for example, when the wife points out the time sequence between the husband's beginning to drink, her own distress, and the adolescent's school failures. In other instances, the practitioner can only make inferences about possible relationships. Sometimes, the idea of circularity helps client and practitioner to become aware of reinforcing problems: the father's harsh authoritative discipline and the daughter's rebelliousness. Often, the practitioner uses his beginning grasp of the client's problems solely as a guide to his own thinking, or he may recognize with the client the existence of related problems with whose interconnectedness he may want to deal when he feels capable of doing so.

In helping the client to understand more clearly about the presenting problem and its characteristics, the practitioner may find useful the following ideas: The presenting problem may represent a solution and not a problem, it may be a symptomatic difficulty, it may constitute the precipitating factor in a crisis situation, or it may be a shared problem. The practitioner may use these ideas about the nature of the client's request to help the client begin to form a cognitive map of his problem situation. When a runaway boy applies for a place to stay overnight or when a mother requests placement, the running away and the placement must be viewed as the client's solution to the underlying difficulty that both he and the practitioner need to understand. The practitioner should clarify this fact with the client. He must say clearly that together they have to define the difficulty before they can choose an appropriate solution since the client's solution is one that may cause additional difficulty. Sometimes, the practitioner may need to go along with the request, arranging for temporary separation or placement or making other environmental provisions until feelings have calmed sufficiently to allow definition of the problem with reasonable clarity.

When a person seeks help because of truancy, stealing, or failure to follow a prescribed diet, the practitioner is dealing with a symptomatic difficulty. This symptom often represents the view of the referring source about the nature of the client's problem since symptoms such as these tend to bring the person to the attention of the school, the doctor, or lay persons. Although the presenting symptomatic difficulty may need immediate attention, the practitioner should, nevertheless, make clear to the client that the symptom indicates underlying stress or imbalance that he and the practitioner need to explore as a basis for deciding upon the appropriate solution.

Whatever the client's initial request, the practitioner usually needs to formulate or reformulate the problem in a way that makes it workable. If the solution requires the participation of other persons in the family, the practitioner helps the client to view the problem as a shared one that can be understood and dealt with only by involving the reciprocal role partner. The idea of a shared problem illuminates the nature of the difficulty. When the client comes in a crisis situation, he may be unclear about the problem that precipitated the crisis; for example, in a marital crisis in which the wife has left home and wants a divorce, what has precipitated the break? When the client becomes involved in a medical crisis, having somehow broken the cast on a limb and thus worsening his physical and financial situation, the practitioner should help him seek behind the crisis for its cause and ask whether the present difficulty bears any relationship to past difficulties since frequently the client's share in producing recurrent crises constitutes the problem to be worked on. Clients who externalize their difficulties by asking for quick remedies often keep the practitioner at a distance to avoid coming to terms with the real problem, usually because it seems so threatening.

The practitioner's reformulation of a difficulty in less threatening terms often makes it possible to begin to deal with it. Family members frequently couch their problems in relation to conflict and angry criticism, which makes it almost impossible to discuss the matter and to work together on a solution. In one such case in which the mother described herself as "controlling" and the children as "rebellious," the therapist's restatement transformed the old theme. His phrasing changed the problem to, "Look how the children's inability for self-control is making you overburdened and helpless. Let's try to help the children increase their self-control."[27] When the client cannot face the fact that he has problems, the practitioner may refer to them as worries. Anger and other unacceptable feelings frequently become discussable when they are diluted.

In the foregoing and in other ways, the practitioner assists the client in exploring the initial request and in defining the area in which they will work. Finally, an understanding of the time factor may add an essential facet to the whole. Is this a recurrent problem, a recent one, or one that has become chronic in nature? The practitioner attempts to develop with the client a beginning cognitive map of his difficulties, although only a few major outlines may be distinguishable in early contacts. When the client comes with an unconscious as well as a conscious problem, considerable time may be necessary before the client is ready to define the nature of the difficulty on which he and the practitioner will be engaged.

Focusing Through Purposive Use of Method

The use of method in a purposeful way also focuses helping because there is a specific purpose for study, assessment, treatment, and the professional relationship. The purpose of assessment is to guide treatment; the purpose of treatment is to improve functioning in relation to the given problem. Characteristically, the practitioner engages the client in telling about himself and his problem. The "telling" itself has a purpose, primarily a diagnostic one: to enable the client to understand more clearly what is making it difficult for him to handle this problem and what strengths he can draw on in self and situation to deal with the difficulty. The practitioner and client usually make better headway when the practitioner can connect the needed information with the purpose it serves. He may ask, "What don't you understand about your medical condition that makes you hesitate to decide on the operation?" or "Have you thought that the way you are looking at your boss's remarks may be making it hard for you to know how to handle them?" Usually, the more clearly client and practitioner see the purpose of shared understanding, the better focused is the study process. When the practitioner engages the client in an overly long explanation whose purpose may have little meaning to the client, the client may react with hostility. He may think that the study facts are for the practitioner's use and not for his own. He may also think that having produced all the information for the practitioner, the practitioner should relieve him of his problem and provide the answers. The practitioner should give considerable thought to the timing of his attempt to focus the study on capacity and limitations in capacity. Usually, he first helps the client to tell his story and unburden himself so that they both can acquire some overall grasp of the present situation. As the problem emerges, however, or as they select the problem, the practitioner can focus the study process in such a way as to connect understanding and doing. It may be impossible for the client to participate in the selection of goals early in the contact if he shows resistance or if what he asks from the agency derives from predominantly unconscious needs.

In a similar way, the necessity to make decisions about what to do and how to bring about change focuses diagnostic assessment. Helpful diagnostic thinking provides a guide to action and can be shared with the client. Whenever possible, the client should get the idea that the necessity "to do better" or to achieve situational change lends purpose to his attempts to understand and leads to the possibility of productive activities. In other words, having begun to see what is holding him back, having begun to see some positives that he can use, he must decide where and how he can begin to work toward a change and what help he needs in order to do so. Similarly, the client should understand that the attempt to handle his problem focuses his planning and carrying through of change. He must identify his successes as bringing him nearer to his goal in problem-solving. Sooner or later, the client should be able to plan next steps and, in some cases, to envisage and carry through a plan that can bring him nearer to a solution of his problem.

The method focus provides a focus on immediate goals. It requires the practitioner to think about purpose in each interview so as to help the client move toward more final goals by well-thought-out steps within his capacity. Purpose is seen as a "planned, purposive mode of procedure, consciously directed toward specific ends." Proximal goals continually change. Frequently, the technique of assigning homework to the client so that he comes prepared to work on some facet of his difficulty contributes to achieving focus and purposiveness.[28]

Focusing Through Use of Principles

In addition to the problem focus and the method focus, three corollaries of the principle of client participation also serve to focus the helping method: beginning where the client is, beginning with the present, and beginning with more outer situational aspects before moving to more inner personal aspects of the problem-situation. All three of these principles provide guides to client participation in the helping process. The principle of beginning where the client is focuses the practitioner's attention on the way the client sees his problem, his unconscious and conscious expectations of help. It requires the practitioner to align himself with the client, to extend help, and to find a place to begin working. It channels the practitioner's efforts into lessening the client's resistance to becoming a client and assuming the client role.

In focusing helping efforts on the present situation, the practitioner and client select for the beginning problem focus a difficulty in the present. The past cannot be changed, but it may be possible to alter the present for the better. Since the purpose of help is to improve the client's social functioning, selecting a present problem around which to improve coping abilities provides the most logical and appropriate way to achieve this purpose in the shortest possible time. Some clients—angry, hurt, and defeated by past experiences—want to engage in endless examination of why they are as they are. Although some ventilation may serve a helpful purpose, the question becomes one of the client's deciding, in view of his past, what can be done to change the present. The practitioner tries to enable the client to accept his past with more equanimity, to loosen its bonds, to find possibilities in the present for new satisfactions that outweigh the satisfaction of reviving the bitter past. He encourages the client to give up repetitive self-defeating patterns of behavior and to consider new possibilities. He continually turns the client's attention, thoughts, and efforts to the present and helps him to perceive new opportunities in the present. In some instances, however, the present problem may lead to one in the past, and the client may be able to settle old issues in a new way.

The principle of beginning to work with more external aspects before proceeding to more internal aspects of the problem-situation has as its purpose the lessening of the more modifiable external pressures with the consequent release of energy and the achieving of immediate success. Success in the present can increase hope and so motivate the client to further efforts toward change. The practitioner can use the principle in two ways: to focus on situational change and to focus on the more external aspects of the client's functioning. Situational change may be brought about in relation to the social systems in which the client functions: family, school, work, and health and welfare organizations. Practitioner and client may identify ways in which the relief of situational pressures, the provision of new opportunities, and increased support may bring changes in the client's functioning. Another way of viewing a situation is to consider the reciprocal role partner or partners as the most significant psychological environment of the client. In this case, the problem is defined as a shared problem, and the practitioner attempts to improve mutual understandings, perceptions, meeting of needs, and handling of role responsibilities. Concerning the client's own functioning, the focus on more external aspects of behavior may lead the practitioner to deal with thinking, perceiving of outer environmental factors, and, in some cases, acting before he considers with the client his feelings, needs, and relationships because these latter functions tend to become involved to a greater extent in unresolved learning difficulties and internal conflict. The client can usually deal more readily with less emotionally weighted aspects of functioning. As he comes to trust the practitioner and experiences some success, he may be able to consider more internal aspects of need, feelings, and relationships.

Wherever practitioner and client start, the practitioner uses the principle of proceeding at the client's pace to focus their work together on what the client is ready to see and is capable of tackling. If the practitioner has an understanding of the client's resistance to using help, the practitioner will be enabled to proceed at the client's pace.

Values and Principles in Method

If social relatedness is accepted as a major value, the method of ego analysis affords a way of realizing the value because the method's goal of adaptation is the goal of the healthy personality. It assumes that the "fit" between person and environment constitutes a "reciprocal relationship" between the two and that processes that change either one can bring about adaptation.[29] This idea guides the practitioner in attempting to strengthen both individual functioning and environmental support for such functioning. The assumption that the ego masters reality and is motivated toward achieving social competence provides the rationale for use of ego and social support to maximize the client's potential for self-direction.

Notes

1. Heinz Hartmann, *Ego Psychology and the Problem of Adaptation* (New York: International Universities Press, 1958), chap. 3.

2. Ernest Greenwood, "Social Science and Social Work: A Theory of Their Relationship," *Social Service Review,* 29:20–33 (March 1955).

3. Sibylle K. Escalona, *The Roots of Individuality: Normal Patterns of Development in Infancy* (Chicago: Aldine Publishing Company, 1968), chap. 3.

4. Leopold Bellak, ed., *Schizophrenia: A Review of the Syndrome* (New York: Logos Press, 1958), pp. 6–34.

5. Stanley H. King, *Perceptions of Illness and Medical Practice* (New York: Russell Sage Foundation, 1962), chaps. 2 and 3.

6. Otto Fenichel, *The Psychoanalytic Theory of Neurosis* (New York: W. W. Norton and Company, 1945), pp. 41–42; and René A. Spitz, *No and Yes: On the Genesis of Human Communication* (New York: International Universities Press, 1957), pp. 53–57.

7. Spitz, *No and Yes,* pp. 45–46.

8. Paul R. Miller, *Sense and Symbol: A Textbook of Human Behavioral Science* (New York: Harper & Row, 1967), p. 57.

9. Erik H. Erikson, *Childhood and Society,* 2d ed. rev. (New York: W. W. Norton and Company, 1963), pp. 72–108; also Bellak, *Schizophrenia,* pp. 34–35.

10. Heinz Hartmann, Ernst Kris, and Rudolph M. Lowenstein, "Comments on the Formation of Psychic Structure," in *Psychoanalytic Study of the Child,* vol. 2 (New York: International Universities Press, 1947), pp. 11–38.

11. Hartmann, *Ego Psychology,* chap. 1.

12. Heinz Hartmann and Rudolph M. Lowenstein, "Notes on the Superego," in *Psychoanalytic Study of the Child,* vol. 12 (New York: International Universities Press, 1962), pp. 42–81.

13. Charles A. Malone, "Developmental Deviations Considered in the Light of Environmental Forces," in *The Drifters: Children of Disorganized Lower-Class Families,* ed. Eleanor Pavenstedt (Boston: Little, Brown & Co., 1967), pp. 132–33.

14. Hartmann, Kris, and Lowenstein, "Comments on the Formation of Psychic Structure."

15. Joshua M. Perman, "Role of Transference in Casework with the Public Assistance Families," *Social Work,* 8:47–54 (October 1963); also, Herbert S. Strean, "Casework with Ego-fragmented Parents," *Social Casework,* 49:222–27 (April 1968).

16. Lawrence S. Kubie, "The Fundamental Nature of the Distinction Between Normality and Neurosis," *Psychoanalytic Quarterly,* 23:167–204 (1954).

17. Benson E. Ginsburg, "All Mice Are Not Created Equal: Recent Findings on Genes and Behavior," *Social Service Review,* 40:121–34 (June 1966).

18. Malone, "Developmental Deviations," pp. 132–35.

19. Benjamin S. Bloom, *Stability and Change in Human Characteristics* (New York: John Wiley and Sons, 1964), chap. 3.

20. Ginsburg, "All Mice Are Not Created Equal"; and Escalona, *Roots of Individuality,* chap. 3.

21. Erikson, *Childhood and Society,* pp. 75–80.

22. Nevin S. Scrimshaw, "Infant Malnutrition and Adult Learning," *Saturday Review,* March 16, 1968, pp. 64–66, 82–83.

23. Quoted in René A. Spitz, *The First Year of Life: A Psychological Study of Normal and Deviant Development of Object Relations* (New York: International Universities Press, 1965), p. 10.

24. Julianna T. Schmidt, "The Use of Purpose in Casework Practice," *Social Work,* 14:77–84 (January 1969).

25. Werner W. Boehm, *The Social Casework Method in Social Work Education,* The Social Work Curriculum Study, vol. 10 (New York: Council on Social Work Education, 1959), pp. 112–13.

26. Catherine M. Bittermann, "The Multimarriage Family," *Social Casework,* 49:218–21 (April 1968).

27. Salvador Minuchin et al., *Families of the Slums: An Explora-*

tion of Their Structure and Treatment (New York: Basic Books, 1967), p. 253.

28. Schmidt, "Use of Purpose," p. 77.

29. Hartmann, *Ego Psychology.*

THREE

The Helping Relationship

The helping relationship provides dynamics of change when the practitioner uses a change process to intervene in the development process. Characteristics of the relationship similar to characteristics in early relationships necessary for development can be used to motivate the client to achieve new learning of more adaptive ego patterns and better ego integration or to motivate his better use of present coping patterns.

THE professional concept of the helping relationship is that of a bond of predominantly positive feeling between the worker and the client. The feeling flows in both directions, and an exchange of feelings—positive or negative—continues for as long as the contact continues, although the feelings of the practitioner differ considerably from those of the client, being more controlled and objective. The feeling bond serves the purpose of furthering, in some way, the client's use of help. It is apparent in the interaction between practitioner and client that the practitioner exerts influence to encourage the client to change. One may then question what makes it possible for one individual to be influenced by another individual and what makes it possible for an individual to take over ideas, feelings, viewpoints, and patterns of operating from another person. Granted that the practitioner offers help, the client must still be willing to utilize the help by accepting the influence of the practitioner. It is generally believed that the characteristics of the helping relationship make the client receptive to the practitioner's influence and serve to initiate or strengthen the client's motivation to utilize assistance. It is proposed here that this motivation results from the qualities of feeling aroused in the client by specific aspects of the helping relationship. How, then, does the practitioner develop these feelings in the client? It is suggested that the client is motivated to use help by feelings of relatedness and a wish to take from the practitioner feelings of trust in himself and in the practitioner, of satisfactions in the relationship and the desire to retain these satisfactions, and a wish to exercise his own initiative. This motivation has particular significance as the major treatment measure for lessening resistance to using help. At any point in their mutual interaction, the practitioner may need to utilize measures to deal with factors affecting the feeling bond between the client and himself.

The method of ego analysis assumes that the practitioner uses the helping process to intervene in the developmental process and to change that process for the better. The changes sought include supporting the developmental process so that the client can use his capacities to cope with present stress, reopening the developmental process so that the client can undo or redo maladaptive learning, and restoring the developmental process that has been interrupted by stress. In this approach, the practitioner uses the helping process to affect the process of growth in the client's adaptive capacities. The helping relationship utilized in the method of ego analysis, therefore, should comprise qualities that tend to enhance growth and to promote ego development.

Childhood development provides useful ideas regarding the nature of a growth-promoting relationship. The child comes into the world as a physiological organism. By the time he reaches adulthood, he has become not only a physiological organism but also a psychological and social being. This development takes place largely in the family. The family relationships that teach a child how to become human and how to function in a human society can be instructive concerning the nature of the helping relationship, the purpose of which is also the strengthening of social functioning. The physical growth of the child occurs as the result of the maturation process—the biological unfolding of inborn potentials according to the built-in timetable of the organism. The musculoskeletal frame grows, nerve circuits that make possible voluntary control of the muscles are completed, centers of higher learning develop, and the individual becomes capable of reproducing the species. Each growth stage represents a potential for new learning, and at each stage the child is ready for certain learning tasks. Even though maturation takes place in a programmed series of steps, these steps still require what Hartmann terms the "average expectable environment which furnishes nurturance, protection, and learning experiences." Without this input, the child may never realize his potential. Malnutrition may stunt not only physical growth but intellectual development. Lack of adequate stimulation and care may set in motion pathological processes that interfere with healthy maturation and development. Physical growth is only part of the story. Ego psychology postulates that the child is born not only with potentials for biological maturation but also with potentials for psychological and social development. The inborn drive and ego potentials also require for their development an average expectable environment.

The development of ego potentials is assumed to result from interaction of the child with other human beings—particularly his parents—who furnish emotional and intellectual food and stimulation in the form of learning experiences. What the child learns or fails to learn serves to develop in varying degrees his inborn potential. From parents, he learns patterns of relating to people—patterns for expressing needs and feelings in a manner harmonious with his culture. He learns to think, to handle himself in social situations, and ways of viewing himself, others, and his world. Food and exercise develop physical potentials. Human relations feed the growing ego by meeting emotional needs and by providing learning opportunities that offer the exercise and kind of stimulation and patterning of ego functions necessary for the development of these functions.

QUALITIES OF THE NURTURING EXPERIENCE

These propositions, however, lead to questions about what makes it possible for the child to utilize these experiences, internalize them, and make them part of himself. What qualities in the nurturing experience make it possible for the child to learn so much from his parents, from other persons, and from experiences with them? Granted the dynamic tendency to learn from other human beings, what conditions activate these dynamics? It is suggested that there are four characteristic inputs on the mother's part that, in the parent-child interaction, set in motion inborn tendencies toward development within the child. Identification, mother with child and child responsively with mother, gives rise to the wish to be like or to take on attributes valued by others.[1] Consistency in nurturing develops trust in what another has to teach and in one's own ability to learn.[2] A balance between satisfaction and frustration provides gratification for achievements in learning; at the same time, however, it also generates enough anxiety to motivate the ego to learn.[3] A balance between passivity and activity in meeting needs furnishes external stimulation and allows an appropriate degree of opportunity for the expression of inner initiative and the push toward mastery.[4] Each of these propositions will be considered here. Following this discussion, it will be demonstrated that use of these propositions provides a method for forming or strengthening the helping relationship. In later discussions of the assessment of capacity, it will be assumed that these same qualities of the nurturing experience are necessary to provide optimum conditions for ego development. A brief explanation will promote understanding of the dynamic role in parent-child relationships of each of these qualities.

Identification

Freud regarded the innate mechanism of identification as of supreme importance in the child's ability to form object relationships and to learn from others through the human tendency to practice actively what has been passively experienced. However, the child cannot identify with nurturing figures unless they first identify with him. Spitz suggests that the formation of the symbiotic relationship shortly after birth becomes possible as the mother regresses and identifies with her dependent child. This identification represents a state of heightened awareness and sensitivity that becomes apparent as she copies the child's facial expressions and sounds. The child then begins, responsively, to copy the mother's gestures and expressions.[5] Therese Benedek discusses in detail the responsive identification between mother and child.[6] It should also be noted that the mechanism of identification implies that the patterns learned by the child as he practices what he experiences can be healthy or unhealthy. If all goes well, however, identification between mother and child becomes a psychological bond and a feeling of oneness. It represents a first step that makes possible internalization of learning from the mother, thus maintaining closeness with her and the use of her ego to support and pattern the child's developing ego.

Throughout the growth periods, the parents give support to the child through the process of mutual identification. The parents, identifying with the child and accepting his learning needs, lend their ego strengths to the child. The child, in turn, feels strengthened and supported as he takes in the nurturing patterns and organizes his own patterning responsively. Similarly, the loss of a person with whom one felt closely identified is felt as loss of support and a loss of a source of inner strength.

With the coming of adolescence and adulthood, identification assumes a more conscious nature. The individual identifies with traits or partial aspects of others with whom he associates. He wishes to be like them since they strike a psychologically harmonious and responsive note in him, and he takes over ideas, feelings, and values because, to some degree, he wishes to pattern his behavior in ways valued by those with whom he identifies. The opposite also holds true. When the individual does not identify with another person, when there exists no psychological bond, no feeling of oneness or empathic sharing in any respect, he wards off the other person and rejects his influence.[7] The wish to be like motivates learning.

Consistency

Consistency constitutes an essential characteristic of the parent-child interaction that is necessary for learning. As the mother gives to the child consistently and dependably, he learns to trust her intentions toward him and to trust that she will meet his needs. This trust frees energy for new learning. Trust, based on the mother's reliability, means that he can trust the dependable model of functioning that she offers since it provides comfort and satisfaction. In effect, the child can trust the mother to teach him. In addition, when the child can begin to understand the recurrent experiences of his world and to find pleasure in becoming organized through internalizing consistent patterns from the mother, he begins to develop trust, not only in her, but also in his own ability to learn how to master. He trusts his capacity to learn to function responsively and harmoniously with his environment and to learn to manage himself.[8] Later, as the child continues to develop, trust carries him through the years of increasing frustration as the parents do not meet all of his needs, hold increasing expectations regarding his learning, and require him to give up, to some extent, his own wishes and ideas. The feeling of trust in what another person has to teach, in that person as a teacher, and in one's own ability to learn provides essential dynamics for learning.

Satisfaction and Frustration

The parent must provide in the relationship a balance between satisfaction and frustration in order to promote learning. When the mother nurtures and gives love, warmth, and protection, the child invests the mother with psychological meaning and interest as a need satisfier. She becomes very important to him.[9] In these conditions of trusting feelings exchanged between parent and child, love comes to have meaning to the child since he has experienced the reality of its rewards. The prize of love becomes another dynamic in learning. The child attempts to master the learning tasks expected of him by the parent and attempts to learn how to conform to expectations in order to retain the prize of love. When, on the contrary, no relationship of trust has been developed, love has no meaning as is evident in the case of delinquents who have no motivation for controlling impulses and for conforming. The wish to earn the satisfactions from being loved or liked motivates learning.

Trust in a dependable and satisfying relationship makes possible the rewards of love. Satisfaction, however, is not sufficient. The parents must also frustrate the child to some extent. Without masterable frustration, the child would never learn. The frustration arouses sufficient anxiety for the child to begin to pay attention to and to try to learn how to master new aspects of his situation related to these frustrations.[10] As the mother increasingly frustrates her growing child, he learns more and more effectively how to operate on the reality principle and to carry his expected age-sex role. Frustration promotes increasing differentiation of ego functions and satisfaction promotes integration. When the child is too greatly frustrated in the parental relationship, he becomes overwhelmed with anxiety, which disorganizes ego functioning.[11] Too little frustration, on the other hand, may leave the child embedded in his dependency and may not provide sufficient incentive for development which, in this view, is a process of differentiation and integration set in motion by learning at the appropriate stage of maturation.

Passivity and Activity

Finally, the interaction must provide a balance between passivity and activity on the part of the mother or parents. Ego theory assumes that learning occurs in response to stimuli from the environment. Parents who provide passive relationships may fail adequately to stimulate a passive child to become interested in his environment and to arouse his "spontaneous interest" in new learning and doing.[12] Other parents may fail adequately to protect the sensitive child from being overwhelmed by the impact of too many stimuli or stimuli to which he is particularly sensitive. The parent who furnishes a balance optimal for the given child sets in motion the child's own capacities for initiative, that is, his ability to channel energy into goal-directed behavior and to utilize trial-and-error methods in learning and in practicing to consolidate and integrate learning. When the parent does too much for the child, the child is not sufficiently encouraged to learn for himself. On the other hand, when the parent does too little for the child, the demands placed on the child's initiative may disorganize him. Initiative is the inner urge to try things out and to invent. It leads to trial-and-error learning and to the invention of new means of problem-solving.

DEVELOPING THE HELPING RELATIONSHIP

The viewpoint of ego psychology proposes that the human environment—particularly parental relationships—furnishes not only the essential learning experiences for the child but also the climate that activates the dynamics of learning. The child's reactions to these experiences constitute learning, and the learning, when it is internalized by the child, can either promote development of ego capacities or hinder that development. If the child can identify with the parent and trust him to furnish a model of consistent patterns, if the parent—through frustration-derived anxiety—prods him to learn and rewards learning with love, and if the stimulation of the parent's expectations of an appropriate rate of learning allow and encourage the exercise of his own initiative, the child can internalize the teaching of the parent and develop his own capacities. This approach assumes that for an adult "with defective ego functioning to learn again is similar to . . . learning in children."[13] If we accept the assumption that human beings tend to learn predominantly from other human beings, and the assumption that this learning involves internalization of ideas, perceptions, feelings, values, and activity patterns from significant others, and if we concede the proposition that certain characteristics of human relationships are necessary for this learning, then we have a theoretical frame of reference that can be used in a method for developing or strengthening the helping relationship. A relationship that possesses these qualities provides the necessary conditions for learning because it initiates inner mechanisms that make it possible for the individual to learn. In this view, learning constitutes a dynamic inner process that is set in motion by qualities in the relationship between the learner and the one from whom he learns. From identification, or the feelings of oneness that flow between the learner and the one from whom he learns, come the dynamic wish to be like and the empathic sharing of feelings and ideas. From the feelings of trust in self and others that flow between the learner and the one from whom he learns comes the dynamic of trusting the one who teaches and trusting self to learn. From the balanced relationship experiences and feelings of satisfaction and of frustration that flow between the learner and the one from whom he learns come the motivating feelings of anxiety that propel the ego toward activity and toward learning, as well as the wish for the rewards of love for achieving new learning. From the balanced experiences of passively receiving and actively doing as a result of external stimulation comes the desire for the use of inner initiative and the use of energy in goal-directed behavior and in new learning.

These ideas lead to the view of the helping relationship as a way of providing the client with an association that has characteristics tending to develop qualities of feeling that motivate new learning and therefore to promote changes that enhance social functioning. The relationship sets in motion dynamics that make it possible for the client to utilize the experiences provided by the helping situation and to accept the practitioner's influence toward improvement of functioning and of problem-solving. The relationship provides the means whereby the external experiences become a process of internalization with resulting increased integration and development of the individual's ability to carry his role. It is pertinent now to inquire about the ways in which the practitioner can achieve a relationship that possesses these characteristics.

Identification in the Relationship

The practitioner starts with the idea that unless he can identify with the client the client cannot identify with him. In order to identify with the client, the practitioner must be able to experience a feeling of oneness with the common humanity of the client. It is the life circumstances that have differed and not the shared human nature. As the practitioner learns about the cultural factors contributing to personality development and as he comes to see this development largely as a result of learning and reactions to learning rather than as a result of innate deficiencies, he can better understand human behavior. An understanding of the life experiences of clients and of the ways in which they affect the realization of inborn potentials makes it easier to accept individual differences. Drama, literature, and art also contribute to an awareness of the variety and complexity of human conditions, the depth and height of human experiences that mold behavior. The practitioner's ability to reconstruct mentally the probable nature of the client's experiences that may have contributed to present outcomes helps the practitioner to identify with him. As Spitz has suggested, identification represents a state of heightened awareness and sensitivity to the other person. In Jerome Kagan's view, it represents a belief that self shares some characteristic of another person or a wish to do so.[14]

On the other hand, the practitioner's own strong defenses against dependency, against particular drives or drive expressions, and against regressive tendencies may interfere with identification. The strong prevailing cultural value of independence has developed in most adults a correspondingly strong need to deny or to minimize dependent longings. The client's dependency can revive this inner problem and cause the practitioner defensively to misperceive the client's realistic dependency needs. For the same reason, the practitioner may see some kinds of dependency, such as dependency caused by old age or by illness, as more acceptable than others, such as that caused by unemployment. When the inner issues have not been well settled, the client's expression of sexuality or aggression in culturally disapproved ways can stir up anxiety in the practitioner and, to some extent, rejection of the client. Since the process of growing up tends to develop strong defenses against regressive childhood patterns of thinking, feeling, and acting, it may be difficult for the practitioner to accept the fact that many clients still use primary process thinking: To wish is to have it happen. It may prove similarly difficult to accept the fact that the client still operates on the pleasure principle and has never learned to utilize the reality principle or the fact that he may never have learned to relate except as a child with his parents. The practitioner must know that the client's problems may arouse anxieties in himself, and he must be prepared to use the ethic of self-awareness. He needs to become conscious of his reactions to the client and to learn to handle them so that they do not interfere with his ability to identify with the client and to perceive him realistically.

The ability to identify with the client is the ability to see the client's world through the eyes of the client, to perceive the way he is thinking and feeling, and to enter into his psychological and social realities. Since many of the modes used by the client now seem foreign to the practitioner, he must be willing to learn from the client. The practitioner begins to identify with the client by using generalizations available from knowledge about persons in similar life situations. He also should become aware of and sensitively learn from this client about his individual uniqueness. These two mental exercises, together with self-awareness, enable the practitioner mentally and empathically to enter into the client's life experiences.[15]

Although the client usually intuits the practitioner's feelings and attitudes toward him, the practitioner's explicit expressions of feelings of empathy and acceptance stemming from the practitioner's identification with the client particularly help to promote identification. The purposeful use of feelings and values by the practitioner constitutes an essential technique for developing the client's ability to identify. Since the client, when first seen, is in some kind of stressful situation, the practitioner begins to develop the relationship by reaching out to the client and using empathy to build a bridge of feeling between himself and the client. Use of empathy constitutes the most essential technique for beginning to develop the relationship. The practitioner may, for example, say that he realizes that the parent feels distressed over his child's difficulty, that the parent is troubled about his relationship problems with the child or with his spouse, or that he can see that the prospect of an operation is worrisome, and so forth. The practitioner's ability to feel with the client begins to lessen the psychological and social gap between them, provides emotional support, and starts to create some degree of the sense of oneness. When the practitioner uses empathy early in the interview situation, it communicates to the client the importance he places on the client's becoming related to him as well as the practitioner's willingness to try to feel with him in his stress. The more the practitioner can, throughout the case, sensitively and intuitively feel with the client in his difficulty and anxiety as he attempts to deal with his problem and to change and the more clearly he communicates these feelings to the client, the more he tends to promote the client's responsive identification with him. Since these feelings probably come from the fact that the client and the practitioner are joined in their efforts to help to improve the client's situation, they provide a source of considerable emotional support.

The practitioner also purposefully communicates expressions of accepting feelings. He finds ways in which to express his acceptance of the client as a person and of the client's differences from himself, while at the same time he exercises his professional responsibility to evaluate the client's behavior as constructive or destructive, as useful or self-defeating. The practitioner can express acceptance of the person in several ways: "I can see that you might feel this way, but"; "I can see that you have had severe provocation, but"; "I realize that endless diaper-washing, cleaning, and care of the children is hard to bear, but." The first part of the communication expresses acceptance of the person and the fact that his behavior was the best that he could achieve; the *but* in the second part of the communication conveys evaluation of the client's behavior. The practitioner frequently uses *but* to suggest that, with the help of the practitioner, the client may be able to find more effective ways of coping or may be able to work on the difficulty that he has been having in the past in order to bring about some improvements in the future. The practitioner should also remind himself that the client does not feel really accepted when he has revealed only the best side of himself. He wonders how the practitioner would feel toward him if he knew how often he hits Johnny, yells at his wife, or has failed at his various tasks. The practitioner is careful not to take the client's tendency to put his best foot forward as the whole story and makes clear to the client that his feeling toward him will remain unchanged if the client can bring himself to talk about other, less socially approved attributes, thoughts, and feelings. Only by empathically putting himself in the client's place can the practitioner visualize the other aspects of himself that the client needs to talk about: the unseen, dark side of the moon. Only through self-awareness can the practitioner face the possibility that, in some instances, his own need to have the client better than he is may block the client's communicating the depths of his difficulty, because the client sees the practitioner as "so different" that he believes that the practitioner could not understand or accept him.

The technique of purposeful use of values may also further mutual identification. The practitioner may expressly communicate his own value position. When the client has failed in one of his major life roles, has become entangled in sexual difficulties, or has been adjudged an offender, the practitioner's clear communication about his value position, based on professional values, may be a beginning emotional bridge to the client. The practitioner may point out that it is not his job to decide on guilt or innocence, but that he believes in the value of commitment to a relationship and of sexual expression within a relationship. He may state that he believes in the necessity for being able to manage oneself in order to make it possible for people to get along together. Children who have been exploited or abused by parents often feel guilty and wonder what the practitioner believes. The practitioner must refrain from condemning the parent, but at the same time he must offer his evaluation of the situation by stating that his prime value is the child's need for protection and care and that this consideration must come first in order that the child can learn how to be a happy person and to get along better.

The practitioner purposefully uses feelings and values to indicate his identification with the person while he keeps himself free to evaluate in a nonjudgmental way the client's behavior as a basis for helping him to change. He thus retains his professional identity as separate from that of the client. In cases of marital conflict and parent-child difficulties, he may also need to make clear the fact that he does not identify with the client against other family members or vice versa and that he is "for" each of his clients. Each individual caught in a relationship conflict usually fears that the practitioner will identify with the other member in the conflict against him. The practitioner also emphasizes his purpose of strengthening the client's identity by making clear that the purpose of helping is to increase the client's capacity to carry his life role, that the client and not the practitioner has this responsibility, and that the practitioner will respect and support his ability to make choices for himself. When the practitioner has been able to develop the bond of identification with the client, he can usually assume that the client has, to some extent, a feeling of relatedness with him and a wish to accept help from him. The practitioner can utilize this motivation as he attempts to influence the client to use this help and to achieve change.

Consistency in the Relationship

In order to develop the client's feeling of trust in the practitioner and in self, the practitioner must provide a sustained and consistently supporting experience. The sustained quality of the relationship can be crucial for clients who have never achieved object constancy or a belief in the permanency of relationships because of experiences with life figures who came and went in an unstable manner. For this reason, the practitioner uses the technique of demonstration since he not only promises to stand by the client but does so in reality. Through self-awareness and self-discipline, he manages his own tendency to start enthusiastically and then to slacken his efforts when the going becomes difficult or to visit haphazardly or irregularly. Frequently, clients test the practitioner's interest and intention to desert them by breaking appointments, by becoming hostile or provocative, or by negativistic behavior, thus using the defense of abandoning before they can be abandoned. The practitioner demonstrates the sustained and consistent quality of the relationship when he continues to go out to clients despite rebuff, continues to offer appointments, and continues to show concern and willingness to help. Since deprived clients, like children, cannot relate to many people, they distrust the need of social agencies to parcel out their affairs and to divide up aspects of themselves for consideration among a variety of persons. The practitioner, therefore, gives attention to the necessity for centering responsibility for giving help in one person whenever this plan seems feasible. Regular and frequent appointments also demonstrate the sustained quality since the client sees the practitioner sufficiently often to reinforce his belief in the fact that he will continue. Until trust has been developed, the client cannot maintain this belief without constant reinforcement from the practitioner's presence.[16] The practitioner also demonstrates consistency and dependability in the way he offers services. His attentive listening in the interview demonstrates interest and concern. He makes few promises and always scrupulously keeps those that he has made. If he agrees, for example, to look up information needed by the client or to secure a resource, he does so promptly; postponing and procrastinating will make the client distrust his dependability. For the same reason, he always keeps appointments and always notifies the client when he cannot do so. As has been suggested, the frequency of the interview is decided by the client's needs rather than by the practitioner's convenience. This demonstration of concern tends to build the client's confidence in the practitioner's reliability.

The technique of the purposeful use of feelings also contributes to the development of the client's trust in the practitioner. When the client becomes hostile or aggressive, the practitioner maintains a consistently positive affect and does not retaliate. Because many clients struggling with their difficulties tend to project their own negative feelings onto the practitioner and to become hostile or difficult, the practitioner may find it hard to accept some kinds of clients or some kinds of behavior. He may discover that he is particularly vulnerable to hostility or insistence. Through self-awareness, he becomes conscious of his human tendency to react with anger, impatience, or anxiety. Acknowledging how he feels, he can then find ways of keeping his feelings out of the helping situation.

Whenever it is realistically possible, the practitioner expresses confidence in the client's ability to better his situation and to improve matters. He also uses his own feelings supportively with the client by expressing courage, cheer, hope, or other feelings that will bolster the client's feelings of adequacy. He conveys, and helps the client to internalize, feelings of optimism about his capacity to learn.

The purposeful use of values can also prove helpful in the development of trust. The practitioner especially needs to explain his value position in relation to confidentiality. He should explain the need for records, the purpose they serve, and the circumstances under which information from the records is made available to other professional persons in helping the client or his family. As a safeguard of confidentiality, most social agencies, clinics, and hospitals require the client's written consent to give out information regarding him.

The practitioner uses the dynamic of the client's increased trust in self and practitioner to encourage the client to accept guidance in learning how to see himself and his situation more realistically and how to deal with it more effectively.

Satisfaction and Frustration in the Relationship

As has been suggested, all clients, to a greater or lesser degree, require some satisfaction for dependency needs, some succor, and some support. When the client can trust the practitioner's support and values his caring, he has become teachable. If the helping relationship provides not only satisfactions but also some frustrations in the form of requirements and expectations, another dynamic will have been added. In Herbert S. Strean's terms, "Focused on the developmental need of his client, the caseworker offers appropriate doses of gratification, frustration, and education."[17] When the client can begin to trust self and practitioner, the practitioner can almost certainly assume that the client has come to value positively the practitioner's liking. His need for "love" from the practitioner motivates the client to try to meet the practitioner's expectations. The practitioner remembers dependably to furnish this reward. He expresses concern for the client's well-being and happiness. By the tones of his voice, he conveys warmth and the fact that he cares, that he considers the client worthy of nurturing. However, he regulates the degree of warmth to the client's tolerance for closeness. He recognizes each achievement by the client and recognizes past and present accomplishments. He shows pleasure at each step forward and sustains the client with continued warmth during the inevitable steps backward that occur in temporary regressions and the failures. He always lets the client know when he is on the right track and doing well.

The client, as he is asked to utilize suggestions for change, will become anxious about the possible loss of the prize of love. This anxiety may motivate him to try to meet expectations for change. For each client, the practitioner must provide the optimal balance between satisfaction and frustration. The greater the limitations in client capacity, the longer the practitioner may have to provide satisfaction for dependency needs before requiring much from the client. He listens, he accepts, he gives, he advises. Gradually, he introduces the reality principle, lessening the giving and increasing the demands. For the clients who have learned to trust and who can identify easily with him, the practitioner can, early in the relationship, voice realistic expectations and can increase these throughout the contact. He always tries to remember, however, that satisfactions and frustrations must balance. The Aid to Families with Dependent Children (AFDC) mother, harassed by the burdens of meeting the children's needs without the support of the father, requires from the practitioner an interest in her own health, well-being, and happiness. In each interview, the practitioner may need to alternate his listening, accepting, and giving of warmth with making suggestions that the client begin to face and work toward realistic changes. Clients who have been progressing well may, at times, need a regressive retreat to the sheltered and comfortable haven of dependency in the relationship before they can advance again. Sometimes chronically ill or dependent clients can function reasonably well if they can return from time to time to the supporting practitioner or agency for refueling.

The practitioner who fails to expect enough of his client

should ask himself whether he needs to keep the client dependent. This characteristic of providing in the relationship some frustration through expectations of growth can be considered the element of authority that is legitimately inherent in the role of the practitioner. Because of authoritative knowledge about what the client needs to learn in order to develop his capacities and because of skill in helping him to achieve this learning, the practitioner has the authority to evaluate need for change and to make some demands for change. Sometimes, practitioners ask too much too quickly and sometimes, too little. Self-awareness should help the practitioner to question whether he rejects the client's dependency when he asks too much too soon. He must learn to be aware of his own need for or fear of dependency or of hostility. Sometimes, the client becomes hostile when the practitioner's expectations frustrate him. The practitioner then responds with increased meeting of dependency needs. The relationship then duplicates the parental one in which the parent feels too guilty to frustrate.[18] If the practitioner preserves the optimal balance between feelings of frustration and satisfaction in the relationship, he can mobilize the client's anxiety over loss of his warmth, caring, and interest by his requests for change. This anxiety represents the inner push toward ego activity, problem-solving, and change. The practitioner can use the client's feelings of discomfort to channel activity into fruitful work and problem-solving; he must remember also to recognize and reward the client's achievement.

Passivity and Activity in the Relationship

The optimum balance between activity and passivity on the part of the practitioner furnishes the right amount of support and encouragement for the client to rally his own forces. The optimum balance varies with the client and usually varies at different times in the case. The client usually requires more activity from the practitioner during early interviews when the relationship has not yet been established and the client is unfamiliar with his own and with the practitioner's role. Moreover, clients who tend to use passive ego patterns—especially deprived and limited clients—may, throughout the case, need a great deal of support and stimulation. Other clients with greater inner motivation and capacity may require a relatively passive relationship. Most clients are somewhere between these two extremes. With the extremely passive client, the practitioner may need to begin the relationship by actively doing for the client. He may demonstrate the actuality that problems can be solved and that one can utilize energy in solving them. He continually draws on his own sources of energy to interest the client traumatized by the continual frustrations of poverty in new possibilities and to encourage him to work toward change. He supportively lends his own ego strengths. When the practitioner shows that he is willing to extend himself for the client, to do for and with him, he may be able to stimulate a responsive activity and initiative in the client. When the client's anxiety has immobilized him, when he is extremely passive and dependent, or when extreme stress has exhausted his capacities, the practitioner may need to take over and do for the client to tide him over the crisis. He utilizes this temporary measure without guilt until the client can become more active. An article on the subject describes these aspects of "direction-finding" and "direction-implementation."[19]

The practitioner also uses various interviewing techniques in an active stimulating manner. It is the frequency with which he initiates in the interview and the way in which he provides direction, rather than the specific technique, that change the balance toward activity. Verbal expressions are probably more active than head-nodding, leaning forward, and encouraging facial expressions. Guiding suggestions, verbalizations for the client, reformulations, and advice are examples of active interviewing techniques. The dynamic that the practitioner attempts to develop through the balance between activity and passivity is the dynamic of initiative. The practitioner uses active techniques by invitations and suggestions that encourage the client to communicate and that guide him in doing so. He uses passive techniques when he listens, waits for the client to begin the interview, and allows silences to develop in the interview. The practitioner hopes to encourage the client to use his own initiative and, to the fullest extent possible, to direct his energies toward problem-solving and change.

The practitioner also uses the technique of explicating the professional value position of self-direction and helps the client to understand its meaning in his case. Some practitioners tend to be too active in the interview situation and some tend to be too passive. Some practitioners fail sufficiently to encourage the client to take beginning steps, perhaps fearing that he will fail or that he lacks capacity, or is not ready. Too great passivity on the practitioner's part often stems from his unwillingness to extend himself on behalf of the client. On the other hand, the tendency toward too great an exercise of initiative activity for a client indicates that the practitioner ought to be aware of his need to have all the answers to a client's questions about how to be a more adequate parent, spouse, or person.

Some clients come to the interview situation having done their homework and are prepared to voice their concerns. These clients need only empathic acceptance, support, and approval to continue working toward change. Other clients would only flounder without active help in focusing their communication and bringing out what is troubling them.

Practitioner's Responsibility

From the discussion of the helping relationship, it becomes apparent that the practitioner can develop the relationship only if he has an ethical commitment to become self-aware and self-disciplined and to use professional values. Working with needful and less-than-adequate clients whose life experiences have ill prepared them to meet their responsibilities arouses emotional responses in the practitioner. Such responses are human and expectable, but he must become aware of his feelings before he can acquire the ability to accept them and to find ways of handling them outside of the helping situation. The practitioner's own needs for success may motivate him to push the client to do well. The practitioner may also push the client toward change in ways that meet the practitioner's needs and not those of the client. He must consistently examine his reactions to his client, to particular clients, and to particular problems, in order to become aware of how to guard against overinvolvement or underinvolvement. When the practitioner overidentifies or underidentifies with the client, he needs to inquire into the reasons.

The controlled quality of the helping relationship and its purposefulness distinguish it from personal relationships. The purposefulness of the relationship lies in the fact that the practitioner purposefully develops it as a way of setting in motion dynamic motivational forces that help the client to utilize help and to achieve change. The purpose of the relationship is to motivate and support the client, and the client is always the center of concern in the relationship.

In the professional helping relationship, contrary to life relationships, the practitioner carries the major responsibility for developing and using the relationship. He consistently goes out to the client and takes responsibility for finding ways for developing the bond or strengthening it and for utilizing the dynamics that it sets in motion. He also takes responsibility for handling problems that interfere with the effectiveness of the relationship. Some problems that interfere with effectiveness derive from transference and countertransference.

TRANSFERENCE

Since all ego functions become patterned, the same tendency applies to the function of the management of object relationships. Individuals tend to use previous patterns of relating and to transfer to the others feelings, attitudes, and ways of relating derived from former significant life figures. These patterns may not be appropriate for the realistic situation. To some extent, the skill of the practitioner, the nurturing, caring quality of the relationship, and the dynamic of identification reactivate feelings, perceptions, and patterns relative to parent figures. To some extent also, this transference may prove helpful since the client endows the practitioner with the power to help him. The client needs to be able to trust the capacity of the practitioner and to identify with his strength and his ability to help. Nevertheless, too strong and powerful a practitioner may promote dependency and passivity. It is probable that some transference elements exist in any helping relationship and that the client tends to project onto the practitioner the qualities that he needs in order to feel secure and supported. However, practitioners tend to keep the relationship reality-based by the various means that help the client to feel that the practitioner is a real person and that keep the client's interest focused on his own situation and not, primarily, on the relationship.

When dealing with deprived clients who must have a stable figure with whom to identify before they can begin to learn and who must first experience satisfaction of dependency needs before they can begin to move on to develop more adult patterns, the practitioner may purposefully deepen the transference. In this event, he may use the relationship as a method of treatment. He provides for the client a positive relationship experience the purpose of which is to develop trust and to free energy tied up in an anxious striving for dependency satisfactions so that the client can begin to master other learning tasks.

Frequently, the practitioner finds that the client has a negative transference or elements of a negative transference toward him. Negative transference reactions tend to stem from seeing the practitioner as an authority figure or as a depriving parent or from endowing him with other qualities and attributes that are a source of the client's hostility toward previous life figures. When the client has a positive transference reaction toward the practitioner, the practitioner uses it as a dynamic to encourage change. However, when the client has a negative transference reaction, the practitioner usually needs to discuss this reaction. He tries to help the client to use reality-testing to separate his past feelings from the present reality.

COUNTERTRANSFERENCE

The practitioner, like the client, is human. The countertransference constitutes the practitioner's transferring to the client attitudes and feelings belonging to his own past relationships. The countertransference becomes evident when he overidentifies or underidentifies with the client. Underidentification springs from the fact that the client arouses negative reactions because of some similarity with a person with whom the practitioner has experienced previous difficulties. In this case, the practitioner unconsciously acts toward the client as if he were that person. He is unable to see the client's strengths or good points, or he takes sides against him or is unable to give warmth and support. When the practitioner overidentifies and tends to see only positives, he may be unable to help the client face problems or to face what needs to be changed. To some extent, overidentification usually comes from identifying the client with some aspect of self and then protecting him as one would wish to be protected. Self-awareness, supervisory help, or consultation may make it possible to correct the countertransference.

COMMUNICATION

The discussion regarding ways of developing the professional relationship should not be concluded without some reference to communication. Communication might be conceptualized as a tool that makes possible the development of the relationship. Communication, both verbal and nonverbal, is the telephone wire over which travel the practitioner's expressions of feelings, values, positive evaluation of the client, and his encouragement of the client's responsive expressions of feelings and ideas. For this reason, the practitioner tends to communicate explicitly his feelings, values, caring, support, and expectations. In giving help, however, he knows that actions speak louder than words. It is not the promise of help but the nature and quality of actual help received that is conducive to trust in help. For this reason the nonverbal communication conveyed by demonstration can often be more effective than words.

Blocked communication will always interfere with the relationship. The practitioner, therefore, consistently attempts to help the client convey his thoughts and concerns effectively, and he attempts always to make clear his own.

In this review of the measures that tend to promote the development of the helping relationship, no attempt is made to imply any time order. The practitioner interweaves the use of these measures, sometimes beginning with one, sometimes with another, and varies their use at different times. He also uses these measures with varying degrees of emphasis depending upon the demands of the given case.

Although the discussion here has dealt only with establishing the helping relationship, it should be observed that some clients cannot at a given time form a relationship with the practitioner. The mentally ill, the convicted offender, the drug addict, and others may find a relationship intolerable. Their fragile ego strengths may make it necessary to deny that they have any problems for which a helping relationship would be necessary. For these and others, a preliminary phase of making contact may be required. The practitioner finds some way to establish contact and then through that contact to begin to develop a relationship. He first begins to form an affective contact with the client in some structured social setting, such as a day-care center. This contact, like the professional relationship, differs from social relationships in that it is still purposeful and, on the practitioner's part, is controlled. The practitioner gauges his giving and the kinds of giving in relation to the client's ability to take at the given time. The purpose of the contact is to handle the client's ambivalence toward closeness and distance in a relationship in such a way that the client can become comfortable with the practitioner. When contact has been established, the practitioner can then attempt to develop a helping relationship.

Notes

1. Samuel Ritvo and Albert J. Solnit, "Influences of Early Mother-Child Interaction on Identification Processes," *Psychoanalytic Study of the Child,* 13:64–85 (New York: International Universities Press, 1958).

2. Eleanor Pavenstedt, ed., *The Drifters: Children of Disorganized Lower-Class Families* (Boston: Little, Brown & Co., 1967), pp. 88–93.

3. Sally Provence and Samuel Ritvo, "Effects of Deprivation on Institutionalized Infants: Disturbances in Development of Relationship to Inanimate Objects," in *Psychoanalytic Study of the Child,* vol. 16 (New York: International Universities Press, 1961), 189–205.

4. Sibylle K. Escalona, *The Roots of Individuality: Normal Patterns of Development in Infancy* (Chicago: Aldine Publishing Company, 1968), pp. 5–8, 238–47.

5. René A. Spitz, *No and Yes: On the Genesis of Human Communication* (New York: International Universities Press, 1957), chap. 7.

6. Therese Benedek, "Parenthood as a Developmental Phase: A Contribution to the Libido Theory," *American Psychoanalytic Association Journal,* 7:389–417 (July 1959).

7. Pavenstedt, *The Drifters,* pp. 132–37.

8. Erik H. Erikson, *Childhood and Society,* 2d ed. rev. (New York: W. W. Norton and Company, 1963), pp. 247–51.

9. Provence and Ritvo, "Effects of Deprivation."

10. René A. Spitz, *The First Year of Life: A Psychoanalytic Study of Normal and Deviant Development of Object Relations* (New York: International Universities Press, 1965), chap. 7.

11. Provence and Ritvo, "Effects of Deprivation."

12. Pavenstedt, *The Drifters,* chaps. 4 and 10.

13. Herbert S. Strean, "Role Theory, Role Models, and Casework: Review of the Literature and Practice Applications," *Social Work.* 12:77–88 (April 1967).

14. Jerome Kagan, "Acquisition and Significance of Sex Typing and Sex Role Identity," in *Review of Child Development Research,* vol. 1, ed. Martin L. Hoffman and Lois W. Hoffman (New York: Russell Sage Foundation, 1964), 146–47.

15. Pauline Lide, "An Experimental Study of Empathic Functioning," *Social Service Review,* 41:23–30 (March 1967).

16. Pavenstedt, *The Drifters,* pp. 64–71.

17. Herbert S. Strean, "Casework with Ego-fragmented Parents," *Social Casework,* 49:222–27 (April 1968).

18. Spitz, *First Year,* p. 148.

19. David Hallowitz et al., "The Assertive Counseling Component of Therapy," *Social Casework,* 48:543–48 (November 1967).

FOUR

Focus on Resistance to Taking Help

Use of ego theory provides related diagnostic and treatment categories of resistance: resistance motivated by not knowing what to expect in the way of help; resistance motivated by conscious positive expectations of the kind of help wanted; resistance motivated by negative conscious expectations of help; resistance motivated by unconscious positive and negative expectations of help. The matching treatment categories are aimed at increasing motivation for taking help by dealing appropriately with the client's expectations.

REGARDLESS of whether the contact between client and practitioner begins face-to-face or over the telephone, it always entails an interview situation, a characteristic that continues throughout the giving of help. It may prove valuable, therefore, to examine the nature of the interview between the practitioner and the client. Members of the helping professions have developed the concept that the interview is an interaction process during which the behavior of the practitioner stimulates a response from the client, which, in turn, stimulates a response from the practitioner and so forth. The idea of reciprocity in the interview situation directs attention to changes in client responses related to the practitioner's efforts, during intake, to enable him to take help. In the helping professions it is generally assumed that behavioral changes result from the interaction of the characteristics that the client brings to the given situation and the characteristics of the situation itself. The client's response to offers of help results both from his own contributions and from those of the practitioner. Both must be understood in order to understand the client's behavior. Ideally, the responses should lead to his increased readiness to accept help in relation to some problem. However, the opposite may occur and the client may resist taking help or using help. Resistance is defined here as client behaviors motivated by discomfort aroused by lack of congruence between the expectations of the practitioner and those of the client regarding help or regarding their reciprocal roles. Support for the propositions that resistance to taking help and resistance to using help constitute the two major categories of resistance will be presented, and related treatment categories for each type of resistance will be proposed.

DIAGNOSIS AND TREATMENT OF RESISTANCE

The proposals which are offered here for understanding and dealing with resistance were developed through the method of analysis of the content of initial interviews as reflected in the casework literature. Analysis showed that the content of casework interviews fell into two major groups: content dealing with the client's relationship to his life situation and content dealing with his relationship to the helping situation, such as the kinds of help the client wanted, his reaction to the help offered, and so forth. This dual focus continued for the duration of the contact. A corollary of this finding leads to the conclusion that the practitioner must focus his attention not only on what needs to be changed in the client-problem situation and how to achieve this change but also on what needs to be changed in the client-practitioner situation. Interaction in the interview situation includes both the client's willingness to take and to use help and the practitioner's ability to offer help in a way that maximizes the client's potential. In the helping situation, problems may develop from the client's relationship to that situation as they have developed from his relationship to his life situation.

In addition to a major focus on the problems, the use of theory in a helping method focuses also on the helping process and furnishes a systematic way of working toward change. Ego and role theories previously utilized in the discussion of the method of ego analysis can furnish a basis for understanding and treating the client's problems related to the helping situation. The principle that the client must participate in the helping process and the corollary that requires the practitioner to engage the client's efforts in working toward change impel the practitioner to examine the meaning of engaging or involving the client. It means that the client, as well as the practitioner, wants change; that the client is willing to begin working toward change; and that the client wants and is willing to use help to achieve change. If the client resists, the opposite holds true. Willing and wanting are related to motivation; it is assumed that all behavior is motivated. In this frame of reference, client willingness to participate in the helping process constitutes a special example of motivated behavior, as does also resistance to participation. Implementation of the principle of client participation requires, among other things, a theory-based method for diagnosing and dealing with the motivational aspects of client behavior in relation to the helping process itself. So long as the client's motivation propels him to ask for help and to remain to utilize help, there is no problem. When, however, his motivation propels him to avoid or to flee from using help, there may be one or several problems of resistance requiring diagnosis and treatment. On the assumption that resistance is motivated, the nature of that motivation should be examined by the use of both ego and role theories.

Ego theory proposes that individuals tend to continue behaviors that bring satisfaction and that avoid dissatisfaction or discomfort. If the client perceives helping as an opportunity for lessening dissatisfaction and for increasing satisfaction in relation to his life situation, it can be concluded logically that he will tend to continue in the helping situation. In a related way, it can be considered that, when the client perceives help as predominantly bringing dissatisfaction or discomfort, he will tend to discontinue. Ego theory postulates that the individual experiences discomfort or anxiety in situations that tax the coping abilities of the ego. Isidore Portnoy quotes K. Goldstein to the effect that anxiety arises when some discrepancy exists "between the individual's capacities and the demands made on him."[1] Similarly, in relation to role theory, we consider that role strain that taxes the individual's ability to carry the role tends to cause discomfort. Specifically, role theory proposes that the assumption of a new role may cause discomfort or anxiety since it may require learning new behaviors to carry the role responsibilities. Because resisting behaviors characteristically propel the client toward avoidance of help, it can be assumed, therefore, that the motivations for the resistance have the nature of discomfort and that this discomfort arises in the interaction process in the interview. No matter what the client brings to the interview situation, resisting behavior becomes problematical only when the practitioner confronts the client with the possibility and actuality of help.

Participation in helping requires the client to assume the client role and then, if he utilizes help, to carry the client role. Assuming the role means that he contracts with the practitioner to become a client of the agency and that he accepts the terms of help and the role responsibilities that require him to become more active in thinking about and in dealing with his difficulties. Carrying the client role requires him to become a user of help, to perceive his problem and the limiting and supporting factors that affect problem-solving, and also to utilize actively inner and outer resources in an attempt to lessen the difficulties that are limiting his coping abilities. His acceptance of the role of client indicates his willingness to try it and to find out what the role entails. Carrying the role requires willingness to learn and to utilize a set of reciprocal role behaviors as a way of achieving some goal of improved social functioning and some changes leading to better problem-solving. Both the taking and the using of help may tax ego capacities and therefore give rise to discomfort. Talking about unpleasant aspects of one's own and others' behavior, facing feelings and examining relationship difficulties, coming to decisions, and trying out new solutions may all be included in the new client role behaviors, which, with the related ego tasks, can set in motion client discomfort in regard to the helping process. From the foregoing formulations derive the two categories of resistance: resistance to taking help and resistance to using help.

However, since not all clients faced with role changes and ego tasks resist taking and using help, the circumstances that tend to set in motion resisting behaviors should be described still more carefully. Discomfort that motivates client resistance tends to arise when "client expectancies and the caseworker's behavior are not congruent."[2] Alfred Kadushin and C.F. Wieringa suggest that interruption of communication and tension or discomfort may arise from "violations" of expectations held by the client. In a similar vein, general agreement seems to exist that "the essence of any social situation lies in the mutual expectations of the participants," patterns for which have been evolved by the culture.[3] The authors of *The Anatomy of Psychotherapy* observe that discrepancies in expectations between client and practitioner result in role strain. Dissymmetry of expectations not only interferes with the therapeutic task, but can actually lead to the death of a therapeutic system.[4] H. Aronson and Betty Overall offer one definition of the concept of expectations as "anticipation of the roles, techniques, and events that will occur in therapy."[5]

Motivation is, thus, the classificatory principle for developing related diagnostic and treatment categories of resistance. It can be hypothesized that the types of treatment are based on differences in motivation and that the treatment measures are directed toward dealing with the given motivation for resistance. When the practitioner understands the motivation for the client's resistance, he may be able to forestall or minimize the resistance by dealing more appropriately and effectively with it by the use of the proposed treatment measures. The treatment measures for handling resistance can all be subsumed under treatment based on ego analysis or treatment for improving role functioning.

The above categories of resistance must be placed on a time continuum because the client's resisting behavior develops as a response to the practitioner's efforts to involve him in taking or using help. It must be recognized, therefore, that what the client brings to the interview situation, as well as the practitioner's efforts, change over time and, as a result, the nature of the client's resistance may differ at different times in the helping process. The client also may manifest the same kind or different kinds of resistance at various times in the life of the contact, and it is necessary, therefore, to specify resistance of a given type manifested by the client at the given time.

Each of the two major typologies of resistance includes four subcategories. In this chapter the first typology of resistance and treatment measures for handling it, together with each of the four subcategories, will be discussed. The second category of resistance and of related treatment measures will be discussed in chapter 7.

Use of the first typology of resistance and its subtypes furnishes a more explicit method for assessing where the client is in relation to taking help and thus indicates what will have to be changed in order to enable him to do so. Significant resistive behaviors of the client constitute criterion measures that indicate the category to which the behavior belongs. Failure to understand or handle indications of resistance may result in loss of the client or in the client's remaining passive while the practitioner does all of the work because he has been unable to involve the client in the helping process. In that event, the client fails to move toward changes in social functioning but, instead, remains in the impasse in which the practitioner found him at the time of application; or he may show regressive movement toward less adequate functioning.

The method proposed here for the diagnosis of the first category of resistance utilizes ego and role theories to assess the client's positive and negative expectations of help, both conscious and unconscious. This method rests on the assumption that when the client has expectations divergent from those of the practitioner, they tend to cause discomfort because of threats to ego capacities or to role strain. This divergence and resulting discomfort motivate the client to resist accepting help and assuming the client role. The techniques that the practitioner uses to facilitate assessment of the resistance include encouragement to the client to bring out his questions and to communicate, exploration in order to ascertain the meaning of behaviors that may be indicators of this type of resistance, probing for information, restating for clarity, and use of treatment measures with observation of the client's reactions to see whether the assessment and selection of the treatment measures was correct.

First Typology of Resistance

The first diagnostic typology of resistance deals with resistance or potential resistance that, at the given time, is evoked primarily by the client's expectations regarding the taking of help or by the client's expectations regarding the nature of help per se—that is, discomfort about assuming the client role evoked by motivations either not understood by the practitioner or discordant with the practitioner's expectations. This category includes four subcategories: A, resistance evoked by not knowing what to expect; B, resistance evoked by conscious positive expectations; C, resistance evoked by conscious negative expectations; and D, resistance evoked by unconscious positive or negative expectations.

RESISTANCE EVOKED BY NOT KNOWING WHAT TO EXPECT

Subcategory A refers to resistance that, at the given time, is evoked primarily by the client's not knowing what to expect in the way of help and by perceptual or cognitive ambiguities about the reciprocal role of client and practitioner that may interfere with mutual understanding and with role complementarity. The client may not know the resources available or the terms of service, or he may misapprehend, expecting that he will not be accepted or that the practitioner will not help, or he may not know what he wants in the way of help, often because of his own ambivalence.

A number of authorities have identified this kind of resistance. Helen Harris Perlman has dealt at some length with ways in which the client's not understanding what is involved in taking help may lead to discontinuance—that is, to resistance to taking help.[6] Herman D. Stein and Richard A. Cloward state that "the more obscure the perception of role, the greater the problems in living it."[7]

The practitioner judges that the client's behavior indicates resistance or potential resistance of this nature when it expresses cognitive or perceptual ambiguity about the reciprocal roles of client and practitioner and about what is entailed in taking help. An assessment of the following pointers may lead the practitioner to forestall resistance by using the first category of treatment measures or to explore more fully the circumstances and nature of the behavior as a basis for dealing with it. When the client does not know what he wants from the agency, including ambivalent wanting, the practitioner usually explores the circumstances that led to the application. Sometimes the client has been referred because his doctor, minister, or some one in his family thought that he needed help. The alcoholic or the mentally disturbed individual may never have done any thinking about the kind of help he wants but simply have come because he was advised to do so. A client may telephone but not want to apply in person, or, in other instances, he may be acting in response to some recent pressure to do so. He may have applied out of spite or anger without having thought through his request for help. Even though the client comes with a definite request, he may become uncertain about what he wants as the interview progresses, an indication that he is not clear about the help desired. Often, the initial interview takes place when the practitioner visits a client referred by someone outside the family because of community pressures caused by the client's social difficulties in school, or court, or home. The practitioner finds, characteristically, that the client has not considered, and does not perceive, the nature of assistance he needs. Whenever the client acts in ways that show his uncertainty about what he expects from the agency, the practitioner realizes that the client is not ready to assume the client role until the practitioner has understood and dealt with this potential motivation for resistance.

The practitioner may need to explore what is preventing the client from deciding what he wants from the agency; frequently this difficulty derives from the client being pulled in two directions. He may not be able to make up his mind whether to accept help and to work toward improving his family relationships or to get a divorce, for example. The client asks for help and then seems to wish that he had not done so. At other times, the client does not manifest ambivalence and can bring out only the side of his wishing and wanting that appears to hide feelings and desires of the opposite nature. In this case, the practitioner explores with the client both sides of the ambivalence and helps the client to discuss his doubts and reservations. He attempts to help the client examine his opposing feelings when he tends to block them out. The practitioner also probes both the reality and the rigidity of the client's ambivalent wishes, bringing them into the open. Sometimes one side of the ambivalence has little substance. In other instances, the two-way pull may completely block acceptance of help until the practitioner has assisted the client to deal with his ambivalence. Throughout the entire contact, the client may need to consider with the practitioner the problem for which he is seeking help, since, characteristically, one problem leads to another problem and the client may feel caught in continuing with the agency unless he is certain that he wants help with the added facets of his difficulty.

Another way in which not knowing may motivate resistance derives from the fact that the client may have little understanding of the agency and the services available. Many clients have only vague ideas about what an agency is like, or they may have misconceptions about it derived from hearsay or from their experiences with other agencies. The practitioner usually explores the client's relevant past experiences as well as other bases for misconceptions. One reason for a client's inability to decide on what he wants may be his ignorance about available services or the terms on which they are available. In other instances, exploration may reveal that the client has a fund of misinformation or partial information that needs correction or supplementation. A client who is referred or a client whom the practitioner visits because of a referral from a court, for example, may confuse the agency with the court or assume that the agency wants to punish him or does not really want to help. In other instances, a probationer or prisoner may be unaware of the choices available to him within the authoritative framework. Lack of clarity about service structure in secondary settings and about the way the practitioner relates to the structure may stimulate resistance. For example, the patient may misperceive the practitioner in the medical setting as an extension of the doctor's authority rather than as a helper. The client on parole or probation, if he is not aware of the way in which the practitioner's services relate to the authority structure, may resist accepting help. The client needs to understand not only the agency but also what taking help involves. Services available to clients today are both diverse and specialized. Their specific advantages or disadvantages, their aim and nature, and the terms of availability may be completely new to the client. The practitioner always stimulates the client to ask his questions and to seek the information he wants.

The client may not understand why he is asked to give information or the nature of the intake or application process. He often manifests this ignorance by the inability to ask questions or to discuss the terms of help, such as the length of time, the steps leading toward improved problem-solving, the involvement of other family members, the cost, and so forth. Ignorance about the realities of becoming a client may later give rise to resistance when he gets home and wonders what he may have let himself in for when he agreed to accept help.

The client may also lack information about, or may misperceive, the nature of the reciprocal roles of client and practitioner. He may express his confusion about his responsibility to participate actively in working toward change by behaviors that indicate either his wishes for or his fears of the practitioner's taking responsibility for providing answers and a magical cure. He may also question how his becoming a client will affect his life roles. He may want to know whether the practitioner will interfere in his marriage, take the spouse's side in the conflict, point out his inadequacies as a parent, or take away his children. When the client is unclear about the enabling and supporting nature of the practitioner's role and the clear differentiation of client and life roles, he may resist becoming a client. Continually throughout the contact, the practitioner needs to be aware of the fact that the client may misperceive their reciprocal role responsibilities and, on this basis, may resist using help.

Sometimes, the client acts as though he has biases or misconceptions about the practitioner. He may show that he expects the practitioner not to accept him with his kind of difficulty or as a person from a minority or class group. He may be passive or unresponsive and seek to establish a distance between himself and his helper. In other instances, he may appear uncertain about the practitioner's willingness to help; he cannot ask if the practitioner thinks he can be helped; or he acts hopeless or discouraged about the possibility of being given help. The practitioner tries to elicit such ambiguous feelings and to explore the basis for them because they offer a potentially serious source of resistance.

RESISTANCE EVOKED BY POSITIVE EXPECTATIONS

Subcategory B refers to resistance that, at the given time, is evoked primarily by the client's conscious positive expectations regarding help that may not be understood or that may differ, to a greater or lesser extent, from those of the practitioner and may interfere with mutual understanding and role complementarity. These expectations include ideas about the way help should be offered, the terms of help, or the desire for a particular kind of help.

Anatomy of Psychotherapy provides formulations that support the proposition regarding this type of resistance for the authors consider that role expectations may be viewed in the sense of wishes and that these wishes may cause differences between client and therapist expectations about their respective roles. The writers attribute the difference to the fact that the very nature of the client's presenting problem —failure in some aspect of life-role functioning—may make for some rigidity and unreality in his expectations of help.[8] The practitioner judges that the client's behavior indicates resistance or potential resistance of this nature when the rigidity and unreality in the client's request make it difficult for him to accept what the agency has to offer and lead to discordant client and practitioner expectations. The following pointers may indicate when there is need for fuller exploration and assessment as a basis for treatment decisions.

The client shows that he has expectations regarding definite kinds of help. These expectations must be understood since they may be more or less impossible to fulfill. The client may ask for a definite kind of help, such as help for the child but not for himself, or help for self but not for the wife. In many instances, he may request a solution, such as placement, telling the wife to stop drinking, specific advice, or some other plan. The practitioner usually inquires into the client's reasons for the request, the circumstances and nature of the problem situation that prompt the request, his previous attempts at problem-solving, and so forth. He investigates the client's willingness to consider other possibilities since this kind of information may help him to judge both the degree of unreality and the rigidity and therefore to decide on appropriate treatment measures. If the client has unrealistic expectations, they may cause resistance when the practitioner cannot fulfill them, or, if his expectations are realistic and the practitioner does not understand or accept them, the client may resist accepting help.

The client also frequently comes with definite expectations as to the way help should be offered and these expectations may or may not be reasonable. The practitioner should understand in detail what lies behind the client's expectations. In some instances, the client's wishes about the terms of help may be completely realistic: He does not have carfare, he cannot commute from a distance for extended help, he has no one to baby-sit for him. In other instances, the client's wishes to exclude the partner from plans for the child may relate directly to anger and to the desire to punish the partner rather than to the realities of the situation. In some cases, the client's expectations derive from cultural values regarding the sex of the practitioner, matters appropriate for discussion with those outside the family, male and female roles, and acceptable sources of help such as church or community. The practitioner attempts to familiarize himself with the client's reality, cultural and otherwise, because failure to do so may lead to lack of congruence in expectations about the terms of help and hence to resistance.

In some instances, the client shows blocking, discomfort, or negative reactions to the practitioner's behavior. When the client shows, in some way, that the practitioner has failed to meet his expectations, the practitioner attempts to understand the basis for these responses in order to deal appropriately with them. The client has a right to expect privacy, uninterrupted interviews, attention and concern on the part of the practitioner, and time to be heard. Frequently, the client may expect something more than talking, some tangible kind of help, such as advice, a possible plan about which he can think, a beginning step he can take to handle problems, or some other concrete form of assistance. The client's feeling that the practitioner has not grasped what he wants can become a potent source of resistance because he may feel that the practitioner has failed him and is not equipped to help him.

RESISTANCE EVOKED BY NEGATIVE EXPECTATIONS

Subcategory C covers resistance that, at the given time, is evoked primarily by the client's conscious negative expectations regarding help that may interfere with mutual understanding and role complementarity because the client distrusts and fears help. The resistance of such clients may be evoked by distrust and by fear of participating in the performance of the reciprocal roles of practitioner and client. The conceptualization of this subcategory derives partly from the statement of Henry L. Lennard and his associates who believe that role expectations may be used in the sense of anticipation and that, in this regard, the client may expect rejection by the therapist because of his previous life experiences.[9] In addition, Nathan W. Ackerman observes that weak, immature, and emotionally handicapped individuals may find their inner selves in conflict with the demands of their social roles.[10]

The practitioner judges that the client's behavior indicates resistance of this nature when the client shows that he doubts that help can result in any positive changes in his problem situation, when he distrusts help, or when he does not want help. The following pointers may indicate when there is a need for further exploration as a basis for decisions about treatment.

When the client shows that he doubts that help can bring any positive results, the practitioner explores to discover the basis for this negative viewpoint. The client may distrust his own abilities or feel overwhelmed, helpless, or hopeless. The situation in which he is caught may be one that seems unmodifiable because of the nature of the problem, the situational pressures, or the lack of support. Some clients distrust the practitioner's ability to help, feeling that he may be biased or may lack appropriate skill. In some cases, the client's distrust characterizes all of his relationships whereas, in other instances, it may derive from his anxiety about his precarious and troublesome situation or about previous unhelpful experiences in a social or health agency. The practitioner must uncover these doubts that motivate resistance to accepting help and that interfere with the client's entering into the contract. Even though the client accepts help, his negative expectations may come to the surface at a later point when the practitioner raises the possibility or advisability of working on more internal aspects of the problem.

Individuals who have been failed by life figures tend to see persons in authority as powerful or withholding or punishing, and they may evidence this distrust in behavior that shows that they have been threatened by the referral or by the need to apply for help. These clients distrust help, often on the basis of previous experiences with other institutions or agencies. For this reason, the practitioner, whenever possible, makes himself familiar with information available from schools, hospitals, courts, agencies, and individuals in the community in order to clarify the nature of the client's previous relationships with agencies or community. At times, the client's perception of his experiences are realistic; at other times, they may be unrealistic. In either case, the practitioner needs to be aware of the basis for the client's negative perceptions. He may also encounter the client who does not want help. These clients refuse to apply for help that has to be initiated through legal or quasi-legal means. The client may be a prisoner required to see the practitioner or a juvenile or adult on probation or parole. He may be a parent referred for neglect, for abuse, or for some kind of difficulty in the community. Frequently these clients have been referred for services previously but have not been willing to ask for help. Knowledge of the circumstances that bring these clients to the attention of the present practitioner is essential. The clients' cumulative past failures in social functioning and in social relationships often illuminate the reason for their distrust and for their weak hopes of bettering life by their own efforts. The practitioner must also understand the defenses which these clients muster to deal with their deep distrust, expectations of rejection, and condemnation and fear of further failure. It is clear that these clients cannot accept help until the practitioner has dealt with their resistance.

RESISTANCE EVOKED BY UNCONSCIOUS EXPECTATIONS

Resistance that, at the given time, is evoked by the client's unconscious expectations of needs and fears regarding help may not be understood or may differ to a greater or lesser extent from those of the practitioner and, thus, may interfere with mutual understanding and role complementarity. Such resistance may be evoked by the client's unconscious expectations of the helping relationship, both positive and negative, based on reactivated or unsolved relationship problems. Theory basic to this proposition comes from several sources. Frances B. Stark states that, during intake, the practitioner should understand both the client's conscious and unconscious requests.[11] She bases her recommendation on the formulations of Nerr Littner who considers that the helping relationship tends to stir up in the client unresolved childhood conflicts. Dr. Littner explains that "these reactivated desires, concerns, and anticipations are now consciously experienced toward the caseworker," and that the worker needs to understand that actually the client is asking for service on two levels. Consciously, he requests help to meet the needs of which he is aware; unconsciously, he tries to persuade the worker to satisfy his unconscious desires, to reassure his unconscious concerns, and to help him to keep both from awareness.[12] In the same connection, John P. Spiegel, writing on the subject of transference and countertransference, states that transference operates as resistance to therapy because of the client's unconscious and unrealistic expectations.[13]

Thus far consideration has been given here to the client's conscious desires regarding help. The practitioner must also be aware of the possibility that the client may come with both positive and negative unconscious expectations. Unless the practitioner understands these expectations expressed in transference reactions, he may be unable to establish a contract. The practitioner may take the conscious request at face value and fail to realize that the unconscious request that the client brings may really be the more urgent one. The practitioner thus conveys the idea that the client's expectations and his own are divergent. The practitioner judges that the client's behavior indicates resistance or potential resistance of this nature when it expresses, directly or indirectly, positive or negative transference reactions based on unconscious wishes or fears directed toward the practitioner. These expectations may, in some instances, be quite different from those the client consciously verbalizes. They may arise at any time in the contact and thus indicate that the client is not accepting the client role but instead attempting to assume the role of child vis-à-vis the parent. The following pointers may assist in identifying this type of behavior as a basis for dealing with the resistance in order to forestall or minimize it.

The nature of the client's pathology shows implications of unresolved relationship difficulties that tend to be characteristic of the specific pathology and that may provide clues to the client's unconscious expectations. The client's disturbed or regressed behavior has similar implications. Clients with various neurotic conflicts, including hysterical and compulsive persons, drug addicts, alcoholics or wives of alcoholics, schizophrenics, or those with affective disorders or personality disorders, frequently convey what they want the practitioner to avoid when they discuss their present relationship difficulties or their previous ones. The client's relationships tend to follow a pattern and therefore can serve as a guide in understanding and dealing with possible transference problems that could cause resistance. Since these patterns stem, to a greater or lesser degree, from fixation to preoedipal object relationships, the client tends to cast the practitioner in the role of parent and to expect from him the same unsatisfying or frustrating relationship. The hysteric fearfully anticipates that the practitioner may undermine his sex role as a spouse or parent; the compulsive is on guard against the practitioner's undermining his need to control. The dependent character with a variety of symptomatologies appears to search continually for a strong protector and ally whom he may also fear and hate because dependency may frighten him. The schizophrenic needs a relationship but wards off any kind of closeness because he cannot trust. The depressed client also struggles with the problem of trust and strong ambivalence.

Frequently, the client acts out with the practitioner his unconscious desires for parental protection, strength, understanding, and support as he describes his feelings or projects them onto family members, the school, court, or social agency. He asks, unconsciously, for protection from the necessity of facing the realities of his situation and his own share in his present trouble.[14] He may attempt to manipulate the practitioner to gain what he wants. In other instances, the client may exhibit strong defenses against admitting his bottomless needs. Because he fears rejection or further frustration, he utilizes provocative, demanding, or rejecting behavior and shows that he expects criticism, derogation, or refusal of help.

The circumstances of referral or of coming for help under external pressure usually cause the client to see the practitioner as a feared authority figure with consequent negative transference reactions. The aged and ill, if they never have been very stout characters, may evidence regression or depletion of ego strengths as they cast themselves on the practitioner's mercy, asking to be told what to do or to be taken care of.

Treatment Measures

The first category of treatment measures is logically related to the first category of diagnosis of resistance. It relates types of treatment to types of resistance. The first category of treatment consists of measures for maximizing the client's motivation for taking help and for assuming the client role: the techniques to minimize factors that interfere with the client's motivation and to strengthen factors that support motivation.

Alfred Kadushin and C. F. Wieringa consider that the practitioner's awareness of the client's expectations enables him to understand sensitively "client tension that results from violation of such expectations."[15] This treatment method is based on the proposition that the more the practitioner tends to increase motivation for taking help, the more he lessens resistance.

The first category of treatment measures includes four subcategories: A, clarifying what the client wants; B, supporting the client's motivation; C, providing external motivation; and D, handling transference motivations.

CLARIFICATION THROUGH EXPLANATION

In order to clarify what the client wants and expects in taking help and the reciprocal roles of client and practitioner (subcategory A), the practitioner gives the client an explicit explanation of the agency—the intake and application process, if any; the services available; and what the client can expect regarding immediacy of service, duration of service, expense, interview frequency, share in problem-solving, share of family members in problem-solving; and particular kind of help that seems related to the client's situation. An understanding of what can be offered may be all that the client requires to formulate his own request more adequately. The practitioner supplements or corrects the client's information. In particular, he explains the client role and its participatory nature as well as his role of practitioner as enabler. He differentiates his role from the client's life roles for which the client has responsibility. The practitioner makes clear that his responsibility is to help the client assume his task as parent, spouse, or wage earner. He may explain the purpose of helping as a way of identifying the problem and of dealing with it better. However, the practitioner may use demonstration before explanation.

Clarification also occurs through demonstration of the helping process. The practitioner demonstrates his willingness to understand where the client is in taking help, his acceptance of the client's need for defenses, and his willingness to find a way to begin working with the client. He demonstrates how he and the client will be working together by his informed awareness of possible psychological, cultural, and environmental factors that may be operating in the client's situation. He especially demonstrates his acceptance of the client and his problem, his interest, his concern, his willingness to help, and his hope of improvement. If the practitioner considers that the client misperceives his intentions, attitudes, or his own role, the practitioner may use clarifying explanations. He also demonstrates his confidence in the client's ability to improve problem-solving and the way he is functioning in relation to his problem-situation.

When the client's not knowing what he wants derives from ambivalence, the practitioner tries to clarify the ambivalent feelings, ideas, doubts, or reservations and helps to strengthen the client's inner perception and observation. He also clarifies the alternatives available and the client's right to decide. He attempts to draw out the side of the ambivalence that the client has trouble in expressing or in perceiving. When the client seems to have thought about only one choice, the practitioner helps him to consider other possibilities. He clarifies the way to make choices through helping the client to weigh the alternatives and, especially, to consider the implications and outcomes of given choices. This essential step should always be taken before the client is ready to enter into the contract to accept help; otherwise, he may feel trapped or unready to decide and thus fail to return because his potential resistance was not forestalled.

Although the client, usually, does not resist participating in finding out where to begin, he may do so if he has predominantly negative expectations of help or unconscious expectations. In this event, the practitioner must usually lessen the resistance before he can clarify the problem focus with the client. Clarification of what the client can expect from the agency, however, may help the client and the practitioner to understand where to begin their work together.

Use of communication to promote clarification constitutes

an essential treatment measure. Clarification depends upon opening up lines of communication. The practitioner helps the client to express his questions, ideas, and concerns. He attempts to communicate clearly and to communicate in both verbal and nonverbal ways. Knowing that what he does and how he does it conveys a message, he attempts to express and to demonstrate to the client his intentions by tones of voice, posture, and attentiveness. The practitioner may, at times, verbalize for the client or recapitulate to clarify what has been taking place between them.

SUPPORT OF CONSCIOUS EXPECTATIONS

The practitioner must, in subcategory B, support, so far as possible, the client's conscious expectations about taking help and attempt to reconcile discordant role expectations regarding the taking of help and the assuming of the client role. Gordon Hamilton has discussed the theoretical ideas conveyed by this type of treatment measure in "Focusing Through the Request."[16] When the client has made known his expectations, he may be a long way from entering into a contract to accept help, for the agency's response to his request may or may not be congruent. This is the time for negotiations that prevent practitioner and client from becoming too far removed from one another with resulting client discomfort. The measures for minimizing or forestalling resistance require the practitioner to relate supportingly to the client's request by making connections between what the client wants and what he has to offer. It requires him to identify some place to begin with the client by attempting to meet his expectations to some extent. The practitioner tries to find a place to start which the client can accept and to reconcile, so far as possible, discordant expectations in a supporting manner.

The practitioner always tries to meet usual client expectations by providing privacy, time to be heard, freedom from pressure, and an uninterrupted interview. If circumstances beyond his control necessitate violation of these conditions, he deals supportingly with the client's feelings and accepts his right to be given service on such terms. He always tries to align himself with the client's conscious goals regarding the taking of help. In instances in which the client's cultural orientations affect his ideas about help, the practitioner may need to clarify with the client the agency's ability to satisfy his expectations as to the sex of the practitioner, where the interviews will be held, what the client feels is appropriate to discuss with someone outside the family, and how use is made of sources of help upon which the client customarily relies. Usually, the agency can find a way to accede to a cultural orientation to taking help.

When the client's expectations seem rigid or unrealistic, the practitioner may supportingly attempt to enlarge and to develop the client's view of possibilities by pointing out new possibilities, by asking him to consider more carefully what he wants in order to understand what it might entail and what might be the consequences. The practitioner, for example, may try to help the client to consider the results of placing a child or of seeking a divorce and to consider other possibilities before deciding to take this action. Frequently, the terms on which the client wants help appear unrealistic or rigid. The practitioner may then attempt to show the client that, in the long run, such terms of help or such a plan for help may defeat the client's own goals or interfere with the possibility of providing assistance.

The practitioner tries to relate client expectations to agency services and to offer service in a way that has meaning for the client and that shows that he has understood and accepted, to some degree, the client's reality. He tries to help the client to regard helping as a way of achieving what he wants, and he also tries to take into consideration the client's wishes regarding the terms of service and kinds of service. In case of discordant expectations, the practitioner attempts to reconcile these expectations. If this reconciliation appears impossible, he may develop a tentative plan that permits later reconsideration. He may set a time for this reconsideration. This plan gives both client and practitioner an opportunity to try things out. In some instances, the practitioner may be able to modify agency policies or procedures in a way that will enable both client and practitioner to enter into a beginning contract and to define a basis for the contract that the client can accept. In other instances, the practitioner must evaluate the client's expectations and the advisability of accepting them as a place to begin when it is impossible to modify them at the time.

SUPPLY EXTERNAL MOTIVATION

The practitioner supplies, in subcategory C, temporary external motivation for taking help by reaching out to the client and using initiative, the authority of skill, and social authority to help the client accept help and assume the client role. These treatment measures aim to provide the motivation for accepting help which is lacking in the client and to initiate the client's role behavior. Kadushin and Wieringa state that unless the client perceives the practitioner as motivated to help him he is unlikely to maintain contact.[17] In her commentary dealing with an article on the subject of motivation in helping services, Margaret W. Millar observes that the practitioner's task is, among other things, to break through, reduce fears, and increase trust in the practitioner's ability and motivation to help.[18]

The practitioner uses his own desire to help to provide external motivation. He represents for the client the motivation of hopeful expectation. He also represents the concern of the community and the expectation of the community that the situation can be improved. He indicates hopeful possibilities and new opportunities for change. The practitioner actively searches for the client's strengths and supports them in ways that increase the client's hopefulness about his capacity and bolster his confidence. He also takes time and patience to develop trust. He allows himself to be tested by the client while he remains consistently warm, supportive, and concerned. He thus attempts to relieve the client's fears of reprisal if he does not meet expectations. Lessening of fear and increasing of trust can diminish discomfort by increasing satisfaction in the client's experience of taking help. These clients require constant reassurance concerning their fears. They need constant demonstration of the trustworthiness and support of the practitioner and the satisfactions that can accrue from help.

The authority of skill enables the practitioner to utilize more than usual initiative in defining the client role and in developing client-family participation through home visits. The practitioner is active in defining the purpose of the visit, in defining the needed changes, in outlining the client's expectations, in finding with the client a place to begin, or in helping him identify some aspect of his problem with which he wishes help. He also uses more than customary initiative in relieving environmental pressures and in meeting immediate needs because these pressures and needs, especially when they have seemed impossible to change, increase negative expectations and resistance. The practitioner, in meeting environmental needs, may exercise considerable leadership in coordinating agency services and in acting as advocate for the client. Relief from situational pressure and the experiencing of greater satisfaction can often increase the client's motivation for taking help, because he now has some basis for positive expectations of help and for hope of change.

When necessary, the practitioner may confront the client with his social authority. Some clients are not motivated to accept help until they are faced with the alternative of court action. Even then, in some instances, the practitioner may need to refer the client to the court before client or his family will begin to move. In such circumstances, the practitioner uses the legal authority of a court order as a first step in dealing with resistance and in making the client accessible to help.

UTILIZE UNCONSCIOUS EXPECTATIONS

In utilizing the client's positive unconscious expectations regarding the taking of help and preventing his unconscious negative expectations from blocking the taking of help and assuming the client role (subcategory D), the treatment measures involve dealing with the transference elements in the relationship in ways that help the client to feel understood and accepted. Annette Garrett states that transference becomes necessary when the client has unconscious emotional problems. She considers that the practitioner should make use of the positive transference as a dynamic motivational force because the parental role with which the client endows the practitioner makes it possible for the practitioner to encourage and strengthen the client.[19] Littner states that he considers it essential for the practitioner to understand some of the subtle interactions in the practitioner-client relationship from the client's point of view, because many of the feelings that disturb the client are unconscious.[20] Casework theory usually recommends utilizing positive transference to motivate the client to take help and to deal with aspects of his reality situation—a treatment measure that tends to keep the transference within bounds. The practitioner usually discusses with the client the negative transference, attempting to dilute or to dissipate those reactions that tend to motivate against the taking of help.

When resistance or potential resistance comes from severe relationship difficulties, practitioners generally attempt to meet at least some of the client's unconscious emotional needs in ways that enable him to see the relationship as satisfying. When the client has experienced the rewards of the practitioner's caring and interest, the practitioner can draw upon this motivation to enable the client to accept help with his reality problem. He makes use of his knowledge of the client's stage of development, of his pathology, and of his relationship difficulties to understand the needs that he expects the relationship to meet and uses this assessment as a guide to what to provide and what to avoid. In most such instances, he develops the relationship before testing the client's ability to recognize responsibility for his problems and to work on them.[21] In this treatment approach, the practitioner expresses understanding and acceptance of the client's needs that had not been understood by parents, and he responds to them appropriately. Frequently, these needs include some that the client is unable to acknowledge or can not express. The practitioner provides the parental support that had been lacking in previous life experiences, the strength of an empathic ally, and psychological protection. He offers psychological support by not expecting the client to give up his defenses until he feels sufficiently bolstered to stop, to some extent, his denial of his difficulties. When the relationship has meaning and value for the client,[22] the practitioner can use the prize, which has now come to have meaning, as a motivation to support the client in accepting his role of client and in working on his reality difficulties. If the stregthening of the positive transference tends to lead to too great dependency, the practitioner dilutes the transference by directing the client's attention to his reality situation and stimulates him to work on it.

In some instances, the practitioner must provide the client with a relationship that avoids his being cast in the negative transference role. The practitioner understands the client's fear of authority figures when the circumstances of his referral indicate that he comes under pressure from legal or semilegal authority or from community agencies, such as the school or court.[23] He understands the client's fear of rejection and criticism when his past experience has shown cumulative failure or cumulative difficulties with the community. When the client has had a long history of dependency or when his characteristic responses show a fear of rejection of dependency needs, the practitioner avoids provoking the client's feelings that his dependency is unacceptable. In other instances, when the client's protests of independence and fear of a dependency relationship make clear what he wants, the practitioner avoids provocation of negative feelings. When the client's pathology shows his fear of closeness, the practitioner is careful to meet the client's expectations of a relationship that maintains contact but at a comfortable distance. In other instances, he may need to elicit the client's negative feelings about the helping relationship and his fears and misperceptions of the nature of the relationship and to use reality-testing to clarify the situation. The practitioner may dilute the negative transference by using the help of other team members and may, at the same time, attempt to strengthen the reality aspects of the relationship by not assuming the negative role that the client tends to expect. For example, the practitioner avoids assuming authority by not inquiring into the way the client is conforming to expectations and reality requirements.

The foregoing theoretical formulations about treatment measures and their relationship to resistance utilize ego analysis and role theory to clarify the client's readiness to take help and to use helping measures that begin where the client is in trying to move him toward assuming the client role and concluding a contract with the agency. The treatment measures proposed include ego-supportive measures for forestalling or minimizing resistance. When faced with resistance that does not yield to these measures, the practitioner may have to confront the client with the fact of his resistance and the nature of his resistance and attempt to help him, when possible, to take a different conscious position toward accepting help.

The goal of the initial interviews is to enable the client to take help by concluding a contractual agreement with the agency when the nature of his problem, the fact that he cannot handle it, and the unsuitableness of referral elsewhere indicate that he needs and can use agency help. Client resistance interferes with developing the contract.

The Contract: First Steps Toward Congruent Expectations

During the initial interview, or interviews, the practitioner attempts to develop with the client a contract regarding the taking of help, unless they have decided on termination or referral. The agreement should identify some immediate goal or goals and set forth a beginning plan for working toward the goals. The plan should make clear some beginning steps toward change, in the way the client is functioning or in his situation, that the client can take together with the help he needs from the practitioner to do so. In developing the contract, practitioners have found it particularly helpful to specify a time limit for giving services because the reality of the time factor encourages client and practitioner to try to accomplish the agreed-on changes without procrastination. They should also agree on the terms on which service is available: frequency of contact, where interviews are to be held, whether other family members will be included, cost, and so on. The client should be aware of what he may expect and should participate in developing the contract, although it may be altered later by mutual agreement.

Notes

1. Isidore Portnoy, "The Anxiety States," in *American Handbook of Psychiatry,* ed. Silvano Arieti, vol. 1 (New York: Basic Books, 1959), p. 309.

2. Alfred Kadushin and C. F. Wieringa, "A Comparison: Dutch and American Expectations Regarding Behavior of the Caseworker," *Social Casework,* 41:503–11 (December 1960).

3. Henry L. Lennard et al., *The Anatomy of Psychotherapy: Systems of Communication and Expectation* (New York: Columbia University Press, 1960), pp. 22–23.

4. Ibid., p. 26.

5. H. Aronson and Betty Overall, "Treatment Expectations of Patients in Two Social Classes," *Social Work,* 11:35–41 (January 1966).

6. Helen Harris Perlman, *Persona: Social Role and Personality* (Chicago: University of Chicago Press, 1968), chap. 7.

7. Herman D. Stein and Richard A. Cloward, "Social Roles: Introduction," in *Social Perspectives on Behavior: A Reader in Social Science for Social Work and Related Professions,* ed. Herman D. Stein and Richard A. Cloward (Glencoe, Ill.: Free Press, 1958), p. 174.

8. Lennard et al., *Anatomy of Psychotherapy,* pp. 23–24.

9. Ibid.

10. Nathan W. Ackerman, *The Psychodynamics of Family Life: Diagnosis and Treatment of Family Relationships* (New York: Basic Books, 1958), pp. 61–62.

11. Frances B. Stark, "Barriers to Client-Worker Communication at Intake," *Social Casework,* 40:177–83 (April 1959).

12. Nerr Littner, "The Impact of the Client's Unconscious on the Caseworker's Reactions," in *Ego Psychology and Dynamic Casework: Papers from the Smith College School for Social Work,* ed. Howard J. Parad (New York: Family Service Association of America, 1958), pp. 73–82.

13. John P. Spiegel, "Some Cultural Aspects of Transference and Countertransference," in *Individual and Familial Dynamics,* ed. Jules H. Masserman, *Science and Psychoanalysis,* vol. 2 (New York: Grune and Stratton, 1959), 160–82.

14. See, for example, Effie Warren, "Treatment of Marriage Partners with Character Disorders," *Social Casework,* 38:118–26 (March 1957).

15. Kadushin and Wieringa, "Dutch and American Expectations."

16. Gordon Hamilton, *Theory and Practice of Social Casework*, 2d ed. rev. (New York: Columbia University Press, 1951), pp. 159–62.

17. Kadushin and Wieringa, "Dutch and American Expectations."

18. Margaret W. Millar, "Commentary," *Social Casework,* 39:136–37 (February-March 1958).

19. Annette Garrett, "The Worker-Client Relationship," in *Ego Psychology,* ed. Parad, pp. 53–72.

20. Littner, "Impact of Client's Unconscious."

21. Warren, "Treatment of Marriage Partners."

22. Sidney Love and Herta Mayer, "Going Along with Defenses in Resistive Families," *Social Casework,* 40:69–74 (February 1959).

23. Robert Strayer, "The Social Worker's Role in Handling the Resistances of the Alcoholic," in *Differential Diagnosis and Treatment in Social Work,* ed. Francis J. Turner (New York: Free Press, 1968), pp. 215–21.

FIVE

Focus on Assessment of Capacity

This chapter explains the facts needed to understand the active patterning that can be expected at each stage of development in each of the six major functions of the ego which have been identified as useful for helping. Understanding of this patterning allows the practitioner to assess where the client is relative to the development of ego functioning. The components of ego identity are also explained and discussed.

SAMUEL Finestone states that the construction of diagnostic classification schemes requires the researcher to make up his mind about the nature of diagnosis (assessment).[1] Perlman identifies three types of diagnosis: dynamic, clinical, and etiological.[2] On a higher level of abstraction, Finestone has developed a concept of diagnosis that includes:

> (1) the location of the difficulty, that is, where it is manifested; (2) the description of the difficulty, that is, how it is manifested; (3) the effective determinants of difficulty, that is, what are the elements in the client and his environment that are maintaining the difficulty and are susceptible to change; and (4) the assets for change, that is, what resources in the person and environment can be enlisted for change.

The author explains that this viewpoint includes in diagnosis not only the location and description of the difficulties toward which treatment is to be directed "but also some formulation of their cause." It is a treatment-oriented view of cause, because it deals with "factors which determine client difficulties and which are alterable by casework treatment." This usage differs from the one which views causes as including "all determinants of difficulty." In this treatment-oriented view, cause signifies determinants of the difficulty which are "effective for change purposes." We find ourselves in accord with Finestone's formulations and will explain the use of ego analysis in this approach to diagnostic assessment. In Finestone's view, knowledge of the preceding four factors provides "an adequate basis for treatment planning."[3]

The earlier chapter on problem focus located the problem or difficulty in some one of the client's major life roles and suggested ways of describing the difficulty in terms of causative factors, resulting effects, duration, and other characteristics of the problem. It was suggested in chapter 2 that the elements in the client that are maintaining the difficulty and that are susceptible to change can be identified by assessing the limitations in the patterning of the ego functions as they relate to the given problem and the limitations in the sense of ego identity. The assets for change in the person can be identified by assessing the coping patterns in the functions of the ego appropriate for dealing with the problem at hand. In a later chapter the elements in the environment will be discussed from a similar viewpoint.

The selection and definition, from among the clustering of role problems, of the problem on which the client wants to work makes it possible to focus the helping method on assessment of client capacity and on those factors that limit his capacity. This assessment is necessary in order to define what needs to be changed in the client's functioning to improve his problem-solving ability. Assessment of the client's capacity requires the practitioner to operate from some theoretical base in order to form evaluative judgments about capacity and limitations in capacity. Much of this assessment goes on in the practitioner's mind during the interview as he appraises what is happening in the interaction process.

After several interviews, the practitioner usually engages

in the more formal activity of organizing and clarifying these evaluative judgments through a written psychosocial dynamic diagnosis. Thus, one can think first of the focus of the practitioner's mental process and second of the joined efforts of the practitioner and client. In this second focus the practitioner helps the client to assess his strengths for dealing with the given difficulty and to identify the factors that are preventing his using these strengths and thereby limiting his problem-solving ability. The practitioner must decide how and to what extent to clarify with the client what it is that needs to be changed in the way he functions relative to his problem. The fact that the healthy ego has already learned, and is capable of learning or strengthening, patterns of active mastery and ways to use them, together with passive patterns to cope and adapt, furnishes a guide to evaluation of the client's capacity. Furthermore, the fact that each of the ego functions is patterned provides a much more distinguishing basis for analyzing social functioning than do global concepts of personality or behavior.

One of the desirable changes toward which helping aims is change in the direction of strengthening or mobilizing capacities and lessening limitations. A clear focus on such change goals requires that the practitioner have some distinguishing way of viewing various aspects of the client's behavior. For this purpose, it is planned here to utilize as the major diagnostic categories of the method based on ego analysis the categories of ego functions discussed in chapter 2, together with the concept of ego identity.

The epigenetic theory postulates that development takes place in stages and that new learning is based upon previous learning and upon the solution of key learning tasks. This formulation calls the attention of the practitioner to assessment of levels of ego development attained by the individual. It is believed, also, that ego functions may develop unevenly, some being more adequate than others.[4] The practitioner can identify expectable steps in progression at each growth stage as outcomes of learning through experiences provided by the "average expectable environment." He utilizes this theory to draw inferences from observed behavior about areas where the individual appears to be fixated, about the learning already achieved and that still to be achieved. The client may have achieved an adequate level of development and need only to have help in acquiring new coping patterns to deal with the present problem. The practitioner also knows that additional basic tasks must be accomplished before the individual can progress to more advanced tasks. Implicit in this approach is the idea of regression. Stress, particularly stress that affects areas of vulnerability or unresolved conflict or stress that is traumatic in nature, tends to produce regression to earlier developmental levels. This regression must be distinguished from regression in the service of the ego, a useful defense that allows the ego to retreat and pause in its endeavors to rally its forces.[5] In other instances, the practitioner sees only a temporary blocking of previously good ego functioning that, if support is forthcoming, does not develop into regression. The ego becomes temporarily immobilized by anxiety. Finally, the individual may have internalized distorted ego patterns that interfere with development and set in motion pathological processes. These distortions require relearning.

The practitioner attempts to discover, in all clients, constructive and appropriate coping methods that they can utilize with his help. In any assessment of ego functioning, the practitioner bears in mind the fact that one or several functions may be more critically related to the given problem than are others, and he will place emphasis on the need for strengthening these functions. Within a given function, some patterns may be more essential than others; for example, in order to deal with increased dependency caused by illness, the client may require support in his use of patterns of being given to and of receiving. When the client comes in a crisis or stressful situation, the practitioner attempts to ascertain his earlier level of role functioning and previously achieved patterns because this information provides clues to abilities that the client, with relief from anxiety, may be able to draw upon or to strengthen. He obtains the same kind of information when the client has regressed because of serious or sustained stress. The duration and degree of the regression, the previously achieved learning, the state of the remaining capacities, and the environmental situation are all indications of the possibilities for reversing the regressive process and mobilizing progressive forces. The practitioner must, therefore, distinguish useful learning presently or possibly available to the client from inadequate or distorted learning. He must also distinguish limitations in capacity related to maladaptive patterning from limitations caused by the need for help in learning new and more effective patterns.

The practitioner bases his assessment of limitations in capacity on the developmental level achieved by the client and on identifiable patterns in each function of the ego which are maladaptive in respect to the problem that the client is trying to solve and which tend to defeat him. For example, the juvenile delinquent may be unable to curb his acting-out tendencies until he has changed the limiting factors in the ego functions related to drive management. In most cases, the predominant characteristics of the patterning of the various functions revealed by the study of present or past functioning indicate the level of development that the client has achieved and the unsolved learning tasks. When the client appears fixated in the preoedipal period, he tends to rely on passive mastery and to have learned relatively few adult active ways of coping. Frequently, the life situation of the client confirms the fact that the environment has not offered appropriate learning experiences. Finally, the practitioner must distinguish, diagnostically, when the client's way of functioning represents a pathological process and distorted learning. These distortions tend to be characteristic of clinical entities and indicate that the client has to unlearn and remedy faulty learning to the extent possible in view of the pathology. In cases of pathology, the practitioner supplements the dynamic diagnosis with a clinical diagnosis.

The following pages discuss, in respect to each function of the ego, how the practitioner draws inferences from client behavioral patterns indicative of capacity to utilize that function in coping, as well as some of the ways in which limitations manifest themselves. However, the practitioner's judgment about the client's ability to achieve new learning and to integrate this learning into his way of operating continually develops as he assesses the client's response to treatment measures, to support, to relief from stress, and to new opportunities. No theoretical framework for diagnostic assessment would be complete without a discussion of resistance; the practitioner needs to understand and to handle resistance at the same time he is assessing and treating other aspects of client functioning. However, the subject of resistance requires extensive consideration and will be dealt with in other chapters.

Although this chapter deals with assessment of the client's functioning, the practitioner must remind himself that situation also affects functioning, providing varying degrees of support and sustainment and varying degrees of stress and of limitations in opportunity. Assessment of situational factors usually takes place concurrently with that focused on the client. The dynamic psychosocial diagnosis includes evaluation of both inner and outer aspects together with their interaction, as will be discussed in chapter 8.

The Function of Perception

As Hadley Cantril points out, perceptions are learned terms of purposive behavior that involve the weighing of the significance of cues. The perceptual meanings assigned to things, symbols, people, and events are built through the individual's past experiences and do not inhere in the stimulus. This learning constitutes the assumptions that perceptually are brought to bear on any situation. Perception helps to develop social constancies in one's relationships with others as one pigeonholes what one is looking for in others—self.[6] This function structures reality by assigning coherent meanings and by selecting the significant from the insignificant. The learned meanings of significance direct the individual's attention and interest to focus particularly on taking in information to regulate his relationships with others. In this case, he pays attention to the ideas, feelings, and activities of other persons and through integration of perception with other ego functions, cognitive and affective, interprets these data with reasonable accuracy.[7] At the same time, he interests himself in many aspects of the outside world in order to find out what it has to offer and to guide his activities so as to deal with reality.

The function of inner perception makes possible self-observation and ability to identify a range of feelings,[8] as well as the related awareness of the effect of own urges, feelings, and activities on other persons. The capacity for reality-testing differentiates cues coming from within from those which come from external reality. It prevents assigning own ideas and feelings to sources outside of self.

Learning should develop perceptual patterns that assign appropriate meanings of danger and pleasure to inner and outer data. In this event, dependence seems safe, authority is seen as reasonable, and sexuality is regarded as based in a relationship of intimacy. Trust in self, the obverse of trust in others, leads the individual to trust his ability to meet social expectations and to carry his sex role.[9]

The healthy individual has learned to channel energy into active patterns, an extension of the early achievements when, according to Charles A. Malone, the child is "exploring personal and interpersonal fields as well as the impersonal; he is making discoveries which assist him in placing and relating himself and his own body to people and to things."[10]

Although perception is largely active, the individual does and can use passive modes as he takes over, in whole or in part, the perceptions of others, of his reference groups, of experts, of the news media, and so forth. To summarize, perception is "a major intervening variable between stimuli and behavior."[11]

ADAPTIVE AND MALADAPTIVE PATTERNS

The client shows that he has achieved healthy patterning of perception when he evidences useful frames of reference for orienting himself to reality, to the social world around him, and, in particular, to human relationships. He sees his problems, his situation, and the individuals with whom he interacts in a reasonably realistic way without significant distortions. He recognizes his need for help and perceives the practitioner as a person able to give help. Based on inner perception, he may be able to use a capacity for self-observation and awareness of his own feelings and motivations; he is prepared to consider his own share in any interaction process and to distinguish his own feelings from those of others. His patterns of reality-testing enable him to separate past from present reality. Active patterning includes the idea that the individual has invested energy in the function of perception and therefore actively seeks to find out the meaning of what is happening between himself and others and the meaning of his own or others' behavior and to find new ways of looking at such events when old frames of reference prove inadequate. Thus, he can accept from the practitioner helpful insights and new points of view.

Therefore, with clients who have achieved a previously adequate level of development, the practitioner bases his positive assessment of capacity on the client's ability to recognize, with support and with relief from anxiety, the necessity for acquiring new perceptual patterns to deal with the present problem. For example, when a couple requests a child to adopt they face problems that tend to provoke considerable anxiety. The practitioner attempts to assess whether, with support, the couple can learn to look inward at the feelings that their new role would stir up, can begin to perceive what the new role could entail, and can learn to see themselves as parents and not as a barren couple. The practitioner also evaluates the couple's ability to learn to see the child as an individual with his own needs, rather than as an extension of themselves or as a way of saving their marriage. Similarly, the practitioner must evaluate the capacity of a AFDC mother accepted for homemaker training to acquire a whole new way of viewing her role, the families she will serve, and the problems she will encounter. The new perceptual patterns must be more objective. In order to make the necessary change, the trainee must be able to use the passive mode and take in, for example, a different way of seeing a parent she had considered lazy but must now see as mentally ill. When the client shows regression from previous good functioning because of serious illness, trauma, or crisis, the practitioner judges capacity relative to the client's ability to perceive connections between his present state and the precipitating stress. The client also demonstrates capacity when he can recognize the necessity to achieve new active or passive coping patterns to deal with his changed situation.

In evaluating limitations in capacity regarding the foregoing ego functions, the practitioner should recall that many clients have never learned how to be self-observant. Research indicates that middle-class parents tend to punish on the basis of the child's intent. In this way, the child becomes aware of, and pays attention to, his feelings and motivations. Working-class parents tend to punish in relation to the immediate consequences of the act and to train for respectability. They teach the child to pay attention to the way others view his acts.[12] From his own experiences, the individual develops a unique perceptual frame of reference in which he views himself and his world, and no two persons' perceptions are the same. In assessing limitations in capacity, the practitioner differentiates clients who have never learned from those who have distorted learning. Many parents have never learned how to perceive the needs of their children or their feelings. They cannot, when asked, differentiate their own feelings and inner urges. However, given new opportunities, they may learn. Their limitations tend to stem from inadequate parental models.

Needs and related feelings, as well as conflict or pathology, distort perceptual patterns in more serious ways. Since anxiety regarding action about what is perceived may arouse a defense of denial, or not perceiving, the practitioner notes when the client blocks out aspects of his environment and has inadequate patterning of outer perceptions owing to experiences of need, frustration, and ego inadequacy, which make him see the environment as dangerous, difficult, frustrating, or distressing.[13] The needful, overburdened parent may not perceive the needs of his children or their good points—only their inadequacies. The troubled adolescent may not perceive that education can open doors to a more satisfying life, particularly if a lower-class background has failed to orient him to the world of work.

The practitioner notes when the client's perceptual patterns appear related to given developmental periods: the need-oriented client who sees everything in relation to unsatisfied need or the client who sees the environment largely as a hostile and controlling authority against which he is in rebellion. Limitations in reality-testing make themselves apparent when the client puts all or most of his difficulties outside of self and attributes them to external events. He is unable to examine his own motivation, wishes, or feelings. He cannot see the effect of his behavior on others, nor does he see why he behaves the way he does. In a related way, he cannot understand the inner motivations and feelings of other people or the fact that they may have a reason for their behavior. Deficiencies in reality-testing also become apparent when the client sees the present through the distorting screen of past experiences, largely unhappy ones. Frequently, the client cannot differentiate his wishes or fears from reality. The client may not be able to separate his own ideas and feelings from those of others and so may attribute to others his own hostility or his destructive wishes.

The worker uses the clinical diagnosis to alert him to possible effects of pathology on perceptual patterning. The conflicted client tends to distort reality. His conflict becomes evident in the aspects of reality which he misperceives. When the client has failed to achieve object constancy, he may see all relationships as temporary, with rejection and desertion as a foregone conclusion. He may view all males as undependable or all females as controlling and destructive. Clients with more severe pathology or personality disorders, borderline characters, and schizophrenics tend to view themselves as weak and helpless and tend never to have achieved realistic patterns for perceiving other persons and their environment. Because of psychosis, the client may have lost the ability to perceive self-object differences and to maintain ego boundaries and may have other serious disturbances in perception, such as hallucinations.

The Cognitive Functions

The various functions related to thinking form mental representations of data furnished by perception, and these functions process the data.[14] Thinking, which begins as sensorimotor experiencing of self that lays down memory traces and develops mental images, progresses to concrete and, later, to conceptual modes of thought. These modes make it possible to deal with a wide range of events on the basis of likenesses and differences. The capacity to classify makes the world more coherent and manageable and promotes the transfer of learning. These cognitive abilities have been based on the acquisition of essential reality concepts in approximately the time sequence described by Paul Miller, who utilizes the formulations of Jean Piaget. These concepts include object, self, time, space, causation, and intentionality —the idea of behaving with intentions toward objects or means-end behaviors to achieve goals.[15] René A. Spitz has shed light on the contribution of this last concept to the individual's capacity to use thought and language for purposes of mastery. When the child identifying with the frustrating parent learns from her the concept of *no* with its inherent assertion of intention, and (according to Spitz) of judgment, he can oppose himself to his parents. In saying no the child can actively practice what he has passively experienced.[16]

Spitz has also theorized that the development of speech organizes thinking.[17] An adequate vocabulary is essential in order to describe the property of things, events, and relationships. Learning promotes holding on to things in memory. As Heinz Hartmann observes, words connect urges and wishes with ideas.[18] Therefore, language makes it possible to substitute words for actions, to use imagination and thought before acting, and so to control impulses and avoid danger. The exercise of imagination opens up new possibilities and solutions.[19] Judgment develops in a related manner. The individual learns to use various modes of communication to get and to give information. He needs to become adept at both sending and receiving messages that regulate personal interchanges.

Experiences in the world of reality give meaning to such concepts as psychosocial causality,[20] choice, and initiative.[21] Although, for purposes of adaptation, the individual passively takes in new ideas and information and is receptive to the thoughts of others, his secondary process thinking utilizes predominantly active cognitive and communication patterns in problem-solving and in dealing with stress and difficulty.

> Intelligence involves an enormous extension and differentiation of reaction possibilities and subjects the reactions to its selection and control. Causal thinking [in relation to perception of space and time], the creation and use of means-end relations, and particularly the turning of thinking back upon the self, liberate the individual from being compelled to react to the immediate stimulus. The intellect understands and invents—it decides whether the individual will accept the event as it is, or will change it by his intervention.[22]

ADAPTIVE AND MALADAPTIVE PATTERNS

The practitioner bases his assessment of cognitive capacity (1) on the client's ability to present a clear and coherent picture of his difficulty and to respond appropriately to the practitioner's verbal communication and (2) on evidences of previous levels of development. The practitioner does not confuse the client's schooling achievement with his cognitive ability. The client gives evidence of capacity when he reaches out actively for information or understanding about self-problem-situation or shows himself receptive to ideas and information from role partners or others. The client's capacity to anticipate may be evident in his past problem-solving or when he can, with help, weigh the consequences and foresee the outcomes of different choices available to him. The client's use of the concepts of initiative, choice, intentionality, and causality becomes apparent as he explains what he has done or can do to handle his difficulty. The client may possess some or all of the foregoing coping patterns. In other cases, anxiety or regression may affect the client's functioning, and the assessment of capacity then depends on the client's acceptance of this fact and of the need to use his previous good patterning to deal with his present reality.

The practitioner pays attention to clues indicative of limitations in the thinking functions. Any or all of the following characteristics may be apparent. Magical, primary process thinking becomes evident when the client, in describing events, presents fragments that stand for the whole or parts of what was said or done without connecting or explanatory content. He partially explains ideas or thoughts without referrents. He confuses words with actuality and reacts to threats as though they have been carried out—a situation that often occurs when marital partners respond to angry words as though they were blows or aggressive acts. He uses magical thinking—to wish is to have it happen—and thus feels that his angry wishes or those of others have done injury. He may, for example, feel that he can stop using drugs when he wants to. His remembrance of events lacks a clear ordering of time and space. He may be confused as to what came before and what came after. As an example, a child in therapy had no concepts of time or space. He thought the moon was nearer to Baltimore than was Washington, since he could see the moon but could not see Washington.

Vocabulary and grammar may also show limitations. The client's thinking remains close to its sensorimotor origins and contains few qualifying adverbs or adjectives. He frequently expresses himself in activities, motions, or gestures without explicit words. His speech contains largely active words such as *get out, shut up,* and *gimme.* He cannot put his ideas and thoughts into words, but instead translates them into actions. He particularly lacks words with which to describe feelings or relationships and can usually discuss only concrete aspects of experiences. The foregoing limitations show that the client has not progressed much beyond early developmental levels, often because of social and emotional deprivation, as with lower-class clients.[23]

He may for the same reason have few reality concepts to guide his thinking. If self and object concepts are blurred, he lacks capacity mentally or emotionally to put himself in the other person's place. He may consider his child a possession. He does not get the idea of choosing, of deciding, or of planning, nor can he use essential concepts to guide thinking and activity. His thinking tends to be concrete: He thinks in terms of what Johnny did today, not of the kind of difficulties Johnny seems to be having. The client shows that choice has no meaning for him when he describes his being told what to do by helping persons or by family, of his being controlled, supervised, or put upon by others, or when he asks the worker to choose for him. He similarly evidences that he has never grasped the possibilities of initiative when his actions show that he considers himself the passive victim of circumstances. He is often unable to use thinking to test possible courses of action or to use his imagination to increase the number of available choices. He may have little ability to use experiences from the past to anticipate, to foresee, and hence to avoid difficulties. Again, this limitation may relate to an inability to conceptualize. Characteristically, the client may not use communication to express ideas or feelings, to give and to acquire information, or to work out problems with those in his family or situation. When the client shows thought disorders indicative of pathology, the practitioner uses the clinical diagnosis to help him to understand this distortion. The client with a personality disorder usually does not use experience to anticipate consequences nor thought to guide behavior. He does not use words and thinking to handle his needs and feelings, nor does he stop to think before acting. If his defenses fail, the schizophrenic may be unable to follow a train of thought, may become mute, or may even manifest delusions.

The Management of Drives, Needs, and Feelings

We never see drives; only the urges and the feelings related to drive tension or drive release penetrate into consciousness.[24] The management of needs or culturally learned drive expressions and the management of feelings include a number of functions. These functions include the capacity to tolerate frustration, to postpone gratification, to find substitute gratifications, to find detour routes to satisfaction when a given route is blocked, to reconcile and synthesize conflicting needs, feelings, or aims, and to handle related feelings.

Since ego theory considers that the acquisition and utilization of psychological and social motivations constitute a learned aspect of the function of drive management and since motivations have implications for helping, some relevant ideas will be summarized here. As George L. Engel indicates, the early experiences of the child center around satisfaction and frustration of bodily needs. Gradually, mental representations of these experiences are built up and to some extent become divorced from the body. These representations include a variety of wishes, impulses, and unconscious standards which, in forms modified by learning, initiate and alter behavior and thought. These psychological constructs or needs include representations of objects in the environment necessary to satisfy needs and toward which the drives are directed with the aim of securing maximum pleasure with a minimum of pain. Ideas about what gives pleasure and ways of achieving pleasure arise from life experiences, thus bringing about psychological and social as well as bodily needs.[25] An understanding of the development of motivational forces in the personality and of the nature of motivations makes it possible for the practitioner to assess and to strengthen innate tendencies in the individual to achieve a more satisfying adaptation to his situation. However, many different viewpoints exist regarding the nature of motivations. A few ideas that appear useful have been selected for discussion here.

Some ideas from *The Roots of Individuality* lead logically to explanations of motivation. Sibylle K. Escalona summarizes the findings of her research dealing with development and adaptation in infancy as "congruent with those developmental theories that emphasize the activation of the organism as the primary mechanism underlying and compelling developmental change."[26] She considers that present-day research tends to emphasize development as a reciprocal process in which "the child's behavior influences the environment and thereby helps to shape the course of his experience and his learning." Experimental studies show that young infants "seek out stimulation" and exert effort in activity for its own sake in spite of obstacles and discouragement from the environment. They tend to pay more visual attention to novel and complex patterns and to become more excited over novel tasks than over familiar patterns and tasks, provided the novelty is not so great as to arouse anxiety. These occurrences have been described as "curiosity, mastery, or an innate drive toward competence."[27]

However, Escalona considers it unnecessary to postulate an innate drive toward mastery or competence but, instead, assumes an innate tendency of the organism to generate spontaneous activities. She considers that searching for and selecting opportunities for action are examples of the "built-in modes of reactivity" of the individual. However, her findings point to differences "in the degree to which they [infants] utilize" activating opportunities provided by the mother, usually in the form of stimulation and other experiences.[28]

The bearing of the foregoing ideas on a concept of motivation can be understood when it is noted that "pleasure in functioning" is one of the developmental outcomes on which Escalona rates the infants in her study.[29] Since her work primarily utilizes psychoanalytic ego psychology as a frame of reference,[30] it can logically be assumed that pleasure in functioning refers to ego functioning. This assumption makes it possible to relate Robert W. White's "sense of competence" with Escalona's concept of pleasure in functioning and with Hartmann's similar ideas. Hartmann states that the healthy individual should learn to find "pleasure in functioning" in the exercise of ego functions or their use for the purpose of adaptation.[31] White believes that the sense of competence, or "effectance," depends on the degree to which the individual feels able to produce desired effects on the environment, achieve goals, and determine the course of his life. He sees these end-seeking processes, the steering and direction of behavior, as being made possible by independent ego energies. He agrees with Hartmann's thinking regarding the autonomous ego and reservoirs of ego energy.[32] White proposes that pleasure in the use and development of ego functioning, or what he terms "output of effective action," tends to occur more often when the child's activities bring about some desired changes in the environment and that such changes, or social responses, tend to reinforce the functioning. As Engel says, "Behavior or mental activity involved in the successful satisfaction of a need itself becomes a source of pleasure increasingly independent of the original biological need."[33] Empirical evidence in *The Drifters* points to the fact that children who experience little success in inducing the environment to meet their needs tend to show relatively poor development of ego functions, little pleasure in functioning, and a poor sense of their own adequacy or competence.[34]

Ego theory inclines to the view that individuals tend to repeat pleasurable experiences. It would therefore seem reasonable that the individual who learns to function effectively would build mental representations of ego activities and goals in relation to the social setting. As patterns of functioning to achieve these activities and goals bring satisfaction, they tend to be repeated, thus channeling energy into the development of the functions of the ego. In this instance, social competence, effectance, and pleasure in ego functioning would represent learned motivations arising out of the innate tendency to initiate activity, the kinds of activating opportunities provided by the environment, and the response of the individual to these opportunities.

The function of managing needs and feelings not only channels energy into ego and social needs but also utilizes defensive and adaptive coping patterns to achieve satisfaction of needs. Developmental learning should teach that the aim of immediate gratification frequently proves self-defeating and brings trouble, while postponing gratification achieves, in the long run, greater satisfactions and, in particular, a new kind of satisfaction from sublimations.[35] The ego therefore redefines pleasure to include future pleasure and learns to operate in accordance with the reality principle. As the ego function of anticipation develops, the individual can give up present for anticipated pleasure and correctly relate "means and ends to each other."[36] In this event, the coping patterns available to the individual will have developed from physiological to ego patterns of taking and getting all kinds of satisfactions—perceptual, cognitive, relationship, and doing. The individual no longer needs to cling unduly to persons or objects, yet he can hold on tenaciously to the pursuit of his goals. He can make his way around obstacles which block routes to gratification and can accept substitutes for pleasures which he cannot realistically achieve.

These active patterns represent a growing confidence in one's own ability to find satisfactions and progressive learning about appropriate ways to do so. Arthur H. Schmale, Jr., considers that affects of helplessness and hopelessness "represent two different types of ego 'giving up'. "[37] The feeling of helplessness derives from the oral period when the child recognizes his dependence on external objects for protection and for gratification. While the affect of helplessness may be revived by experiencing the loss of external sources of supplies, in states of prolonged deprivation the individual's lack of trust and of self-confidence may interfere with the achievement of autonomy. He has a feeling of deprivation resulting from the loss of gratification from others. According to Schmale, the affect of hopelessness stems from the oedipal period. "The child's pleasure in making a sexual identification and in being accepted by the parental objects as having an identity similar to the parent of the same sex gives rise to a feeling of hope"[38] in his own ability to find gratification from objects of his own choice. Failure to resolve the oedipal conflict interferes with achieving autonomy and results in a feeling of despair because the individual feels incapable of finding satisfactions for himself.[39]

The foregoing discussion of affects should make clear the fact that healthy development emphasizes the acquisition of active patterns of finding enjoyment and of directing aggressions in constructive and socially approved ways, while it also teaches passive modes of being gratified by others. The individual should have learned to accept his feelings and to utilize them in coping and in holding on to or letting go of feelings appropriately.

The effective solution of key learning problems in each developmental period has meant that major energy has not been tied up in maintaining defenses but has been available for handling the ongoing tasks of adaptation. The defenses can be utilized flexibly, are appropriate to the reality situation, and serve a primarily adaptive purpose. Indeed, they often represent a synthesis of attitudes and once-defensive behavior into the adaptive functioning of the ego.[40]

ADAPTIVE AND MALADAPTIVE PATTERNING

The practitioner assesses competence in drive management partly on evidence of the client's previously achieved patterning. The individual who has learned a predominantly active patterning for handling needs and feelings is hopeful about his ability to maintain a predominance of satisfaction over frustration in carrying life roles. In asking for help, the client does not show an affect of helplessness nor an expectation that help will not be forthcoming—evidence of minimum conflicts around dependency. Since he has channeled energy into ego functioning from which he derives pleasure through achieving social competence, he manifests this motivational force in his ability to participate actively in problem-solving. He has established inner controls and patterns in accordance with the reality principle, taking into account future gains in formulating his goal and patterns he can utilize in considering solutions to his difficulties. Since neither his needs nor the related feelings provoke undue anxiety, he can discuss them and attempt to deal with them with a minimum of defensiveness. He has, however, adequate useful defenses. His passive patterns bring gratification in such areas as receptive taking in from others, watching sports or television, being outdoors or in pleasant surroundings, and so forth.

The anxious client caught up in stress or trauma may fail, temporarily, to use his previous effective patterns. The husband, feeling guilty about his wife's hospitalization for tuberculosis, may impulsively buy her gifts he cannot afford or may indulge the children because of similar inability to handle his feelings. In fact, any new situation or problem may require new patterns for handling the feelings aroused by the change. Often because of changing circumstances, such as the loss of a job, the move to a new location, or illness, disability, or loss of a family member, the client finds old patterns for securing need satisfaction no longer work. The practitioner bases his evaluation of capacity on the client's ability to recognize the connection between his new life situation and the demand it makes on him to redefine his needs in terms of ones that are readily achievable. The client also demonstrates ability when he can accept the necessity for finding new patterns, passive or active, for handling needs and feelings. The task becomes more difficult when he has developed maladaptive patterns for dealing with grief, anger, or despair. Relevant examples are the troubled mother who displaces her anger at her alcoholic husband onto the children and the husband who has lost his job and projects his feelings of inadequacy onto his wife by saying that she thinks he is no good or by withdrawing to deal with his guilt.

When the client has regressed because of serious illness, handicap, or trauma, his patterns for handling the change may become more limiting than the change itself. When he can no longer carry the role of breadwinner in his previous manner or pursue active patterns of bowling, gardening, or camping, he may fail to recognize the avenues to satisfaction that remain to him. Because of regression, he may have invested psychic energy in bodily and dependent needs and have decathected ego and social needs. He may have resorted to completely passive patterns of need satisfaction as seen, for example, in the stroke patient who expects his wife to wait on him continually. The wife may become involved in the regressive pattern because she is happy to have found in her husband a child to mother.

The practitioner often becomes aware that the client has been using maladaptive patterns to handle conflicts about dependency, authority, or sexuality when the defensive patterns no longer work. A client who has been pushed to become independent too early in life may, using the defense of denial, have become intent on striving to achieve and unwilling to depend on anyone. The limiting effect of these patterns becomes evident when illness, job loss, or serious stress requires him to take dependently from others or to accept weakness or dependency in spouse or children. The limiting effects of the client's usual way of dealing with authority often become apparent when he attempts to train and discipline his child. In a similar way, the child's behavior often shows the parent's inability to deal with sexuality, reflecting the parent's unacknowledged delinquent wishes or other conflicts related to sexuality.

The practitioner notes client behaviors that indicate maladaptive patterns for handling needs and feelings that derive from the client's severely deprived childhood, as is especially true of many lower-class clients. The needs which the client expresses may be primitive ones, characteristic of early life periods. His desires are largely physical and he seems to be seeking a strong protector, parent, or ally. His needs may be inappropriately related to life roles and his affect is one of helplessness. In other instances, he appears to have little hope of his own ability to secure life's satisfactions. When the client's needs indicate preoedipal fixation, he usually has developed little frustration tolerance or ability to function according to the reality principle. He defines pleasure as immediate gratification—a characteristic of clients with personality disorders who act impulsively. Such a client is unable to translate needs into words and to use words instead of actions to deal with needs. He cannot use thinking to deal with needs by imagining outcomes of behavior and possible choices available to him in handling needs. He has few ego needs, and he has not learned to take pleasure in adequate ego functioning. He may not enjoy mental activity or seeing or hearing interesting things. He may find little satisfaction in achieving in socially valued ways. He may never have learned patterns of finding ways of securing substitute satisfactions or better satisfactions in the future. The practitioner uses the clinical diagnosis in the case of clients with personality disorders, borderline characters, and psychoses to understand that the client may be able to use only the motivation of "what is best for me" and of finding ways of operating with less pain and more pleasure. These individuals have never learned to channel energy into ego functions to a desirable degree nor to acquire patterns for achieving success, and their motivations remain the largely narcissistic ones characteristic of early development.

Other clients, although they have learned to operate according to the reality principle, may use patterns that, to a greater or lesser extent, fail to bring them satisfaction, sometimes because of role requirements that they do not understand how to handle. Often, the client's pathology, such as personality disorder or borderline character, shows that he consistently uses self-defeating patterns.

In some instances, the client's defenses appear to be characteristic of early life periods or to represent a regressive solution for learning tasks which he could not master and about which he is still conflicted. The client's defenses may appear seriously weakened by pathology or heightened by present stress and anxiety.

The Management of Object Relationships

The management of object relationships serves to regulate the individual's relationship with other persons. It is the single most important function of the ego because it enables the child to become human.[41] Through utilizing the mechanisms of identification with loved objects and internalization of their characteristics, he learns from others and brings his maturing new capacities under the control of the ego.[42] The loved persons, by rewarding and punishing, reinforce learning.[43] Erikson postulates that relationships which promote healthy functioning have the quality which he terms mutuality. Each partner learns to get what the other has to give and each needs to give what the other needs to get. In order to achieve mutuality, the individual must learn trust, the foundation of all relationships, and must learn patterns of mutual regulation.[44]

These patterns include ways of achieving and of regulating closeness and distance and of maintaining intimacy without loss of individuality. Moreover, the development of satisfying relationships depends on learning patterns of receptivity and responsiveness to the needs, ideas, wishes, and feelings of the partner. Healthy development should teach a belief in object constancy, which makes possible commitment to an enduring relationship, and should teach patterns for handling separation anxiety and experiences. These experiences include changes in and loss of significant life figures. Owing to the inevitability of frustration as well as gratification from relationships, the individual's patterns should include ways of dealing with likenesses and differences between self and others. Tolerance of others springs, to a considerable degree, from satisfactory resolution of the oedipal conflict and from identification with the parent of the same sex with the resulting acceptance of other human beings and of one's own humanity. A well-developed relationship capacity means that the individual has learned to value the prize of love.

ADAPTIVE AND MALADAPTIVE PATTERNING

The practitioner considers that the client's active patterning of management of relationships shows capacity when he can invest himself and his feelings in developing and handling relationships with other persons, when he can endow the mental image of these persons with trust and pleasure, and when he can hold onto these images with considerable permanence. He also manifests this ability in the way he relates to the practitioner. Because in his life situation he respects the individuality of others and also has a clear sense of his own individuality—because he can manage both closeness and distance—he does not fear engulfment by the practitioner. He has acquired a variety of patterns for relating to others as a child, as a sibling, as a peer, as a spouse, as a parent, as a worker, and as a friend. He can handle the ambivalence aroused in his relationship with the practitioner with whom he utilizes patterns of receptivity and responsiveness. He also demonstrates his ability to learn from the practitioner and other persons. Therefore, he can continue to develop the quality of his relationships and the quality of being human.

Any change in family composition, health, and well-being may require the client to find ways of managing relationships different from those that worked well in the past. The coming into the home of an elderly or ill relative, the loss of a family member, or the disablement of the breadwinner entails giving up old patterns and finding new ones. The single parent must discover new sources of adult companionship. He relates to these individuals differently from the way he did when he was dating before marriage. The deserted wife must now develop with the children patterns of giving and receiving that help the children to deal with their sense of loss of their father. All the family members may need to realign their roles when the father becomes incapacitated, in order to help him retain as much responsibility as a spouse and parent as he is able to carry. Clients in such circumstances as the foregoing show relationship capacity when they can use previous good ability to achieve new learning and can accept the necessity for doing so. Their task becomes more difficult when they have acquired maladaptive patterns, such as when the mother invests everything in caring for the ill relative and neglects her relationship with husband or children. Similarly, the man who loses his job or becomes handicapped may feel inadequate to handle marital or parental relationships. He may withdraw, abdicate responsibilities, or show only passive receptive tendencies and fail to reach out to his wife and children. The working-class male is particularly vulnerable to this kind of reaction because his sense of adequacy depends so heavily on his work role.

The practitioner observes limitation in the management of object relationships in the way the client relates to the practitioner and in the way he handles life relationships. Learning tasks basic to object relationships may never have been achieved by the client.[45] Through his discussion of his relationships with spouse, children, and others, the client evidences inability to trust and his expectations from others of only unkindness, deprivation, and disregard of his needs and feelings. Frequently the client's history of a deprived childhood explains his lack of trust. He may never have had a stable mother figure or may have been deserted repeatedly. In other instances, he may show that he needs to keep the role partner close and is unable to allow individuality. Other learning failures become evident as the client shows that he expects rejection or abandonment because he seems unable to commit himself to any permanent relationship and needs to reject or to leave before he can be rejected. This fear prompts him to break appointments and to test continually the practitioner's constancy. Some clients seem unable to accept ambivalence in a relationship either on their own part or on the part of others.

The practitioner notes evidences of the client's incapacity to establish patterns of mutual regulation, both to give and to take, and to use patterns that bring him satisfaction and give satisfaction to a role partner. In other clients appear evidences of poor fit; the client has difficulty in sharing understanding, perceptions, feelings, problems, decisions, and activities. This difficulty may stem from conflicting cultural patterns for handling role responsibilities and securing satisfaction and from role expectations which are culturally different from those of the partner.

The practitioner assesses the development achieved by the client. He determines whether he has ever been able to form a satisfying relationship and the nature and extent of his unresolved learning problems. The nature of the client's life relationships may be seriously distorted by pathology. The practitioner understands not only the schizophrenic's fear of closeness but also his great need to be able to define the difference between self and object and to use the practitioner as a stable object who helps him do so. The practitioner also realizes that the client with a personality disorder tends to use patterns of exploitation as he manipulates and maneuvers for his own self-interests in his relationships with family and with the practitioner. The borderline client fears loss of separateness in a relationship and needs continual assistance in self-definition.

The Executive Function

Executant competence is the ability to affect the environment through the use of bodily apparatuses and sense organs in the service of the ego to carry out goal-directed activities. This function makes it possible to decide and to act effectively and in ways which demonstrate social competence. Spitz comments on the pleasure the child experiences in discharging drive tensions through activities which become increasingly goal-directed.[46] According to Engel's discussion of Jean Piaget's theory, the individual develops a capacity for goal-directed behavior by progressively developing an ability to experiment with ways of influencing the environment and by finding new means-end behaviors.[47] The individual learns mastery of his body and how to use bodily skills and abilities to explore and manipulate objects and to affect others. As a result, he develops what Charles A. Malone calls "a concept of the self as active."[48]

Through learning appropriate sex-age patterns of work and play, the individual achieves effective patterns for carrying his social roles. Executant ability is manifested in task orientation, setting of goals, perseverance, and pride in accomplishment. The individual acquires a sense of competence and a sense of satisfaction in active mastery when he can achieve success through appropriate role activities.

ADAPTIVE AND MALADAPTIVE PATTERNS

The client demonstrates appropriate active patterning of executant ability when he can decide, make choices for himself, and select a course of action. His executant ability is also apparent when he can plan and organize activities without prolonged indecision and can persist in pursuing these activities in the face of difficulty.[49] These capacities are available to the client in dealing with his present problem and situation.

The client with executant capacity reveals this fact in the way he has carried his life role. The breadwinner has had stable employment, which shows that he can invest energy in work and that his work gives him both pleasure and a sense of completeness. However, he does not place undue emphasis on success to bolster shaky self-esteem. The spouses share their activities, complementing each other in the management of home tasks and responsibilities. They enjoy doing for and with each other and engage in joint decision-making. As parents, this couple clearly distinguishes task responsibilities that are appropriate for parents from those that the children should perform. The mother is active in behalf of her children but shows no need for sacrificial giving or overdoing, thus removing appropriate responsibilities from the children. The parents allow the children to participate appropriately in family decisions without feeling threatened. The client who has achieved executant competence has set goals for himself toward which he works steadily. The family also has goals and works as a unit to achieve them because the parents teach these patterns to the children.

Anxiety caused by stress, trauma, or by hopelessness and discouragement may interfere with the client's use of previously adequate patterning of executant ability. He may seem immobilized—unable to decide or to take beginning steps to do something about his difficulties. With relief from anxiety and support, the client may be able to use his previously adequate ways of coping. The regressed client shows that he has lost hold of previous activity patterns, as evident in clients who have been hospitalized for serious mental or physical illness. For example, the family of a cardiac patient may contribute to the regression if they overprotect the ill family member and fail to help him to resume doing things for himself as soon as possible. Inappropriate management of medical regimes may also contribute to loss of executant capacity unless the patient is taught, for instance, to administer his own insulin, manage his diet, and so forth. The patient may become afraid of resuming activity unless the physician emphasizes what he can do. Lack of appropriate physical therapy, physical rehabilitation, and other services to teach the handicapped client new activity patterns may contribute to his remaining more disabled than necessary.

In evaluating limitations in executant capacity, the practitioner should remember that individuals vary constitutionally in activity patterns. Some individuals tend to be much more active than others, although, as they develop, they seem to approach the mean in this regard.[50] Life experiences in the environment may provide more stimulation and opportunity for the development of patterns of activity for some persons than for others, particularly the patterns of role behavior taught in the culture. The practitioner draws upon information about cultural differences to understand the lower-class father's tendency toward passive patterning of his parental role, the lower-class wife's inability to share actively in decision-making with her husband, and the tendency in working-class and lower-class families to have a sharp division of parental responsibilities rather than a sharing of joint endeavors. The practitioner evaluates the effects of this cultural orientation on the functioning of reciprocal role partners. Similarly, role strain between marital partners may derive from cultural conflicts regarding appropriate role activities for each.

In many instances, the client may never have learned active role behaviors as parent or worker nor have had any stable adult role models that he could internalize—a fact that becomes apparent through examining the client's life story and the way he now handles role responsibilities. The client may never have learned to invest interest in doing or to find activities rewarding.

Some clients with emotional conflict relating to carrying life roles suffer from inhibitions in role activity, as may be evident, particularly, when the individual holds on to his childhood and resists growing up. Such immature individuals tend to experience difficulty in taking responsibility for making decisions or responsibility for actively carrying out decisions. Other clients cannot passively rely on help from others in making decisions even when they should appropriately do so.

The client's role functioning may reflect his serious pathology. The schizophrenic often sees doing as a requirement imposed from without. He may never have learned to invest energy in activities like work or carrying home responsibilities. He feels put upon when he is faced with realistic role expectations because he has never experienced satisfaction from these activities. As a result of his life experiences he seems to say, "These adults ask so much and give so little." The borderline client and the client with a personality disorder have internalized distorted role models and frequently those role models that reflect the client's view of himself as still a child unable to function without his parents. He asks to be told what to do; he can neither make decisions nor follow a consistent course of action.

The Integrative Function

The capacity to learn and to integrate new patterns into ego functioning exemplifies the integrative or synthetic function.[51] As indicated earlier, some frustration is essential to learning. As the individual experiences frustration or a situation in which previous coping patterns will not work, the resulting stress arouses anxiety that motivates him to find new patterns and new solutions. The learning tasks at each growth stage give rise to usual stress and motivate new learning, thus resulting in the differentiation of ego functions. Solution of the tasks promotes integration on progressively higher levels, with increasing mastery. As Lawrence S. Kubie observes, all ego functions become patterned, but the normal individual is able to learn and to change the patterns to meet the changing nature of the reality situation. The integrative function of the ego, which overlaps all other functions, makes this learning possible. Pathology, according to Kubie, results in a repetitive self-defeating pattern poorly adapted to reality. The repetitive nature of the pattern derives from the fact that it is not under conscious control but springs from predominantly unconscious motivations. The problem has been repressed and become unconscious; it is never solved.

Instead, it gives rise to repetitive behavior characteristic of the conflict at the time it was repressed early in life. The gratifications sought in this behavior symbolize early needs. They symbolize the earlier insatiable and unrealized childish gratifications. In contrast, when energy is not tied up in conflict and when the motivations giving rise to behavior derive largely from conscious sources, the individual can flexibly learn and adaptively change his behavior patterns to fit reality. He can then integrate these patterns into his total functioning.[52] The more conflict that ties up psychic energy, the less energy is available for new learning.

The integrative function also enables the ego to reopen issues, to redo and relearn earlier problems on a higher level, to heal trauma, and to engage in restitutive efforts. This function becomes apparent in the way the individual handles severe stress, such as the cumulative difficulties of poverty; belonging to a minority group; or the loss of such ego tools as sight, hearing, or bodily parts. The grief work and the final efforts toward restitution constitute the ego's attempts at healing. For example, the adolescent who has to give up previous identifications with significant persons replaces them with new objects in his peer groups; loss of a child often motivates parents to adopt one or to give birth to another baby of their own; deprivation and frustration move the individual to restitutive efforts to make up for the difficulties by being good to himself and finding other ways of securing compensatory satisfaction. Pathology tends to limit capacity for new learning, to a greater or lesser extent.

However, the practitioner cannot usually evaluate the capacity of the client to learn and to change except as a result of helping efforts that offer the opportunity for new learning and that motivate and support the individual in his efforts to learn. The method of ego analysis provides a way of strengthening the client's capacity to learn and to increase his conscious control of behavior.

Ego Identity

To avoid having the discussion of ego functions appear to fragment an understanding of ego capacity, the concept of ego identity will be utilized to explain how, through the sense of identity, the individual integrates all of his ego functioning and achieves a feeling of wholeness and relatedness, both within himself and in respect to his place in society. The achievement of a sense of identity depends upon several related achievements which include a sense of continuity, commitment to work and sex roles, social confirmation of worth, a feeling of self-esteem, and an amalgamation of previous identifications with significant persons.[53] However, the process of identity formation is an ongoing one, continuing throughout the life cycle.

Continuity gives the individual a sense of relationship between his past, his present, and his future. Having learned dependable patterns of ego functioning in the past, he can draw on these to cope with the present and can look forward with hope to being able to meet social expectations. He acquires a sense of inner goodness and of being reasonably well able to live up to his ideals and values. He also views himself as competent and effective.[54] Beginning with inner trust, the individual progressively learns to value his body and to consider himself as lovable, as reliable, and as worthwhile. A body image, derived from a dependable and intact body, contributes to the individual's self-concept.

Each role that the individual carries evokes different aspects of the ego in a different way.[55] The carrying of social roles requires utilization of all ego functions and, especially, the executive function in role behavior. Each new role changes the individual's sense of identity, adding new ego patterns and changing others. Loss of a role brings a sense of loss of some aspect of identity. Social roles, therefore, also connect the individual with society and the world of reality and carry forward the concept of continuity between self and society. The social appraisal of his worth and the appraisal by his peers of his ability to carry life roles will always remain, for most individuals, a major aspect of the image that they internalize in their sense of identity and the confirmation that they seek in order to validate their sense of self-esteem.

The identifications made by the individual throughout his lifetime form the core of his personal identity. Identifications assume major importance during adolescence and young adulthood when the individual should be able to combine these identifications in a unique way to form the essence of his own identity. Faulty or negative identifications can result in the identity confusion apparent in many of today's alienated youth. The adolescent shows his weak sense of identity in the aimlessness with which he pursues life plans.

The practitioner judges that the client has achieved a sense of identity when he has achieved patterns of ego functions that have enabled him to deal effectively with the demands of living. In addition, he is comfortable with his own body, values himself, and seems sure of his own worth and dignity. He has achieved, or believes he can achieve, a place in society through carrying sex and work roles. He shows no confusion over his sexual identity and no need to bolster his identity with symbolic success or pseudoachievement in order to feel adequate.

The client manifests failures in identity formation when he expresses low self-esteem, lack of self-trust, or expectation of rejection or of being considered unworthy of help. Marital partners frequently defend their poor sense of identity by resisting the giving in to the other partner and continually asserting independence. If one accepts the formulations of Arthur Schmale that were discussed previously, an affect of helplessness indicates the possibility of identity formation that has advanced little beyond early childhood since the individual has not developed reliable patterns of mastery and still feels dependent on someone else to satisfy basic needs.

Similarly, an affect of hopelessness suggests the possibility that the available ego patterns may stem from late childhood and a preoedipal identity.

On the other hand, various kinds of trauma may disturb a previously well-formed identity. Loss of a sexual organ or bodily part changes body and self-image from intact and reliable to damaged and unreliable. The cardiac patient, for example, demonstrates his threatened sense of identity when he compulsively engages in push-ups against medical recommendations. On the other hand, a patient whose long-standing defect has been corrected by surgery may have trouble in developing a healthier body image. Congenital defects may contribute to a poor body and self-image, particularly if the parents view the child as inadequate. Giving birth to a defective child who cannot confirm the identity of good parent, in addition to the related social role difficulty, usually results in the parent's loss of identity through lack of social confirmation or loss of self-esteem.

Any serious failure in social role functioning as spouse, parent, or worker tends to cause a negative social evaluation of the individual and to confirm his own negative or shaky identity. Loss of a social role or a role change always changes identity to some degree and may mean loss of identity. The client frequently projects his own feelings of worthlessness on others and believes that family and friends consider him inadequate.

In many instances, the practitioner can infer negative or poor identity formation from the life circumstances of the client that failed to provide any stable figures with whom to identify. Serious conflict or pathology means that part of self is unacceptable, resulting in loss of a sense of wholeness with concomitant weak identity formation. Compulsive pregnancies in or out of wedlock, fathering many illegitimate children, or engaging in sex exploits demonstrate weak sex identifications. Erik H. Erikson's concept of identity confusion calls attention to individuals who have never achieved a firm sense of their own individuality, have achieved mainly negative identifications, have no concept of their place in a world of work or their place in the family, and have not been able to commit themselves to significant social roles.[56] The motorcycle culture exemplifies the young male who bolsters his shaky masculine identity with reckless performance on his powerful motorcycle that represents an extension of self. Past history shows that many of these youths grew up with successful, cold, critical fathers with whom they could not identify and who weakened their sense of masculine worth.

The Superego and Moral Character

The roots of superego formation lie in the early use of identification with the parent and internalization of parental characteristics. Authorities suggest that the parents' warmth and use of love and consistency in discipline facilitate the learning of guilt over lapses from moral expectations. When the parent uses aggression, he tends to provoke anger and to reinforce aggression in the child, and he fails to provide a model of control.[57] Lawrence Kohlberg believes that identification with the parent of the same sex forms the basis for the individual's wish, not only to be like his parent, but to grow up and become a parent. This idea sheds light on the difficulties of today's youth who have elected to "cop out" and cannot face what growing up entails. The parents' warmth in taking the role of teacher, based on identification, promotes the child's identification with the parent and prepares him for adolescence. In addition, positive affectional relations promote the child's ability to take the role of the other and develop his capacity for warmth and empathy.[58]

In the resolution of the oedipal, as the child identifies with the parent and internalizes his functions of warning, guiding, rewarding, and punishing, the superego functions and guilt become part of the child's character structure. The core of moral character lies in the capacity to identify with another human being, to feel at one with him, and to share vicariously in his feelings and experiences and, thus, to become able to empathize with other persons, and to feel remorse for transgressions against others. Because the individual has identified with the role of parent, he wants to grow up and to reverse the passive position of childhood through active doing and giving to the coming generation. He thus becomes ready to learn how to pass on to the next generation a feeling of trust, a sense of inner and outer order, and a concern for and consideration of others. He accepts his common humanity and takes into account the effect of his behavior on others, particularly if he has been so taught by the parent. Kohlberg also contributes the idea that moral strength—or the ability to resist temptation and to live up to the internalized moral norms—consists largely of ego strength. As the individual develops foresight, can predict the long-range consequences of his actions, weighs probabilities, and defers gratification, he can deal with moral issues. In particular, the capacity for empathy and for concern over the effect of one's behavior on others increases moral strength. Kohlberg quotes Piaget to the effect that role-taking in peer groups teaches "logical principles of justice" as a necessary "condition of social relationships." Kohlberg believes that the child's participation in group activities helps him to internalize the moral values of parents and the culture since it helps him to relate these values to the "social order and to his own goals as a social self."[59]

The client's moral strength is demonstrated in several ways. He shows that he has internalized from his parents and his culture a set of moral values and that he uses them to guide his behavior. He has expectations of himself that are neither too lax nor too excessive. He can trust himself to act in ways that contribute to social relationships with family and friends. The patterning of his ego functions makes it generally possible for him to live up to these expectations in the ways in which he deals with the realities of his life.

Notes

1. Samuel Finestone, "Issues Involved in Developing Diagnostic Classifications for Casework," in *Casework Papers from the National Conference on Social Welfare* (New York: Family Service Association of America, 1960), pp. 139–54.

2. Helen Harris Perlman, *Social Casework: A Problem-solving Process* (Chicago: University of Chicago Press, 1957), pp. 171–80.

3. Finestone, "Issues," pp. 141–43.

4. Robert P. Knight, "Borderline States," in *Psychoanalytic Psychiatry and Psychology: Clinical and Theoretical Papers*, ed. Robert P. Knight and Cyrus R. Friedman (New York: International Universities Press, 1954).

5. Heinz Hartmann, *Ego Psychology and the Problem of Adaptation* (New York: International Universities Press, 1958), p. 58.

6. Hadley Cantril, "Perception and Interpersonal Relations," *American Journal of Psychiatry*, 114:119–26 (August 1957).

7. Charles A. Malone, "Developmental Deviations Considered in the Light of Environmental Forces," in *The Drifters: Children of Disorganized Lower-Class Families*, ed. Eleanor Pavenstedt (Boston: Little, Brown & Co., 1967), pp. 127-28.

8. George L. Engel, *Psychological Development in Health and Disease* (Philadelphia: W.B. Saunders Company, 1962), p. 124.

9. Erik H. Erikson, *Childhood and Society*, 2d ed. rev. (New York: W. W. Norton and Company, 1963), pp. 247–54, 263–66.

10. Charles A. Malone, "Guideposts Derived from Normal Development," in *The Drifters*, ed. Pavenstedt, p. 94.

11. Stanley H. King, *Perceptions of Illness and Medical Practice* (New York: Russell Sage Foundation, 1962), p. 32.

12. Melvin L. Kohn, "Social Class and the Exercise of Parental Authority," *American Sociological Review*, 24:352-36 (June 1959).

13. Pavenstedt, *The Drifters*, pp. 62–4, 126–29.

14. Paul R. Miller, *Sense and Symbol: A Textbook of Human Behavioral Science* (New York: Harper & Row, 1967), p. 259 and chap. 10.

15. Ibid., chap. 9.

16. René A. Spitz, *No and Yes: On the Genesis of Human Communication* (New York: International Universities Press, 1957), pp. 49–59 and chap. 10.

17. René A. Spitz, *The First Year of Life: A Psychoanalytic Study of Normal and Deviant Development of Object Relations* (New York: International Universities Press, 1965).

18. Hartmann, *Ego Psychology*, pp. 14–15.

19. Anny Katan, "Some Thoughts About the Role of Verbalization in Early Childhood," *Psychoanalytic Study of the Child,* vol. 16 (New York: International Universities Press, 1961), pp. 184–88.

20. Miller, *Sense and Symbol*, pp. 253–4.

21. Erikson, *Childhood and Society*, pp. 80–91.

22. Hartmann, *Ego Psychology*, p. 60.

23. Martin P. Deutsch, "The Disadvantaged Child and the Learning Process," in *Mental Health of the Poor: New Treatment Approaches for Low Income People*, ed. Frank Riessman, Jerome Cohen, and Arthur Pearl (New York: Free Press, 1964), pp. 172–87.

24. Herman Nunberg, *Principles of Psychoanalysis: Their Application to the Neuroses* (New York: International Universities Press, 1955), pp. 45, 189–90; and Engel, *Psychological Development*, pp. 123–25.

25. Engel, *Psychological Development*, pp. 112–16.

26. Sibylle K. Escalona, *The Roots of Individuality: Normal Patterns of Development in Infancy* (Chicago: Aldine Publishing Company, 1968), pp. 517–18.

27. Ibid., pp. 7–8.

28. Ibid., pp. 510–13.

29. Ibid., chaps. 3, 12 and pp. 509–18.

30. Ibid., p. 10.

31. Hartmann, *Ego Psychology*, pp. 46–7.

32. Robert W. White, "Competence and the Growth of Personality," in *The Ego*, ed. Jules H. Masserman, *Science and Psychoanalysis*, vol. 11 (New York: Grune and Stratton, 1967), pp. 42–58.

33. Engel, *Psychological Development*, p. 68.

34. Pavenstedt, *The Drifters*, chaps. 4, 6, 7.

35. Heinz Hartmann, "Notes on the Reality Principle," *Psychoanalytic Study of the Child*, vol. 11 (New York: International Universities Press, 1956), pp. 31–53.

36. Hartmann, *Ego Psychology*, p. 43.

37. Arthur H. Schmale, Jr., "A Genetic View of Affects: With Special Reference to the Genesis of Helplessness and Hopelessness," *Psychoanalytic Study of the Child*, vol. 19 (New York: International Universities Press, 1964), p. 287.

38. Schmale, "Genetic View of Affects," pp. 299–300.

39. Ibid., pp. 287–310.

40. Hartmann, *Ego Psychology*, chaps. 1, 2.

41. Miller, *Sense and Symbol*, chap. 7.

42. Sally Provence and Samuel Ritvo, "Effects of Deprivation on Institutionalized Infants: Disturbances in Development of Relationship to Inanimate Objects," in *Psychoanalytic Study of the Child*, vol. 16 (New York: International Universities Press, 1961), pp. 189–205.

43. Spitz, *First Year of Life*, chap. 7.

44. Erikson, *Childhood and Society*, pp. 72–97.

45. Pavenstedt, *The Drifters*, pp. 64–71.

46. Spitz, *First Year of Life*, p. 123.

47. Engel, *Psychological Development*, chap. 8.

48. Charles A. Malone, "Guideposts Derived from Normal Development" and "The Psychosocial Characteristics of the Children from a Developmental Standpoint," in *The Drifters*, ed. Pavenstedt, pp. 101–102, 113.

49. See, for example, Clyde Kluckhohn and Henry A. Murray ed., *Personality in Nature, Society, and Culture*, 2d ed. rev. (New York: Alfred A. Knopf, 1953), pp. 24–26.

50. Escalona, *Individuality*, chap. 2.

51. Joseph C. Solomon, "Ego Mastery and the Therapeutic Process," *American Journal of Psychotherapy*, 12:650–59 (October 1958).

52. Lawrence S. Kubie, "The Fundamental Nature of Distinction Between Normality and Neurosis," *Psychoanalytic Quarterly*, 23:167–204 (1954).

53. Erik H. Erikson, *Identity, Youth and Crisis* (New York: W. W. Norton and Company, 1968).

54. Pavenstedt, *The Drifters*, pp. 93, 115–117.

55. Nathan W. Ackerman, *The Psychodynamics of Family Life: Diagnosis and Treatment of Family Relationships* (New York: Basic Books, 1958), chap. 4.

56. Erikson, *Identity, Youth*, chaps. 4, 6.

57. Wesley C. Becker, "Consequences of Different Kinds of Parental Discipline," in *Review of Child Development Research*, ed. Martin L. Hoffman and Lois W. Hoffman, vol. 1 (New York: Russell Sage Foundation, 1964), 169–208.

58. Lawrence Kohlberg, "Development of Moral Character and Moral Ideology," in *Review of Child Development Research*, ed. Hoffman and Hoffman, pp. 383–431.

59. Ibid.

SIX

Focus on Increasing Capacity and Lessening Limitations

In respect to the foregoing functions of the ego and ego identity, this chapter explains treatment techniques for increasing capacity and for lessening limitations.

SINCE ego psychology assumes that ego functioning makes possible the mastery of self and environment, helping based on the method of ego analysis takes as its goal increasing the client's conscious control of behavior and ability to handle his life situation. This method embodies and puts into practice the social work values of self-realization and self-direction by providing a language that makes it possible to define with the client in nonthreatening terms (1) what he needs to change in order to cope and (2) ways of changing, in relation to learning. The practititioner uses his analysis of the client's coping patterns in each ego function to help him become aware of adaptive patterns he can strengthen and of maladaptive ones he needs to change. The functions of the ego provide treatment categories that are logically related to those used in diagnosis. When the practitioner strengthens the client's coping abilities, he thereby strengthens his capacity to achieve a more satisfactory life and to exercise greater self-direction because he understands better, perceives more clearly, and can act more appropriately to achieve social competence and the valuing of social relatedness. Ego analysis provides a method of intervention in the developmental process. The practitioner uses this method to support the developmental process when stress threatens to disturb it, to reopen the developmental process when the client evidences failures in learning, and to restore the developmental process temporarily interrupted by demands with which the ego was unable to cope.

The treatment measures and techniques fall in three groupings: The practitioner allies himself with the client and lends his ego strengths; he serves as an identification model and teaches in order to develop new strengths in the client; and he supports and encourages the client to use his own ego capacity. Helping the client to divert his energies into more personally satisfying and socially acceptable channels constitutes one of the major aspects of these treatment measures. The practitioner also tries to help the client develop an environment that is less limiting and more supporting. With any client, the practitioner may use all of these measures. Probably to a greater extent than has been realized, the practitioner lends his own good abilities. He shares knowledge and understanding with the client, particularly in relation to the behavior of self and of others. He continually shares his perceptions of the meanings of what the client, family, and others are doing, saying, or feeling. The practitioner also uses his feelings in ways helpful to the client, frequently acting for and with the client and giving direction, advice, and guidance.

The practitioner continually teaches and often consciously serves as an identification model. Whenever he finds capacity in the client, he encourages and supports the client in using his own abilities. Treatment techniques and measures used in the method of ego analysis encourage active coping and the progressive psychological process through the client's acquiring of new learning, his strengthening of old learning, and, to some extent, his undoing of previous faulty learning. The practitioner helps the client to strengthen coping abilities in all ego functions and to lessen the use of ineffective patterns in those functions most essentially involved in solving the given problem. This goal may require bringing about changes in a single ego function or in groups of functions.

The Cognitive Functions

The practitioner can help the client to understand the ways in which thinking and talking contribute toward problem-solving and to apprehend that being aware of his problem-situation opens the way toward mastery. In a related way, the client should understand what changes are needed and how to achieve them. The thinking activities that the practitioner tries to mobilize or to develop include reality-based rational thinking; labeling, word formation, and use; concept formation and conceptual thinking; anticipation or the exercise of judgment; the giving and getting of relevant information; and the use of communication in problem-solving. Agreement between practitioner and client that the problem is a shared one—shared with the reciprocal role partner—indicates that their thinking and understanding are congruent and that help should be given to both clients in ways that will promote their joint thinking.

LESSENING LIMITATIONS: RATIONAL THINKING

Patterns of reality-based rational thinking form one of the base lines from which practitioners usually start, and these can be mobilized or strengthened in most clients. Heinz Hartmann regards thinking as an autonomous function that develops relatively independently of the drives and that tends to become less involved in conflict and conflicted feelings than do some other functions. Therefore, asking the client to discuss his ideas about what is happening and what he is doing tends to mobilize his efforts. The practitioner guides the client regarding what is relevant and then helps him to put his ideas together in some coherent form through using such techniques as recapitulation of the interview, summarization of progress or lack of progress, reformulation of ideas and information either during or at the end of the interview. He brings the client back when he tends to wander and stimulates the client to consider relevant aspects of the situation or of his problem-solving activities. He encourages the client's orderly assembling of ideas: "Try to get a clearer picture," "Can't we clear up some of this fog," "Let's get down to brass tacks," "Let's deal with the nitty gritty business," or, "It seems to me you are leaving out a lot of things." With the regressed client or one immobilized by anxiety, the practitioner frequently starts by stimulating the patterns of active thinking about the problem-situation, thus initiating the progressive process. As an example, a practitioner encouraged the client to question why he needed to become involved repetitiously with an older woman and so destroy his marriage.

With clients who have poorly developed egos or so-called borderline character disorders or with schizophrenics, encouraging the client to talk and to think about his daily doings enables him to get a better picture of how he is operating.[1] He begins to include many details previously overlooked as the practitioner takes him mentally through such steps as what exactly happened or did not happen before the children went to school; what was the sequence of events when the husband came home; what the client said or did or did not do that led to the boss' getting angry with him. In helping any client to develop a cognitive map of his own or others' functioning in relation to his situation, the practitioner encourages him to be specific and definite about details since foggy generalities usually obscure the reality. The practitioner can also help the client to think about what he could have done differently and about better ways of achieving his purposes. Moreover, the cognitive maps of role partners who share a problem should agree in order to furnish a similar basis for working toward change.

The use of rational thinking may require helping the client become aware of ideas about which he had been only partly conscious. Sometimes trauma, anxiety, or strong feelings push ideas out of consciousness. The practitioner, realizing this tendency, may participate with the client in some key life experiences in which he faces a reality situation. He can then better help the client to acknowledge this shared reality. He may, in the medical setting, accompany the client to physical therapy, to the brace shop, or to the coffee shop; he later can help him to admit to ideas about his disability. Participating with the mother in observing a child in nursery school can help her to bring out her ideas about the child's difficulty and how to deal with it. The actuality of experiences shared with the practitioner may enable the client to admit unpleasant ideas into consciousness and to regard thinking as necessary to realistic planning. Thinking about what will be involved in assuming a new role helps to prepare the ego to handle the role. Sometimes, also, the practitioner suggests a little homework, something the client can think about and be ready to discuss at the next interview. This technique can be used when the client seems unready to think about some aspect of his situation during the present interview.

LESSENING LIMITATIONS: LABELING, VOCABULARY

Closely related to rational thinking is the development of word formation and correct labeling. Words and terms correctly used can make it possible to describe the properties of events, situations, and behavior and to understand them. Labeling provides a first step toward mastery. Learning to label correctly the symptoms of the illness furnishes a measure of control to the mentally ill client and to his role partner by enabling them to discriminate between health and illness. Cardiac patients and other physically ill patients can find out how to differentiate symptoms of excessive fatigue or impending diabetic coma from less important or unimportant physical manifestations. Parents and family members may come to appreciate the fact that use of correct terms can improve understanding of their own and others' behavior. For example, the child's desire to explore, to experiment with aggression, or to find out about anger is not necessarily defiance but may be a step in learning autonomy. The mother's setting of limits is not a hostile act, but protection.

For clients with poor cognitive functioning, improvement of verbal ability may constitute one of the most difficult helping tasks. Frequently, the lower-class deprived client has never learned to describe feelings or relationships; he thinks and talks in concrete terms. The practitioner usually begins by increasing the client's capacity to describe and discuss concrete aspects of living. Moreover, since the thinking of many of these individuals has not advanced much beyond the sensorimotor stage and relates to acting, they can begin to describe "doings" of themselves and others. Because nonverbal clients may not at first grasp the need for increased verbal ability, the practitioner often attempts in the interview to teach appropriate verbal expression. For example, he helps the client to find words that convey his meaning, or he reformulates the client's communication for purposes of clarity. Using the techniques of joint interviews, of family sessions, or of home visits, he may verbalize more clearly what family members appear to be saying or what they may be communicating nonverbally. When the practitioner accompanies the parent to a school conference or clinic visit, he may put into words salient aspects of the experience and encourage the client to respond. Because the nonverbal client especially lacks words with which to describe feelings, the practitioner may begin to help him to do so when the relationship is sufficiently strong. It may take time before the client trusts enough to express intangible concerns.[2] Some individuals have little ability to differentiate kinds of feelings and, hence, to discuss them. The practitioner, therefore, may inquire whether the client's present feelings are the same as or different from those he felt on another occasion when he discussed feelings. If the feelings are different, the practitioner should elicit how they are different. In presenting his own ideas about family relationships, the practitioner needs to remember that deprived clients tend to think pictorially; therefore, drawing word pictures can help the client begin to think about relationships and about less concrete aspects of behavior. Moreover, when the client uses primary process thinking, either because of regression or of developmental failures, the practitioner needs to help him in distinguishing the word from the reality and the wish from the happening. He may comment as follows: "Angry words do not have the power to destroy because they are only words." "Wishing to injure one's children is not the same as having it happen." "Many people wish things but do not necessarily give way to acting out the wishes."

LESSENING LIMITATIONS: CONCEPTUAL THINKING

In the guiding of human behavior, the formation of reality concepts may be more crucial than has been realized. Clients caught in early growth periods may have formed few usable reality concepts because they are mental representations of consistent characteristics of experience. For some clients who have never formed concepts of object or of self or have lost them because of regressive processes, this forming of object or self-concept may be the place to begin. The practitioner attempts to represent, perhaps for the first time, a stable, consistent object with clearly defined ideas, attitudes, feelings, and abilities, including the ability to act. Perhaps the ability to act is one of the factors that account for the effectiveness of techniques that use acting. For example, the practitioner may begin to help the schizophrenic by engaging with him in various activities on the ward or in groups; in one treatment plan the practitioner scrubbed the bathroom and did housekeeping chores.[3] Perhaps for the same reason, the homemaker, the public health nurse, or the indigenous worker who rolls up her sleeves and participates with the client in some activity quickly assumes meaning as a significant life figure because these individuals act in relation to the client. The child first develops a mental representation of mother as an object through her doings. Participation in the daily activities of clients in the mental hospital or in an institution for disturbed, retarded, or delinquent youngsters is relatively easy. Probably other practitioners should consider how to find ways of doing with the client that begin to define the practitioner as a person. One practitioner started this process by bringing a tool kit to the home to repair broken furniture. Others have shared the family meal, helped the client find a house, or participated in group activities and, in these ways, strengthened the client's mental grasp of himself as a person in relation to another person.

In whatever way he makes himself real to the client, the practitioner must also help the client to separate his own ideas from those of others. He encourages the client to bring out his own thoughts and, in appropriate ways, to differentiate them from those of his mother or wife or from the ideas of experts and authority figures. Since many lower-class, socially and emotionally deprived parents do not see their children as individuals, in home visits the practitioner can encourage the parent to individualize the children. The practitioner calls them by name, finds ways to share the child's concerns and interests, and supports the parent in identifying the child's good points and particular needs. The weakness of the client's subject-object reality concepts usually extends to authority figures whom these clients tend to view as unhappy replicas of their parents. The practitioner should always help the client to see teachers, judges, and doctors as real persons by explaining about them, their responsibilities, and their function and by fostering interpersonal communication.

Another reality concept that may have little meaning to

the client is that of choice. Many clients who have gained this concept may need to have it consciously strengthened as they face such major decisions as planning divorce, relinquishing a child for adoption, entering a home for the aged, or consenting to an operation. The practitioner points out that the client does have a choice. For other individuals, especially for those who have lived in poverty, life experiences have never taught the possibility of choice or what is involved in making choices, particularly in regard to their own behavior. They have learned that one gives in to authority and to superior power, but they have not learned that one can consciously choose what to do and not to do. One practitioner taught choice in buying by playing a game in which he and the client made out an imaginary shopping list. With the previous consent of a supermarket and general merchandise store, each "shopped" and then compared items they had collected. In this way, the practitioner taught the client how to compare labels, prices, and quality and to choose wisely. The concept of choice can be useful in many aspects of home management, of handling children, and of finding and keeping a job and can be taught in relation to the reality aspects of living and of exploring the neighborhood or community to find new resources or opportunities. Often, clients think that no possibilities for choice exist, when actually there may be many. For example, a young veteran who felt himself caught in the necesssity to marry a girl about whom he had considerable unconscious guilt could decide to pursue his educational goals when he was faced with the fact that he could choose. When the client tends to act blindly, the practitioner can point out that he has made a choice and ask if he had thought out this choice beforehand. He can ask the client if, in retrospect, he could have considered another course of action and could have weighed which course would have been better.

The concept of choice becomes crucial with the impulsive acting-out client and contributes to the development of other ego functions necessary for increased self-control. The practitioner tries to keep in the forefront of consciousness of such an individual the idea that he did have a choice and that he could choose in relation to acting by using thought. Concepts of cause-effect relationships and of choice reinforce each other as the practitioner asks the client to examine what he could have chosen to do and to compare results. The client with a poorly developed ego may only be able to grasp the idea of choosing what is best for him on the basis of judging what causes him pain and trouble. Others can understand only the idea of choosing to let others make decisions or to carry for them those responsibilities that are beyond their capacity. For example, they allow the doctor to decide when an operation is imperative, allow a child-caring agency to assume guardianship of the child, or allow the practitioner to decide about the feasibility of some plan. The practitioner only encourages the client to use the passive mode when he has clear diagnostic indications of the necessity for the choice and of the client's inability to choose.

The related concepts of discipline and of inner control are also mental ideas that the client may never have learned if his life experiences have taught that authority comes solely from outside self. Some parents equate discipline with power and engage in a power struggle. Other clients equate discipline with hostile aggression and are afraid to set limits.[4] If the client shows some confusion about concepts, the practitioner can clarify conceptual differences and can help the client understand the need to acquire a mental image of the behaviors related to each concept. What does the parent do and say when he disciplines or when he sets limits? When the client has poor cognitive ability, the practitioner may have to teach a concept using various techniques that help the client experience the meaning of the concept. He then makes the learning conscious. Such techniques include use of the homemaker or an indigenous worker who demonstrates and then discusses the meaning of appropriate discipline or the use of group experiences in which group members try out their ideas and arrive at a clearer shared understanding of the meaning of an idea, such as setting limits. Observation in a child development center, where the mother sees appropriate methods of teaching inner controls, demonstrates this idea that later can be talked over with her.

Similarly, the concept of initiative or of intentionality becomes real to the client as the practitioner stimulates him to try things out and to take first steps and then encourages the efforts that he makes on his own. The fear of failing prevents many individuals from trying out new ways of doing—a fact that vocational and rehabilitation counselors especially need to recognize. In one instance, the client only grasped the idea that the initiative he must use must be his own when, after his first failure, the rehabilitation counselor told him that only he could decide what he was capable of doing and wanted to do and that the counselor would not push him. Often, the practitioner can clarify with the client the reality of his not being able to decide until he has tried out possibilities. Sometimes only through use of trial and error can the client give up unrealistic plans or find that a plan is more realistic than he expected. If the practitioner discusses with him the fact, for example, that many people change job plans and vocational goals or their ways of handling their affairs before they find the one best suited to their needs and abilities, the client may be able to accept the value of experimenting. A related useful concept states that one seldom progresses in a straight line but must learn to tolerate temporary setbacks, to pick up the pieces, and to go on. If fear of failure has been a life problem, the client may not be able to grasp the concept of initiative until he has used inner perception to consciously deal with this limitation. In any given case, the practitioner may identify such additional key concepts whose reality the client needs to experience, understand, and use as interaction, relationships, clean home, happy children, work, play, giving and receiving, and a host of others.

Conceptual thinking provides a way of bringing order into

the problem-solving situation. When the client is not using his conceptual ability to understand the situation, the practitioner may help the client to generalize and so to form a more coherent idea of his difficulties.[5] Some parents can begin to be more objective about their problems in relationship when they view them as problems of fit or see the interaction between themselves and their child as a pattern of circularity with child and parents contributing to and reinforcing the pattern. Married couples may find illumination in the idea that the behavior of each one influences that of the other and that they need to develop patterns of mutuality, of receptivity, and of responsiveness. Stress and crisis appear to be concepts that have helped to organize the client's and the practitioner's thinking in a way useful for problem-solving. Although many clients cannot develop an ability for conceptual thinking, the practitioner may formulate for them. Deprived clients, particularly those who depend upon public assistance, may think that their only problem is lack of money. Although lack of money is a factor, the use of money may also contribute to their pressures. In this instance, the practitioner helps the client to conceptualize his limitations as the need to learn the use of inexpensive recipes, meal planning, budgeting, comparative shopping, credit buying, and second-hand furniture and clothing resources.

Conceptual thinking about relationships may prove the one that the client is least able to grasp. Because many lower-class, deprived clients tend to think in images, the practitioner can draw word pictures and generalize about patterns of behavior through the use of these pictures. A number of problems concerning discipline control could be pictured in some questions such as: "How do you help a child to learn to be good—by being the big boss or by being a teacher?" "How do you show love to a child—by a warm hug when he comes home from school or by acting as though you are not glad to see him?"

JUDGMENT

Because behavior always has consequences, the practitioner helps the client to grasp this idea and to anticipate. He strengthens the client's capacity to judge by clarifying for him the necessity to foresee the consequences of one course of action as contrasted with those of another. He fosters the client's ability to see consequences in relation to the effect of his behavior on self and on others. He helps him to take account of the future. Most clients can develop a capacity for evaluating consequences by learning to weigh the pros and cons and to consider the effects of various courses of action. The practitioner may need to engage the client repetitiously in the process of anticipating results in relation to the way he functions concerning the problem he is trying to handle.

Frequently, the technique of anticipatory guidance strengthens the client's capacity to anticipate the future and to use judgment in planning for it. The pregnant wife and her husband find anticipatory guidance particularly helpful as the practitioner enables them to visualize what will be needed for the coming baby, such as housing, equipment, and financial outlay. In many instances, the couple needs preparation for the emotional experience of parenthood and help in their readiness to receive an additional family member. They should also be assisted in bringing into the open the possible problems that the birth of the new baby may entail. These difficulties may include the necessity for the wife to stop work or for the husband to interrupt his schooling. Parents need particular help in preparing a child for such an experience as hospitalization. A mere booklet does not suffice. Preparation includes not only appropriate information about what to expect but also clear foresight about what the new experience will entail and the reactions it may evoke. Similarly, when the individual faces discharge from the hospital or institution, it is essential that he be given a chance to discuss his anxiety and other feelings, to face intellectually the possible problems, and to have help in thinking out in advance how he plans to meet these problems. When anxiety or lack of experience limit the client's ability to foresee the difficulties that he may encounter, the practitioner should share his knowledge about what the client may face. In other instances, the experience of visiting the scene of future endeavors may prove helpful. For this reason, practitioners often arrange for patients in a mental hospital to visit factories, stores, or other work settings to prepare them for return to the work world. The parent should take the child to the hospital, foster home, or institution as preparation for the separation experience. Sometimes more than one visit is needed. Following the visit, the client should discuss the experience with family and practitioner, as appropriate, in order to work through anxiety and to find answers for questions. Mothers benefit from anticipatory guidance about future developmental needs and problems of their children. In this way, they can prepare themselves to deal with these changes and assimilate their anxiety to some extent. Well-baby clinics and pediatric services should furnish this guidance.

LESSENING LIMITATIONS: INFORMATION-GETTING

Learning how to acquire and to give information involves communication and thinking. Frequently, the practitioner begins by asking what the client understands or does not understand about the problem. He does so particularly when the communication of experts from psychological, medical, legal, educational, or bureaucratic domains about technical matters and complicated policies have generated some bewilderment in the client's mind. He assists the client in identifying the needed information as a basis for thinking about the situation. Sometimes he can point to misunderstandings or explain professional or bureaucratic language.

He can also clarify with the client essential information needed as a basis for decision-making or planning in regard to a particular problem. In the case of a medical or psychiatric condition, the client should be informed of how the condition affects capacity to function in his major life roles both in the present and in the future. He should also be informed of the nature of treatment, the purpose of treatment, and the possible outcomes. Both role partners need to have the same essential information. Parents have stated that adequate information about their congenitally retarded child was a powerful factor in their ability to deal with the problem and that lack of information contributed to their confusion and distress.[6]

Often clients receive information from professional persons when they are anxious, ill, or exhausted. This state adds to their inability to grasp what they are told. In addition, many individuals lack the verbal ability to ask questions, are intimidated by authority figures, and, because of ignorance, do not know the kind of information needed. The technique of having these clients list the questions they want answered or of going with them to an interview, during which the practitioner stimulates and supports communication, can increase their ability to get information. In other instances, it may become obvious from the client's story that he has not consulted appropriate sources of information but needs to do so. The practitioner then strengthens his perception of the necessity for understanding and identifies with him the most appropriate source for securing information. Some individuals find it hard to accept new ideas, and they may require help in understanding the necessity for using the passive mode of receptivity. New ideas can be threatening as can, also, the necessity to give up old ideas or misconceptions and misinformation. Frequently, the practitioner makes the client aware that he must work consciously to achieve the pattern of accepting ideas and information from others.

Most clients require help in understanding social resources. Pictures can be used to prepare children for entering homes or institutions, followed if possible, by one or more visits. The mother can be taught to use dolls and play activities to prepare a child for his coming operation. The practitioner encourages the adult client to visit institutions, the rehabilitation center, and so forth. Often he goes with the parent and child, and he may accompany the adult on his visits, using the shared experience to increase the client's mental grasp of the events taking place and the structure of the agency. Following such visits, he may use the technique of reviewing the experience verbally and of encouraging the client to express his ideas. In general, the better developed the client's cognitive capacities, the more explicit is the practitioner in helping the client to identify what needs to be changed and to acquire new and more active patterning, or passive patterning, as the need may be. The more that mental illness, conflict, or lack of previous learning experiences limits functioning, the more the practitioner tends to use techniques of providing new experiences and then techniques of explicating the new learning to the client. He helps the client consciously to affirm the new learning and the need for continued learning.

LESSENING LIMITATIONS: COMMUNICATION

In almost all cases, the practitioner tries to increase the client's communication ability and his recognition of the fact that communication helps him in problem-solving. He uses, for this purpose, techniques of joint interviewing, family sessions, and home visits. As he listens to a mother's communication, he can clarify for her that she is conveying a double message or an unclear message. In family and in joint sessions, the practitioner tries to help family members to differentiate "noise" from interchange of personal messages and to put nonverbal communication into words. He helps them to see that each is a sender and a receiver of messages and therefore must both listen to messages and also convey clear messages. He may encourage socially deprived clients to arrange for family meals and then, through these experiences, show them that such group activities can be used to teach children how to share ideas and feelings with each other and with parents. When the thinking of the client has moved little beyond the sensorimotor stage, the practitioner can sometimes begin to get across the idea of communication as doing. The authors of *Families of the Slums* describe a situation in which the practitioner posed the question, "What could you do to make your mother talk to you?"[7] Similarly, he may ask such questions as, "What do you think you are doing to give your child the idea that he can get away with anything?" "What can you do to give your husband the idea that you would like him to be more affectionate?" The practitioner helps the client to separate the cognitive from the affective content of the message. Frequently, the idea part of the message never comes across because tones of voice and language convey the kind of feelings that tend to make the receiver close his ears.

The Functions of Perception

The practitioner tries to help the client adopt the viewpoint that the ways in which he sees himself and his problem guide his activities—what he does or does not do—and therefore his problem-solving. He supports the client in identifying the changes needed so that the client can more consciously control and utilize perceptual ability. He tries to strengthen or to develop the patterning of outer perception, of inner perception, and of reality-testing. The practitioner handles perception and concept formation in a related way since each function can reinforce the other. The parents' grasp of the concept of discipline should be increased by helping them to learn how to view their own behaviors that have a coercive quality or that fail to exercise appropriate, benign protective power. Other clients may need to perceive the distinction between behaviors that teach and support the child's learning of inner controls and those that fail to do so. The role partners' perceptions of their shared difficulties usually do not agree, but they must achieve reasonable congruity in order for both partners to work in the same direction rather than at cross purposes. Elizabeth C. Stevenson suggests strengthening the alliance between parents by helping them to perceive their "automatic responses" to the child and to "gain control of their own behavior when they see its negative results."[8]

Frequently, the client has well-developed perceptual ability and a realistic but insecure outlook in some aspects. The techniques of early and continuous encouragement and reassurance from the practitioner may enable him to see that he is on the right track. Sometimes the practitioner can serve as a sounding board, allowing the client to verbalize his perceptions of problem-situation and solutions and to discover in the process that he rejects some views, strengthens others, or can make better sense out of the whole. In these instances, the client can usually accept the fact that increased self-confidence in his ability to see things clearly is the change toward which he should work. Other clients with reasonably well functioning egos can strengthen their capacity for outer perception when the practitioner uses the technique of sharing his own perceptions based on professional expertise and experience. Many clients welcome a new way of perceiving things or an objective viewpoint. Early in the case, the practitioner may give the client his professional opinion about the problem. Some mental hygiene clinics consider it essential to do so because otherwise the client cannot make an informed choice about whether or not he should accept treatment. Frequently, as the client becomes engaged in problem-solving, he can accept the necessity for getting new light on his own and on others' behavior and for gaining a new perspective. Parents may ask for a professional view of the child's behavior or of his own or others' functioning. The practitioner can then help the client to differentiate perceptually the important from the unimportant aspects of the situation. The practitioner may give the parents an explanation of the child's behavior that emphasizes learning tasks or needs that represent a push toward development, that is, a dynamic rather than a genetic viewpoint. In other instances, the practitioner may suggest that the picture indicates the need for medical or psychiatric evaluation, or that it falls more within the range of normality than the client has hoped or thought.

LESSENING LIMITATIONS: OUTER PERCEPTION

In many instances, the client's usually well functioning perceptual ability has become obscured by strong feelings, particularly anxiety aroused by crisis or by long-continued stress that makes objectivity difficult. Characteristically, work in such instances involves enabling the individual to perceive the anxiety-provoking aspects of the situation over which he had drawn a veil. To relieve anxiety, the practitioner gives the client a way to view his situation. In particular, crisis and stress with resulting ego insufficiency or helplessness arouse anxiety. The client may not clearly perceive the steps leading up to the present crisis or the way in which the present difficulty has stirred up feelings related to a previous, similar unresolved problem. In other words, he may not perceive the predisposing and precipitating stresses. Structuring the situation cognitively and perceptually may give the client a way of handling and understanding the crisis or stress.[9] The practitioner can use joint interviews or family sessions to help clients become aware of how their behavior affects others. One practitioner present at a family quarrel in front of the ten-year-old son, who was doing poorly in school and who had begun sucking his thumb, helped the parents make connections between their bickering and the boy's regressive behavior. Another practitioner arranged a conference between a disabled father, mother, and two teenagers in relation to the male boarder with whom the mother was having an affair. She had refused to put him out of the house until confronted with the perceptions of her husband and daughters about the destructive effects of the boarder's presence.

Role perception and culturally conflicting perceptions of one's own and others' roles may constitute another limiting factor with which reasonably well functioning clients may need assistance. Adolescents may benefit from help in developing a frame of reference in which to see their socially expected role behaviors in the sex role, work role, or in-school role. Cultural learning in the family and in reference groups always affects role perceptions. Parents who come from different family backgrounds—either of class, of ethnic group, or of region—may have divergent views about what to expect of children in various growth periods, about how to socialize a child, and about how much freedom and dependence to allow. They may not agree on who should provide the discipline. Each may see his own role differently from the way in which the reciprocal partner views it. All cultures teach what needs are acceptable and how they may be gratified. This learning may affect the way in which the clients view parental or marital roles. In addition, family members carrying reciprocal roles may perceive their responsibilities in ways that cause conflict, and they should be helped to realize that this is a shared problem. The practitioner then has two or more clients. The technique of joint interviewing may make it possible for the partners to face their difference in role perception and find a way to reconcile these differences or to compromise. Conflicts in role perceptions may also arise between client and community. Ethnic and class reference groups may define roles in ways that result in a poor fit between the client and the core culture. If the client can accept the need for change, the practitioner can use, under appropriate conditions, techniques of acculturation to improve fit between client and community, or he can, at least, help the client carry his role more harmoniously with the core culture. Whenever role perception affects problem-solving, the client may experience relief when the source of the difficulty has been identified as lying in learned orientations. He may then be able to work toward changes in order to bring about compromises or to resolve the difficulty.

The client's limiting perceptual patterns may spring not from cultural divergences but from difficulty in using the passive mode and in being receptive to the perceptions of other family members. This limitation means that the clients should recognize that they have a shared problem on which the partners need to work. With encouragement, parents and child, husband and wife, mother or father may become aware that they should work to achieve sensitivity to another person's perceptions regarding the problem-situation and to utilize these shared views. The practitioner usually uses the technique of joint interviewing and supports the partners in confronting each other with perceptual distortions and with failures to see and hear cues sent out by the partner. He helps them to achieve greater perceptual congruity.

Many mothers, particularly if they come from a lower-class or deprived background, have never learned a frame of reference that gives meaning to the child's behavior. They cannot pick up cues that indicate need, anxiety, or other feelings, or else they misperceive behavioral cues. The technique of having such a mother observe her child in a child development center can be used to encourage her to take an interest in new ways of viewing her child and to teach her to interpret cues. She can be helped to learn that doing so makes it possible to respond appropriately and to get along better with the child. Movies of desirable and undesirable parent-child interaction might be used to teach parents how to see what is happening or what should happen between themselves and the child and to see the differences in outcomes related to different child-rearing patterns. Some experiments in family therapy utilize a one-way screen to enable some family members to see interaction between other members of the family.

Individuals who have not moved far beyond early developmental periods particularly require help in learning new patterns of active outer perception. An example is the need-oriented client who tends to view all his experiences in the frame of reference of frustrated, early dependency needs. When such individuals become parents, although their vision is unimpaired, they do not "see" their filthy children, dirty clothes and home, or disorganized living. They go out but remain practically strangers to the world outside their doors. They seem never to have invested meaning and interest in other people, and so they tend to see their children as possessions and scarcely to distinguish them as individuals. They have never invested interest in or secured pleasure from perceiving the various provisions for community living, such as stores, playgrounds, and health and welfare resources. Instead, they tend to see all aspects of their surroundings as frustrating rather than as sources of satisfaction.

These clients need someone with whom they can identify to teach a different perceptual frame of reference. When the practitioner uses the technique of providing a homemaker, they tend to see her as someone who, for the first time in their experience, offers friendship and companionship. A homemaker who serves as an identification figure can often teach these clients a new way of perceiving themselves, their homes, housekeeping, and the external community. The client may begin to trust himself to receive satisfaction and to trust the external world to give satisfaction. When the homemaker helps the mother to paint walls, hang curtains, decorate, or keep the house clean, the mother finds meaning and pleasure in her surroundings and perceives them very differently. When the homemaker helps her to find new resources, the mother may see her community as offering pleasant possibilities and opportunities and herself as able to utilize these opportunities. When the mother learns to prepare family meals and engage in such family activities as birthday celebrations or trips to the playgrounds or the zoo, these activities and her own new capacities take on significance and pleasure.[10] For mothers with greater ability, the use of group experiences in housing developments, neighborhood centers, or schools can serve the same purpose because, through sharing their problems or discussing them with a leader, the participants come to take a new view of themselves and their situations. Otto Pollak suggests the use of joint and family sessions, especially for clients with character disorders, to improve their perception of the effect they have on others. By identification with the practitioner who listens, such clients often begin to listen to each other in joint sessions.[11]

Sometimes the client uses a selective pattern of outer perception. He may pick out only aspects of his experiences which support his inner pathology or conflict. For example, he may see only negative aspects of self and others, which reflects his inner unresolved difficulties. In this case, the practitioner may try to teach a more positive outlook. When the mentally ill or disturbed client has ventilated about all of his wife's failings, the practitioner asks, "What about the other side of the coin?" When the client talks only about his failings or difficulties, the practitioner suggests to him that he is overlooking the positives. "What about your good qualities?" or "Hasn't something gone well with you this week?" When, for example, the client hallucinates by hearing footsteps, the worker can suggest that he is, perhaps, lonely and wishes that someone would visit, thus emphasizing the ego aspects of this disturbance in perception. The practitioner can engage clients and families with low self-esteem in actively searching to perceive strengths. One such example mentioned in *Families of the Slums* describes the use of a technique in family interviews in which the practitioner selects the positive, healthy aspects of each member's communication and ignores the negative, hostile segments. He teaches family members how to view self and others in a more positive way.[12] In other instances, the reverse is true and the client tends to pick out pleasant and successful facets of his behavior and to overlook his failures and difficulties. The practitioner then inquires about these failures and suggests that the client is seeing only part of the picture and, perhaps, the part that makes him more comfortable. He helps the client to identify and change consistently ineffectual patterns of perceiving.

The client with low self-esteem stemming from a poorly developed ego, or one whose functioning has been seriously affected by pathology, tends to be inner-involved and have few patterns of active outer perception. He tends to shut out a world that he considers hostile, dangerous, depriving, or unmanageable. Because of regression, the severely mentally or physically ill client usually ceases to use previously acquired patterns of paying attention to the outside world and may be unable to resume active patterning of perception even when he has improved in health. The technique of setting up a therapeutic environment in a hospital or in an institution serves to orient the patient and to keep him interested in finding meaningful ways to relate to the new situation in which he finds himself. However, some observers have noted that the patient in a mental hospital, having learned to pay attention to the hospital environment, begins in a few months to withdraw interest from the outside world. One hospital reports that this shift of interest takes place in three to six weeks and, at that time, the staff members begin to turn the client's attention to his family and to discharge plans and problems.[13] Similarly, when the mentally ill client remains in the community, the practitioner tends to encourage discussion, observation, and understanding of daily experiences in the environment. In order to lessen the client's focus on inner perception, the practitioner discourages discussions of symptoms and illness. When such clients have regained sufficiently adequate ego functioning, the practitioner can strengthen interest in the outside world and healthy perceptual patterns.

Whenever the practitioner, through various experiences, teaches a more active patterning or a different patterning of external perception, he can, in most instances, make these changes conscious at some point in the contact. He may say, for example, "Now you see the difference in your children and in your home." "Now you see how much more happiness you get from happy children." "Now you see how capable you are and how many more ways you can find for managing your job as mother." "Now you can see how much more satisfaction you get when you can look on the bright side." "Now you have been able to see some of the difficulties you have having, and your seeing these difficulties makes it more possible for you to know what to do about them."

LESSENING LIMITATIONS: REALITY-TESTING

Frequently, clients with reasonably well functioning perceptual capacity have difficulty in reality-testing in situations that cause stress and anxiety. In probably the majority of cases, the practitioner helps the client to do reality-testing. Feelings of ego inadequacy and strong needs or wishes tend to promote a view of the world as one wishes it were, not as it is. Reactivated memories and feelings related to earlier situations interfere with ability to examine the present situation realistically. Faced with crisis and stress, the individual searches for a way to view the situation and remembers experiences from his own past or from that of others because present experiences tend to reactivate previous feelings and memories related to similar events.[14] The mother who has had a traumatic experience with an unstable husband sees what she fears: The son is becoming a replica of the father. The regressed patient in the hospital who experiences dependency on the powerful physician or nurse perceives them as parent figures endowed with his early ambivalent feelings. Anxiety and strong feelings or needs related to the present situation may affect the client's ability to distinguish what he wishes or fears from the actual reality. When the client has achieved generally good ego functioning and the memories that he projects onto the present lie in the preconscious, he can be helped to recognize that the past and the present are not identical. He can learn that wishes and fears are not the same as the reality. The technique of generalizing about the effects of anxiety and stress on perception often enables the client to accept his difficulties in reality-testing and to see the need for change. In other instances, the practitioner confronts the client with a factual review of the situation and points out how these facts do not agree with the client's view.

With the regressed or conflicted client, the practitioner may only be able to help strengthen reality-testing without the client's full awareness of the nature of his difficulty. However, if the practitioner attempts to improve the functioning of the client with serious pathology, he will, of necessity, need to engage the client in reality-testing to lessen the effects of the difficulty on the client's grasp of reality. For example, clients fixated in early periods of development tend to see authority figures and other adults as parent figures, projecting onto them omnipotence and power and, quite usually, hostile, aggressive, withholding, or punitive attitudes. Similarly, they see themselves as weak, small, and childish victims of circumstance. Their weak sense of autonomy makes them fear engulfment. Depending upon the level of fixation, clients may regard dependency experiences with particular distrust, may view all relationships as an arena for the battle to control, or may see sexuality and the role of male or female as frustrating and as a source of unpleasant, difficult experiences. One such client brought up in institutions and reform schools had tattooed on his arm, "Born to fail." Progress for these clients may occur when the practitioner identifies for them their patterns of perception and uses the technique of the well-directed question to ask whether these views are really true and whether experiences or attitudes that the client expects will necessarily occur. He tries to get the client himself to question whether this kind of repetitive experience and the way he is looking at things may mean that he is not really seeing things as they are. The practitioner may need to show the client how the distorted perceptions, their effect on the way the client acts, and the resultant reactions of others are connected. If he can get the client to accept the need for change, he can also begin to connect new perceptions with improved problem-solving: The client will act differently and so will receive different reactions from others. The client then becomes aware of the fact that his repetitive patterns of viewing reality may not have furnished an adequate guide to dealing with reality and may have brought about recurrent difficulties.

With seriously ill and disturbed clients and those with poorly developed ego functioning, the practitioner may continuously engage in reality-testing, attempting to help the client separate what he wishes things were or what he fears from the way they really are in order to enable him to see reality more clearly. Such clients may not achieve insight into the early sources of their difficulties. In the case of hospitalized patients, if the doctor or nurse spends time in full explanations to the patient of the medical situation, they dilute the patient's transference reactions of intended injury or hurt. When long hospitalization or incapacity has brought on considerable regression or when the medical situation has reactivated dependency or authority conflicts from early parental relationships, the client may act out his negative feelings by attempting to defeat the doctor's or rehabilitation counselor's efforts to help him. In this case, the physician may need to assert his identity as a physician and to make clear to the client that his activities will only defeat himself, not the physician.[15] To avoid such an impasse, the helping persons in medical and rehabilitation settings should realize that the more they take the superego role, seeming to ask the client to do as they wish by following their regime or plan, the more they arouse his ambivalent feelings toward parent figures. Practitioners will do much better to ally themselves with the client's ego and inquire not how the client is getting along in following their advice but how he is progressing in his ability to face the facts of his condition and what he needs to do about it. Joint efforts will then be directed toward dealing with what is getting in the way of the client's ability to do reality-testing.

LESSENING LIMITATIONS: INNER PERCEPTION

With support, many clients can look inward to perceive their own share in the problem, although they are not usually able to be introspective in the early stages of treatment. The less conflicted the client and the better developed his ego functioning, the more easily can he do so. Clients who never progressed beyond early growth stages may never have learned to perceive their own motivations or feelings, far less to observe with any objectivity how they are functioning. However, with even these clients, the practitioner may attempt some development of inner perception through the technique of questioning or of probing, which tends to encourage the client to think about why he is behaving in a given way. The practitioner tries to increase the self-observing capacity of the ego in an attempt to increase conscious control of behavior and this kind of change may be taken as a conscious goal with the client. Rubin Blanck recommends use of joint or group interviews to enable the client to make "his own discovery about the effects of his behavior on himself and on others."[16] Depressed individuals who turn anger inward may become more comfortable when they can perceive anger as an acceptable and universal feeling. They then can be helped to become aware of their feelings and to find more constructive ways of expressing them. A changed perception of guilt, rejection, hostility, or ambivalence may be necessary as the practitioner offers his own perception of the acceptability of these feelings and explains that other individuals generally experience similar reactions to similar life situations. Sometimes he suggests as homework that the client try to listen to himself or observe himself and his feelings in relation to the problem situation. Such suggestions might include, "Try to listen to yourself when you correct Johnny." "Try to see what your feelings are when your husband won't listen to your worries over Johnny." "Try to see what it is that you do or say that starts the argument."

The development of insight through an increasingly active patterning of inner perception usually requires long-time treatment except in crisis situations. However, practitioners in medical settings have long been aware of the fact that hospital admission tends to reactivate separation, dependency, and authority conflicts, and fears related to past experiences. Operations stir up castration fears or conflicts about helplessness and bodily intactness. Loss of body functioning or body parts arouses feelings related to body image basic to ego identity. Current formulations from crisis theory have provided an underpinning for practice experience, which demonstrates the fact that crisis situations tend to bring into consciousness past experiences that the client has not been able to handle and with which the present crisis is integrally related. This fact often makes it possible for the client to redo previously unresolved learning problems as he obtains insight into the connections between an aspect of his present functioning and his previous inability to handle a similar experience.[17] The client learns to perceive why he finds it hard to handle the present situation and, on this basis, is able to see the need to handle the new experiences in a different and more realistic way.

Management of Needs and Feelings

Appropriately active and passive patterns for handling needs and feelings usually bring to the individual (except in cases of trauma, loss, or overwhelming situational limitations) a reasonably favorable balance of satisfaction over frustration. They also make it possible for him to carry his life roles so that he contributes to a similar balance in his relationship with others. The client must become aware that life roles should bring pleasure and gratification and see the possibility of working toward obtaining maximum satisfaction with minimum pain. With this end in mind, the practitioner engages the client in trying out patterns that contribute to improved problem-solving. In case of a shared problem, role partners must consider not only their own but the partner's needs and feelings, attempting to achieve a workable balance of gratification for both. The practitioner may turn the client's attention to changes needed in any or all of the following functions: the aims or needs that motivate him; the patterns used for achieving these aims and for gratifying the needs; the patterns for handling the feelings related to satisfaction or frustration of need; and the coping patterns, both defensive and adaptive, used by the client to handle conflict and anxiety.

LESSENING LIMITATIONS: AIMS AND NEEDS

The practitioner often becomes acquainted with the motivational forces in the personality through the conscious and unconscious demands that the client makes upon the practitioner, upon those around him, or upon himself. The practitioner must understand both conscious and unconscious expectations. The unconscious motivations include the unresolved childhood need to be protected and passively gratified, the need to be relieved of responsibilities, and the need to rely on someone else to settle life's issues and to handle life's problems. Characteristically, individuals bring to present life situations remnants of early, partly conscious, childish needs. Depending on the client's capacity, he may be enabled to see that these needs cannot possibly be satisfied and to search for more adult needs and more effective routes to gratification.

The client's needs become most problematical when they interfere with his meeting the needs of others—spouse or children. Most commonly, practitioners encounter the client with strong dependency needs that seem almost bottomless. Actually, inability to find ways of meeting the needs makes them even more overwhelming. The practitioner usually begins by "feeding" these clients through giving warmth, support, concern, and showing that he values the individual. He also gives his own efforts, goes out to visit, makes small gifts, and helps to secure provisions for basic necessities from all available sources. As he gives, he tries to elicit a trusting response from the client—trust in the practitioner and trust in self as worthy of nurturance. The practitioner also begins to teach more active patterns of need satisfaction. As suggested by Ludwig L. Geismar and Jane Krisberg, the practitioner teaches social skills and helps the client learn how to secure required supplies and help from various community resources.[18] Many lower-class or deprived clients have never learned effectively how to get better housing, jobs, or health care.

The second lesson regarding need satisfaction learned in childhood is learning how to give in order to get. The child accomplishes this task as he internalizes the image of the mother who provides dependable gratifications. For the deprived, the practitioner must provide this image. He also serves as a role model of how to get. He demonstrates in the home those ways of expressing to the children the warmth, care, comfort, and interest that evoke similar responses. He suggests such patterns to adult spouses. By identification with the practitioner, the client learns new patterns that serve to bring him the dependency gratifications he desires. The practitioner also attempts to help the client become connected with new sources of enjoyment from church, community centers, and various other groups. These opportunities assume special importance when the reciprocal role partner who usually serves as a source for some satisfactions has a limited ability to give or when he is missing, owing to unmarried parenthood or a break in the family. As he gratifies, the practitioner also remembers to frustrate to some extent in order to teach frustration tolerance. Actually, placing increasing responsibility on the client himself to find new routes to gratification accomplishes this purpose. When the client has learned that he must give in order to get, he may be able to develop a reasonably comfortable balance between satisfaction and frustration.

With all clients, the practitioner encourages the investment of energy in ego functions and in the securing of functional pleasure from success resulting from increased mastery and from the realization of ego and socially valued aims which brings approval and recognition. He helps the client to direct his energies in more fruitful and less self-defeating ways. He expresses pleasure when the client can understand better, see more realistically, and act more competently. In one way or another, he helps the client to experience the possibility and satisfactions of social competence and to develop a need to direct his own life more satisfactorily. He encourages the client to feel more gratification and enjoyment in his improved functioning and attempts to set with the client small immediate goals that the client can achieve. The memory of the accomplishment of these goals spurs him on to hope for further achievement. As Thomas M. French postulates, present opportunity and memories of past successes provide a realistic hope of future success. This hope, together with discontent about the present, motivates goal-directed behavior.[19] The practitioner always helps the client to remember previously effective coping and emphasizes progress or small gains because the client, in his general discouragement, may overlook them. At specific times, he reviews with the client the course of their work together and encourages him to affirm for himself the progress he has made. This kind of summing up is a technique characteristically utilized at the time of termination of contact. Throughout treatment, the practitioner encourages the client to increase his conscious positive expectations of self and of his ability to define for himself what he wants. He stimulates the client to achieve socially valued aims that bring more certain rewards than do those that he may have internalized in the past; that is, the client learns to operate on the reality principle. When the practitioner gives the client hope of being able to change things for the better, he strengthens the ego aim of mastery and improved capacity to cope.[20] Client social action groups serve a similar purpose by providing satisfactions from carrying an active citizen role and from being able to effect some changes in client conditions.

Dependent clients with primitive needs learn best through experiences and through the technique of demonstration, which teaches new possibilities for gratification if the practitioner remembers that such learning is made possible through becoming related to a person or persons who give consistently and dependably. The client becomes more teachable as he achieves trust. Diminished anxiety about immediate needs frees energy for new learning. Through the mechanism of identification, through the human tendency to practice actively (giving or doing) what he has passively experienced (being given to or helped), and through the desire to hold on to the rewards of love that now have meaning, the client begins to learn. The childlike client who has been taught to mother and to stimulate the baby appropriately by a protecting mother figure in the home gains approval of clinic personnel, family, and friends. She finds pleasure in the baby, who begins to thrive and to reward her efforts by his smiling and happiness. She begins to need to give as well as to get and to find pleasure in being like the effective mothering figure with whom she has identified.[21] By teaching these clients new motivational patterns, the practitioner makes them aware of the new sources of pleasure from more adequate social functioning. The client learns to obtain pleasure from seeing a well-organized, pleasant home and happy children who do well in school, from the relationship responses of a more contented husband, and from participation in new activities in the community. The practitioner supports these clients in internalizing these needs and in valuing these needs because of the gratification that comes from achieving them. Sometimes, the more mature role partner can encourage and reward the learning of more adult ego motivations by the less mature partner.

LESSENING LIMITATIONS: NEED SATISFACTION PATTERNS

Active patterns for handling needs may be disrupted by changes in the life situation, may be only partially successful, or may never have been learned. Practitioner and client together should give careful attention to ways in which situational changes can interfere with the previously adequate patterning and change the balance for the client from satisfaction to frustration. Several financial setbacks or increasing financial strain caused by growing family burdens may bring a narrowing of interests and activities so that all life centers in work and home, with consequent impoverishment of pleasures. Working-class families who live on the edge of poverty are particularly vulnerable to this type of stress. Moving into a higher-class or lower-class neighborhood because of upward or downward mobility or moving to a different region or to a rural area from an urban one or vice versa can mean loss of friends, and of recreational and social resources. To these individuals, life seems to be closing in. In one such instance, the family had lost their car that they could no longer afford, and the father's semiskilled job paid less than did a previous one in the city from which they had come. His angry outbursts at the family stemmed from his sense of increasing frustration. The practitioner helped the family to plan picnics in a nearby park and to budget for an occasional movie for the parents. Through his instigation, the children and parents joined recreation and church groups.

The practitioner should usually help clients consciously to face the fact that changing circumstances have brought loss of satisfactions and should engage them in finding new routes to happiness. Frequently, he may have to strengthen the client's cognitive ability, helping him to acknowledge the facts of his changed situation. In other instances, the client's anxiety may interfere with perception. Selma Fraiberg gives an interesting example of a mother with a celiac child who was helped to perceive that her inability to feed the child blocked her need for successful mothering and that he child's frustration over the monotony of his diet increased her own unhappiness. Once she could perceive her own and the child's mutual needs and the necessity for changed patterning for meeting these needs, she engaged enthusiastically in experimenting with recipes that gave the child a varied diet that he could enjoy and that, therefore, increased her own enjoyment.[22]

Changed patterns for handling needs include the use of sublimation and the finding of new interests or objects or sources of gratification. This achievement may entail role changes, finding new roles, and new friends and associates. Rehabilitation centers, sheltered workshops, and vocational training or retraining programs teach new role patterns that can bring new rewards. Group experiences often support parents of children with emotional difficulties or devtlopmental problems in finding ways of handling their roles that bring them less frustration and more satisfaction. Church, recreational and social groups, hobbies, and volunteer work offer fresh outlets. The practitioner may connect the newly blinded person to resources for learning how to care for himself, to get about, and to do household chores. The deaf client may be able to learn lipreading. Clubs and groups for handicapped persons and for the elderly offer a chance for companionship. Many older persons find great pleasure in such volunteer activities as being foster grandparents. The single parent often discovers congenial friends in a Parents Without Partners group.

Frequently, the client's usual patterns have failed to bring true satisfaction and may even have been self-defeating. In one such example, the practitioner pointed out to the husband that he could never accept compliments, that he was certain his promotions were undeserved, and that he had a need to spoil the good things that came his way. This young adult, aware that this way of operating was not working well either in his marriage or in his work, was able consciously to strive for and accept the rewards he had earned. In another instance, the father, an unskilled laborer, was helped to weigh his need to discipline harshly against his need for a son who could get along well in school without rebelling against all authority. The father chose to find more effective methods of discipline.

When the practitioner engages married couples in examining their shared problem, one or both partners may have to consider the needs they bring to the marriage and to seek the causes of dissatisfaction that may lie in the attempt to gratify inappropriate needs or to utilize inappropriate patterns for handling the needs. Sometimes, one partner fails to understand the other's needs.[23] For example, one practitioner pointed out to the couple that their usual angry bickering prevented both of them from discussing and dealing with their mutual unmet needs. In another instance, the wife was unable to say no to her husband or son, and her only way of handling their criticisms was to feel hurt and guilty. In both instances, awareness of the pattern led eventually to a beneficial change. If the less mature partner can be encouraged to try out more adult behaviors, then his ability to achieve new learning will partly depend on the other partner's rewarding and encouraging these efforts so that they become more gratifying than the previous childish patterns. The more healthy partner can stimulate, support, and respond warmly to attempts of the less mature partner to change. The practitioner uses individual, joint, or multiple client interviews to enable the clients to identify patterns that do not work well and to learn to use those that lead to complementarity, a mutual meeting of each other's needs.

In cases of serious pathology, the client's needs and the ways in which he deals with them reflect his pathology. The individual with partially adequate or inadequate ways of handling need tensions usually engages in repetitive, self-defeating efforts that bring him pain and difficulty. Included in this group are impulsive acting-out persons, individuals with personality disorders, and delinquents. These individuals have usually lacked a consistent parental figure who was sufficiently trusted, so that the prize of love which could have made them teachable has little meaning. The parent or parents have frequently failed to represent stable models; therefore, the individual could not identify with the parent and internalize the parental functions of control. A satisfying relationship is the place to begin with such clients. The longing for dependency satisfactions and for a strong protector must be gratified before the client can begin to learn to tolerate tension and anxiety by facing some of his limitations. The client must begin to trust sufficiently to identify with the practitioner. Because many such individuals require help in learning to relate to another person and to admit that they need a relationship, the practitioner must attempt to develop and strengthen the ego function of object relationships. The client must also perceive him as stable and as offering an acceptable model since he neither retaliates nor punishes and he cannot be seduced to condone antisocial behavior.

The client's achievement of trust may make it possible to strengthen active patterning for handling needs. First the client is made aware of his previous patterns through strengthening cognition and perception. The acting-out client needs to grasp cognitively the ideas of choice, to perceive the consequences of impulsive behavior, and to use thinking to understand his fears, wishes, and dissatisfactions. He needs to be helped to put his urges into words and to think or to talk about them before he acts. He can, in a connected manner, be helped to face the fact that he can weigh choices and foresee consequences.[24] The client's capacity for reality-testing must be strengthened by his learning to distinguish wishes and magical thinking from what really is. He should learn to perceive the patterns derived from pathological needs as self-defeating or as bringing trouble and to perceive the possibility of more successful patterns as he experiences the use of choice, foresight, and new ways of operating. In some cases, the practitioner helps the client to find patterns that offer more constructive ways of meeting his pathological needs. The individual who has never learned patterns of managing needs and feelings must often experience some changes before he can consciously affirm the need for change and take as an ego aim the securing of more satisfaction with less pain.

LESSENING LIMITATIONS: HANDLING FEELINGS

Work with the client on redefining his needs and the routes to gratification so that they are more in keeping with reality and on handling his feelings takes place in a related way. The techniques of generalizing and accepting and, in some cases, of verbalizing for the client often make it possible for him to express such feelings as guilt, anger, pain, loss, grief, and inadequacy. Sometimes, the practitioner should clarify with the client the fact that no one can really accept blindness, deafness, or similar traumatic blows of fate; he should acknowledge that fact and face his feelings honestly. This acknowledgment constitutes the first step toward mastery of the problem. Constructive patterns for handling feelings that the client can be encouraged to strengthen or to learn include ventilating and sharing of feelings with the role partner, friends, family, clergy, or other appropriate individuals and the channeling of feelings into appropriate doing that tends to relieve anxiety.

Especially following trauma or crisis, the individual may use repression and denial to deal with unbearable feelings. Unless he is given prompt help, he may be unable, later on, to use feelings. The practitioner must help him to understand the necessity for being able to acknowledge his emotions. Some parents who have believed that they should not express anger at the children become more comfortable in acknowledging their honest feelings when the practitioner helps them to realize that they have a right to them. Moreover, the practitioner often finds that the parent's guilt over his own anger makes it hard for the child to learn to deal with anger. When parents become aware that their previous patterns did not work well for themselves or for the child, they may be able to change them. Lower-class clients may particularly require help in learning to talk out feelings instead of acting them out. In joint or family sessions, clients can perceive maladaptive patterns. One practitioner helped a family to see that the parents handled their hurt feelings and disappointment by reacting to the adolescent daughter in ways that hurt her. The adolescent, feeling unloved and unwanted, reciprocated by doing what she knew would hurt her parents.

Characteristically, borderline and schizophrenic clients fear their emotions. Only when the relationship is secure and the client's anxiety has diminished does the practitioner approach the matter of feelings. For example, one practitioner suggested to a schizophrenic client that blocking was one way of handling feelings but that there were other ways.

Irving Kaufman proposes that with borderline clients, treatment should begin by demonstrating feelings and by generalizing about their acceptability. Later, these clients may be able to talk about their feelings and learn ways of dealing with them.[25]

LESSENING LIMITATIONS: DEFENSES

In general, the practitioner attempts to strengthen the defenses that work well for the client and to lessen the use of restrictive or crippling defenses. In the case of a severely crippled arthritic who refused a wheelchair because she wanted to try to continue to get around by herself, her defensive denials of disability and dependence had served her well. She had continued to be self-maintaining despite disintegrated and painful joints. The practitioner aligned himself with the client and helped her work out the plan she wanted. When the defense or defenses that the client uses prove defeating, the practitioner may utilize the technique of getting behind the defenses to the feeling and the needs that the client is defending against. Examples of situations in which this technique may be appropriate include those in which the client is defending against involving himself in a relationship and denying that he needs affection and that the relationship has any meaning or value or those in which the client uses compulsivity as a defense against hostility. In using this technique, the practitioner sometimes verbalizes and expresses acceptance of the feeling or need and encourages the client to use thinking and talking as patterns of bringing into the open and making more conscious the feelings and needs against which he has been defending. Later, the client may be able to ventilate and express affects. When the client can use a more appropriate pattern or one that is more adaptive, the defense may become less necessary and he may have more available energy.

In working with the neurotic client, the practitioner helps

him to secure more satisfaction with less pain. His energy is tied up in conflicts around dependency, authority, sexuality, or related needs and in maintaining defenses against the anxiety aroused by conflict and by ego inadequacy to solve it. These clients can usually function reasonably well with diminished anxiety, a change that they usually want to achieve. For this purpose, one or more of the following techniques may prove effective. Whenever possible, the practitioner strengthens useful defenses and channels energy into achieving positive coping patterns. Individuals who are beset with doubts about masculinity or femininity but seem to wish more than they fear an appropriate sex role identification may benefit from the support, which perhaps they once lacked, of a parent figure who perceives them as masculine or feminine and who values these qualities. When the practitioner encourages the client's identification with the masculine or feminine role in marriage, in parenthood, or in work and helps him to internalize the practitioner's concept of him, he may strengthen the wish and lessen some of the anxiety caused by fear. The practitioner also strengthens the client's defenses by engaging his interest in appropriate activities that offer group support and shared pleasure with other men or women.

When the fear of appropriate sex role identification appears stronger than the wish, as with women who have strong aggressive masculine drives or with men who have strong passive receptive longings, the practitioner may redirect the defenses. This technique may prove useful with individuals who have used compulsivity as a regressive defense against conflicts related to sexuality. The practitioner helps the client to perceive the unacceptable part of himself as an asset and to perceive the fear as acceptable. This nonjudgmental attitude helps the client, through identification, to become more accepting, less guilty, and hence less anxious. He can then channel his energy into activities that express his previously anxiety-provoking needs and that utilize it constructively. The practitioner encourages the client with a need to control to find such useful activities outside the home as group activities and business ventures that utilize management capacities. Women with a strong aggressive drive often do well when they go to work or learn a profession. They can then hire full or part-time help or make family arrangements that relieve them, to some extent, of the homemaking chores that arouse anxiety and conflict. The emotional balance of a male with a greater than usual feminine component can be improved when he learns to choose work and other activities that meet this need constructively. The field of male nursing, service occupations, the garment industry, food industries, cooking, waiting on tables, or food processing frequently offer satisfying jobs for these individuals. Sometimes, the practitioner can improve the balance in the family by suggesting that the husband assume more of the household tasks or, in some instances, that the wife seek employment. In other instances, the balance in the family can be improved by advising the wife to assume more direction and control, to exercise more initiative, and to take a more active role rather than to expect the passive husband to do so.

Vocational and rehabilitation counselors should be aware of the unconscious meanings of work and the purpose that work serves in handling conflict. They should use this understanding to supplement aptitude tests in helping the client choose appropriate training goals. One client, trained as a power machine operator but who never used his skills, confessed that he disliked this "feminine" occupation. He was successful when he was helped to select a trade that for him had masculine connotations—one that helped to bolster his struggle to resolve the oedipal bind to his mother.

Serious pathology may, in some instances, weaken the client's defenses with consequent breakthrough of fantasies and primitive needs. The practitioner then attempts to strengthen the defenses, helps the client do reality-testing, and strengthens all aspects of ego functioning. He focuses attention on ways of dealing with reality and turns interest away from symptoms. In other instances, the practitioner should encourage the client to use a passive pattern of handling needs and feelings. Occasionally, a spouse or parent in the client's environment can take responsibility for providing firm external controls and can help the client to manage his needs better. The client can be encouraged to accept advice, to talk things over with this relative, friend, or guardian, and to use the judgment of the other person when his own seems less adequate. In this event, the individual in question may serve as an external superego for the client, a technique found particularly useful for clients with personality disorders.[26]

The Management of Object Relationships

The client's management of object relationships, the key function in individual adaptation, can be strengthened by improving the patterning in the functions of regulating closeness and of regulating distance from other persons and in the functions of receptivity and responsiveness. The ability to regulate closeness depends upon having achieved basic trust and object constancy and upon having used that learning to achieve intimacy. The individual can invest in a relationship and can commit himself to one. The capacity for regulating distance in a relationship depends on how well the individual has solved the learning task of autonomy. He can relate to others without fear of engulfment and yet has no need to hold on, unduly, to another person. The function of receptivity in a relationship is based on the individual's capacity to identify with other human beings and to take from them ideas, perceptions, and feelings. He can allow others to have needs and to act without being threatened. The function of responsiveness enables the individual to respond appropriately and realistically to his role partners without distortions because he needs to give as well as to get.

LESSENING LIMITATIONS: REGULATING CLOSENESS

Clients who have achieved the capacity to trust may lose this ability because of changes in their life situations. When the ill or handicapped client feels that he can no longer trust his wife or friends to care about him, the practitioner helps the client to do reality-testing and to distinguish his own feelings from those of others. The practitioner may need to show the client that his defense of withdrawal helps to create the very situation that he fears and prevents him from finding out whether his loss of trust is justified. A client who had undergone a colostomy operation and could no longer work in a restaurant showed his loss of trust in his relationship with the practitioner. He complained that his friends would not want to associate with him any longer and that they would feel he was unclean. He continually broke appointments with the practitioner who always offered another appointment. The practitioner's consistent acceptance helped to restore this client's ability to trust. When parents lose mutual trust following some disappointment in their life, the practitioner may be able to restore this bond. He may make connections for them between their distrust and their feeling that life or the partner has betrayed them.

Because the individual must continually redo the lesson of trust, many marital partners find themselves at odds because they have not been able to enter trustingly into this new relationship. Parents who distrust their child may be reflecting distrust in their own parenting. Whenever role partners show mutual distrust, the practitioner makes these patterns evident to them. He often uses the technique of confrontation in joint or multiple interviews in order to help the clients realize the destructive effects of this pattern. Many clients can benefit from seeing why they distrust when the practitioner uses probing and questioning techniques that help the clients to consider the reasons for their feelings. He encourages them to try out trusting patterns and to realize the rewards that accrue from this change. For example, on two occasions when her husband lost his job, the wife left him and returned to her parents. She became overly dependent on them and on the two children who manipulated her and refused to listen to their father because "he probably won't be around long." The wife, who had blamed the family difficulties on her husband's job loss, was helped to see that her own distrustful separations had disturbed her husband's trust in her and the children's trust in both parents. If the client has not achieved object constancy, the practitioner helps him to see how he continually provokes rejection. He encourages the client to question the inevitability of desertion and to do reality-testing in relation to his exchanges with his partner. The practitioner may use confrontation to show him the self-defeating consequences of his relationship patterns, as in one instance in which the client used flight and moved from place to place to avoid the disappointment he feared.

When the client has never learned to trust, the practitioner may attempt to teach trust through the use of the relationship. He offers a relationship experience that has the qualities lacking in the early life relationships. He empathically understands why the deprived client expects nothing but pain and frustration at the hands of others and so uses the defense of hostility or flight to protect himself from hurt. He gives consistently to these clients in ways they can understand. He gives material things; he goes with the client to look for a house or to buy a piece of furniture. He arranges for the client and the children to be driven to the clinic. When parental criticism has lessened trust in self and others, the practitioner not only refrains from negative comments but builds the client's confidence in self. He voices his belief that the client can become a more adequate spouse or parent, and he gives a great deal of recognition to any past or present accomplishments of the client.

The schizophrenic has never learned trust and the borderline client may show considerable impairment of this capacity. The practitioner recognizes that neither client can regulate closeness and takes responsibility for developing a relationship that helps to bridge the client's feeling of isolation, yet demonstrates interest and concern rather than warmth. As the client can begin to trust, he is encouraged to seek contacts in social activities and to handle relationships at home or at work without withdrawing.

LESSENING LIMITATIONS: REGULATING DISTANCE

The client with previous good patterning may need to acquire new ways for managing distance between himself and the partner following divorce or separation. Some clients fail to develop sufficient distance. For example, one AFDC wife allowed her husband from whom she had separated to visit at any time, to be disruptive in his criticisms, and to interfere in her handling of the home. The practitioner helped her to set up a contract with her husband concerning the times for visits and her rights to manage the home without disruption from him. Another practitioner helped both parents to see that their pattern of undermining each other with the children, while maintaining distance in the separation, seriously disturbed the relationship of the children with each parent and had caused the six-year-old son to become disturbed and act out in school.

If the client has failed to master the lesson of autonomy, he may have trouble in allowing his partner appropriate independence while, at the same time, being able to assert reasonable independence and individuality for himself. Clients manifest this kind of difficulty when they see any kind of giving in as threatening their sense of autonomy.[27] They may tend to see their children as possessions and to hold on to them in controlling ways. They also hold on to parental or marital relationships. One AFDC client made clear her fear of loss of autonomy when she said that social workers had always told her what to do and she expected this practitioner thought he knew better than the client how to manage her children. The practitioner refused to let the client seduce him into making choices for her, even the choice of accepting help. Instead, he continuously stimulated the client to talk about her feelings and ideas and respected the client's decisions. The practitioner must realize that clients who have not learned autonomy fear they cannot survive on their own. He, therefore, helps them to learn patterns of activity that enable them to carry their roles with greater competence. For example, one client from an ethnic group in which extended families tend to prevail, seemed unable to manage her children without constant advice and interference from her mother; yet she greatly resented her dependence on her mother. The practitioner encouraged her to separate her own ideas from those of her mother and to distinguish what she wanted from what her mother thought she ought to do. He supported the client's ability to think for herself, to use her own feelings as a guide, and to internalize the practitioner's confidence in her capacity as a mother. Later, this client and her husband established their own home. As these clients develop competence, they have less need to hold on to or to fear engulfment in a relationship. The practitioner's respect for the client's wishes and feelings, his perception of the client's unique qualities, and his consistent rewarding of achievement lessen the sense of helplessness, build confidence, and develop a sense of autonomy.

LESSENING LIMITATIONS: RECEPTIVITY

Apparently all human beings come into the world with a longing for human relatedness. The ability to manage object relations depends, to a considerable extent, on the ability to become related to another human being through the mechanism of identification and a feeling of empathic sharing. It has been suggested that an essential part of the core of moral character lies in the capacity to empathically take the role of other.[28] The practitioner increases mutuality between role partners by helping them to become more tolerant of each other's weakness, by encouraging them to identify good qualities in each other, and by strengthening capacity for mutual support and shared satisfactions. He may also attempt to strengthen the identifications of role partners with each other by engaging them in an attempt to understand and to perceive each other as individuals. The practitioner may encourage greater self-revelation, or he may use his own empathic identifications to help each partner to share feelingly in the way the other experiences life and the relationship. This effort may involve helping the clients to see how their own ideas, perceptions, needs, and feelings get in the way of receptivity to those of the partner. He helps each to see things from the viewpoint of the other, to become more accessible and willing to listen, and to accept ideas, views, and feelings. In one instance, an American wife was helped to understand her Puerto Rican husband's loneliness and need for acceptance that repetitiously drove him to give up his job and stand on the street corner with his Puerto Rican friends. She stopped her angry outbursts and became more supportive.

The practitioner himself demonstrates listening in joint interviews as he is receptive to his clients. He encourages the client who always needs to be self-sufficient to be more accepting of dependent receiving. In some instances, the client's inability to identify with wife or child comes from his fear of weakness or dependency. When he sees these feared traits in them, he identifies them with the unacceptable part of himself. A realization of this pattern may make it possible for him to accept his wife and child as individuals and to identify with them more positively.

Many delinquents and the client with a personality disorder tend to ward off other persons and to be unable to feel little except suspicion and hostility toward them. With such individuals, the practitioner must start to develop the function of object relationships by making some positive connectedness between the client and another person—the practitioner. He must help the client to abandon his denial of humanness and help him to experience a consistently gratifying and trustworthy relationship. When the client learns from experiencing dependable caring that he will not again be disappointed, he may be able to trust and to value the exchange of human feeling with the practitioner. On this basis, he can begin to identify with a giving person and to value the gift of love. A strong positive identification with the practitioner helps to lessen the client's hostile negative identifications with his parents. The client may then internalize, through identification with the practitioner, patterns of warm feeling. The client may later be able actively to practice what he has passively experienced and to feel with and for another human being. Identification includes ability for empathic sharing of feelings, ideas, and experiences.[29]

The schizophrenic, on the other hand, shows serious and permanent impairment of the function of object relationships. He cannot identify until he has learned to trust in some degree. The practitioner may use the technique of group experiences to increase the client's ability to take the role of the other, since he knows that children learn to do so largely through membership in peer groups.

LESSENING LIMITATIONS: RESPONSIVENESS

Finally, the individual has progressed from a biological to a biopsychosocial being when he can place sexuality in the framework of a relationship of mutual tenderness and trust. Lower-class and working-class clients frequently see sexuality in physical terms and many males have never learned either to express tenderness in the marital bond or to ask for affection from their spouses. In one such instance, the practitioner was able to help the couple improve their relationship only after he elicited the fact that when they said they wanted to achieve a more affectionate relationship, the husband meant more frequent sex relations and the wife meant more exchange of expressions of warmth, interest, and caring. The practitioner suggests to the client the possibility of increased satisfactions from finding ways to show concern, kindness, and consideration to the role partner as well as the value of teaching this view of sexuality to the children. He encourages patterns for securing love and for responding to expressions of love. He teaches the parents to show interest in what their children do and say and to praise their achievements. As clients learn patterns of responding, they find that these patterns work better for themselves and for others.

In the way the practitioner listens and responds appropriately in joint interviews, he demonstrates the value of this way of handling relationships. He accomplishes the same thing when he responds courteously and objectively to whatever the client is expressing or acting out. He may go with the client to an interview with school, hospital, or agency personnel and demonstrate effective ways of dealing with another person's communications.

The practitioner always attempts to bring about greater compatibility between role partners by enabling them to develop mutual regulation patterns that lead to greater mutual satisfaction. He helps them to find better ways to communicate about shared difficulties, to try out new patterns, and to support each other in making mutual changes.

The Executive Function or Executant Competence

Reliable activity patterns promote reduction of anxiety because they lessen ego anxiety related to helplessness. In case of loss of previously adequate patterns, the client should become aware of the purpose that they had served in enabling him to cope and the reasons for his present anxiety. This understanding frequently motivates him to find changed patterns. If previous patterns have been inadequate, the client should, at some time, be helped to question their adequacy in securing role rewards and satisfactions with a minimum of pain. The practitioner supports and develops executant competence by strengthening the functions of decision-making, of planning and carrying through activities to implement decisions, and of handling role responsibilities.

LESSENING LIMITATIONS: DECISION-MAKING

The practitioner can involve the client actively in securing the information needed for decision-making, in rational thinking about the pros and cons of the decision, in perceiving realistically the situation relative to the decision, and in anticipating the consequences of deciding or not deciding. He should elicit his ambivalent wantings and not wantings. All functions of the ego may require strengthening in order to promote decision-making. The client should also be encouraged to use the passive mode appropriately and to involve those most concerned in making major decisions. For example, whenever possible, grown children should include the elderly parent in planning that concerns the parent's future. Both spouses should make decisions regarding the future of their marriage and of their life together. Both parents should unite in decisions that concern their children. When the client appears incapable of deciding because of severe pathology or other limitations, the practitioner encourages him to use a passive pattern and to shift responsibility to appropriate persons, such as the physician, the stronger role partner, or other individuals in his environment.[30] In some instances, the necessity to decide reactivates old patterns of denial, of flight, or of avoidance. If possible, the practitioner should bring these patterns into the open and clarify the nature of responsible decisions, which involves consideration and weighing of the welfare of all concerned and evaluation of possible outcomes. Only through experiencing a new way of deciding does this concept have meaning and value. A decision is a decision to act or not to act.

LESSENING LIMITATIONS: PLANNING AND CARRYING PLANS THROUGH

Role rehearsal is one of the measures that the practitioner uses to assist the client in planning and following through on a decision he has made. The practitioner takes the client through the steps in the required role activity. He may help the mother plan how to tell her daughter that she was born before the mother's marriage. Relatives who decide to take a patient home need help in planning and in managing this step. The practitioner should explain the physical layout and concrete application procedures when the client plans to apply to an institution, home, or agency. The court procedures for relinquishing guardianship of a child should be made clear in addition to the way in which adoptive parents are chosen. The client who has finally braced himself to apply for a job may have more success if the practitioner helps him to form clear expectations about what will be involved in filling out an application form, in explaining his qualifications and limitations (prison record, disability, lack of experience), and in asking questions about what will be required of him. He can be prepared for the possibility of no opening and helped to distinguish this response from outright rejection. The technique of role rehearsal has also been called anticipatory guidance. The technique of preparing clients for relocation for the purpose of finding new employment possibilities is clearly described elsewhere.[31] Many clients who misperceive their own limitations or those in the environment need help in reality-testing to avoid unrealistic planning regarding vocational goals, their own future, or that of others.

LESSENING LIMITATIONS: ROLE PATTERNS

When, as a result of mental or physical illness, the individual has lost his customary patterns of activity, restoration of active coping patterns is essential to prevent loss of social competence. The client's previous activities have been organized around major life roles which he can now fulfill only partially, or not at all. In many cases, role changes may entail the loss of old patterns and the acquisition of new ones. The client must cognitively acknowledge the fact of the change and may do so more easily if the practitioner generalizes about the idea of self as active and about the reliance that is customarily placed on patterns that make coping possible. He helps the individual to perceive how threatened he feels by the loss of his previous dependable ways of functioning and to express anxiety about this feeling. This kind of situation occurs when the parent finds that he must, because of death, desertion, divorce, or prolonged separation, manage without a spouse. He must reorganize his role functioning and consciously engage in the search for and use of more appropriate patterns. He can profit from understanding that he cannot be both father and mother and that the child cannot be elevated to the role of the missing parent. He requires guidance in reorganizing his patterns and those of the children and in finding substitute activities that, to some extent, fill the vacuum left by the missing partner.

Severe mental or physical illness, including the hospitalization experience, usually results in loss of customary patterns for carrying life roles. The present emphasis on the therapeutic environment in the hospital has as one of its purposes the restoration of the executive function. Hospitals use various techniques to accomplish this purpose. Some have instituted activity programs or have encouraged the better-functioning patient to help those who do less well. This technique involves the reversal of the passive position to the active position of giving and doing and carries excellent therapeutic implications. Other hospitals engage the patient in active doing by using the technique of interesting him in performing various social roles.[32] This doing also provides an opportunity for opening up communication with the practitioner and promotes the thinking, talking, and doing with someone else. One mental hospital offers activity programs that develop "skills and talents—verbal and nonverbal, technical and social" and play skills. The patients go to movies and discuss them; they engage in work projects, in walks, and in games, all of which help to restore previous abilities. This hospital realizes that the patient may not be able to maintain his activity when he leaves the hospital, in which case he will again regress. It has developed after-care facilities to support the client in making the necessary adjustment in the community and in handling the transition from the hospital to a living situation. The hospital reports that staff members engage the client in problem-solving, in decision-making, and in organizing, planning, and managing life activities. They supplement discussion sessions with activity sessions that practice aspects of living with which the client is having trouble, such as grooming, recreation, or relating to the community. These centers use various techniques, such as role-playing, trips to the community, and group sessions.[33] Many children's hospitals try to prevent regression and loss of previous good functioning by using play that helps the child to act out his anxieties and to deal actively with the hospital experience. Many hospitals and clinics emphasize giving the patient active responsibilities for his own care and treatment, thus reversing the trend to passivity.

In his family and life experiences, the client usually learns socially acceptable and appropriate role behaviors, except that situational changes or his own development may present him with a role for which he is completely unprepared. Parents who give birth to a severely handicapped child or those whose child becomes ill or disabled need empathic support in facing their feelings of frustration, anger, and guilt as they acknowledge the fact that nothing in their life experiences has prepared them for handling this present role. The practitioner should furnish them with explicit teaching about appropriate ways of carrying the role of parent of a handicapped child. He should explain to the parents of a blind child ways to prevent stimulus deprivation, to keep the child related to the mother through the reassurance of her voice and touch, and to orient him in space and time. If parents fail to understand how to accomplish this stimulation, the child may lie passively in his crib, and the mother then perceives him as not only blind but also mentally retarded. Parents with a mentally retarded child may need help in training the child. This training is an ongoing process as the child's development brings new problems from time to time. The father of a seriously ill or handicapped child may benefit, if he tends to withdraw and to leave all responsibility to the mother, from being shown ways of becoming involved in the child's care. He can help to put on braces, share in assuming much of the physical care of a boy, and share in discipline, recreation, and other activities. He can particularly take responsibility for bringing the child to the hospital or to the clinic. In order to carry their parental roles appropriately, the parents of a handicapped child must understand the child's condition, perceive realistically his capacity, and develop a healthy relationship with him. Usually, parents see the child as more disabled than he is, in which case they overprotect him; or they tend to see him as less disabled, in which case they expect too much of him. In other words, they need a clear perceptual frame of reference in which to view their handicapped child and one that is realistic. This perception paves the way for learning to handle their parental roles.

In considering the teaching of a more active patterning for carrying roles, the practitioner must remember the fact that clients who have never learned appropriate patterns can usually do so only through the mechanisms of identification and internalization. In this case, he needs to give considerable thought to the provision of a suitable object with whom the client can identify. He needs a role model. In the case of a strong negative identification with parents, such as that of the neglectful mother or the abusive mother who has hostile ties to her own neglectful or abusive parents, the practitioner must serve as an omnipotent figure who can protect and furnish consistent gratification. The stronger the negative tie to the figure in the past, the more the client needs the practitioner to serve as a new model. This need for a model proves especially true when the parents of the client live nearby and reinforce old patterns because they continue to exert control and try to use the client to support their own negative perceptions of reality, as is true of many slum families. The practitioner can combine use of himself as an identification figure (or of herself in the case of the mother) with the use of a homemaker or other person in the environment. Sometimes, the practitioner starts with the homemaker with whom deprived clients can more easily identify and then proceeds to develop the client's identification with himself. A male practitioner or a Big Brother may furnish a stable role model for the adolescent boy.

A severely handicapped male client who struggles with a damaged body image often finds it difficult to identify with the strong, well, masculine rehabilitation worker who reactivates all his anxiety and negative feelings. In one such instance, the client did better with a female counselor. An amputee can successfully encourage a new amputee to identify with him as a person who has found a way to manage his handicap. Blind counselors have proved similarly helpful because the blind person conceives of them as furnishing an acceptable model that he can use in finding a way to handle his own problems. Frequently, the same purpose can be served by groups, such as groups for diabetic patients or groups for parents who, in struggling with poverty and life in the slums, share similar problems.[34]

Because the teaching of more active patterning has been referred to in a variety of connections, only a few additional instances need be mentioned. Lower-class fathers tend to define their roles as breadwinners and to have not learned to share parenting with their spouses. They need to understand the role of a father and to be helped to find enjoyment and reward in being a concerned and interested parent. Mealtimes when feelings and ideas are shared or work on home projects with family members can bring new satisfactions. Fathers can find pleasure in taking youngsters to the ball game or to see where daddy works. Involving the parent in teaching his child appropriate patterns provides one of the best techniques for teaching the active parenting role. Fathers can understand that a boy needs to know what the work world is like, that he wants to find out what his father does because he strives to be like his father, and that this learning readies the boy for eventually going out into the work world. Mothers can be encouraged to teach the daughter cooking, sewing, and other homemaking skills. Often, in order to do this teaching, they themselves must learn. In one interesting experiment, the mother was engaged in teaching language skills to her two-year-old child because research indicated that, at the age of two, the lower-class child begins to fall behind in this respect. The mother was given stimulating materials and guidance in their use. The materials required her to engage in interaction and verbal exchanges with the child. Helping the parents to teach the child can, therefore, accomplish a dual purpose and may break patterns of passivity handed on from generation to generation. In particular, the lower-class parent needs to see himself as a teacher of his child and to learn this role in helping the child learn inner controls. In helping clients to maintain active patterning, it is important for the practitioner to attach them to groups that can sustain them through social recognition and group support after termination of services.

Integrative Function

Probably the essential meaning of ego theory for helping lies in the integrative function that overlaps all others. Support of the integrative function means that the practitioner focuses the client's attention on ways in which he can improve problem-solving by new learning, by strengthening, or by correcting old learning. He helps the client to acquire the practitioner's confidence in his capacity to change and to find better ways of handling his situation. This approach also focuses on new possibilities in the present and implicitly emphasizes health rather than pathology because the practitioner holds out the hope of improvement and encourages the client to reopen old issues and make new attempts for solving, synthesizing, or reconciling conflict. One characteristic conflict that the client continually faces and that the practitioner helps him consciously to resolve is the conflict between progressive and regressive functioning, with the practitioner emphasizing progression. The strengthening of the integrative function means that the practitioner's goal is to strengthen the client's conscious control of behavior through learning new ways of coping that are better related to the demands of the client's reality situation.

Identity

The practitioner helps the client to deal with the trauma, difficulty, loss, and ego inadequacy that threaten his sense of identity. Whenever the practitioner individualizes the client and makes clear that he is trying to understand the client's individual needs, perceptions, capacities, and limitations, he strengthens the client's sense of identity. For example, one practitioner succeeded when others had failed when the client who was receiving public assistance realized that the practitioner had grasped an essential aspect of his individuality. He accepted help after the practitioner noticed his excellent verbal ability, inquired about it, and learned that he was a college graduate. Realization that the practitioner was interested enough to see beneath old age and dependency restored this client's sense of identity. Throughout the contact, as the client becomes better related to his life situation and to those around him, his sense of belonging and of having a place in society strengthens identity. Many clients can verbalize the fact that they feel lost and inadequate. The entire helping process that strengthens ego-coping abilities contributes directly and indirectly to strengthening a sense of identity.

The practitioner enhances the client's sense of inner continuity when he helps him to develop dependable and effective patterns of ego functioning. He promotes the client's feeling of wholeness when he enables him to accept aspects of himself or of his past and more capably handle his conflicts. The experience of success makes it possible for the client to relate past, present, and future because he can accept his past and look forward to the future with more hope. When the practitioner supports the client in regaining reliable patterns lost through stress and trauma, the client usually can also regain a sense of identity.

The practitioner's strengthening of ego patterns usually leads to improvement in the client's ability to carry his social roles. As a result, he achieves a clearer sense of identity as a parent, a spouse, a child, an adolescent, a worker, or a citizen. The practitioner helps the client to internalize his belief that the client can learn to handle his roles more effectively. He tries to make clear to the client the ways in which improved role functioning help him to feel related to his community and win for him social rewards. Vocational counselors attempting to help lower-class adolescents achieve a sense of identity through finding a place in the work world should realize that these youngsters are usually unfamiliar with the work role and job possibilities. They require information and experiences, such as work-study programs, before they can become interested in trying out a work role.

Since identifications form the core of the client's identity, the practitioner provides a stable identification figure either in himself or through using other role models. He always attempts to loosen the bonds of negative identifications. Whenever possible, he tries to remove barriers that prevent the youngster from identifying with the parent of the same sex. Many youngsters from minority groups, from the culture of poverty, or from single-parent families, however, lack suitable role models in the family. To deal with this situation, one practitioner organized a touch football team and another one led a scout troop. In this way, they were able to help the adolescents to identify with an adult who represented a new way of getting along in society. Solomon Kobrin has discussed the possibility of working with semidelinquent gangs to change the gang culture to one that is positively related to society at large.[35]

Strengthening Moral Character

Research suggests that working-class parents subscribe to the same norms as do middle-class parents but lack the ability to effect the desired outcomes in the child. Parents can profit from understanding the fact that the father's influence is as important as that of the mother, and more important for boys, and that consistency in the expectations of the parental coalition promotes effective learning by the child. Wesley C. Becker also suggests that the practitioner can help parents learn appropriate patterns of reward and punishment, patterns of clear and consistent conveying of expectations. When the parent represents a faulty role model, because of defective superego or seductiveness, the child cannot change until his situation is altered.

In the case of adults with rigid superegos, the practitioner may help to relax superego controls that, because of guilt and anxiety over unacceptable aspects of self, interfere with the individual's ability to face what needs to be changed. However, in the majority of cases, the client lacks the ego strengths suggested by Kohlberg. In the relationship, when the client identifies with him, the practitioner can encourage empathic feeling with and for other persons in the family and elsewhere. He can strengthen ego functions, especially the ability to perceive the effect of one's behavior on others, the ability to defer gratification, to foresee, and to plan on the basis of anticipation of outcomes. Adolescents also can frequently benefit from help in affirming standards and values for themselves. In the case of the client with a personality disorder, the practitioner attempts to provide external controls that serve to set limits and to restrain impulsive acting-out behavior.

Notes

1. Richard Stuart, "Supportive Casework with Borderline Patients," *Social Work,* 9:38–44 (January 1964).

2. Kenneth Dick and Lydia J. Strnad, "The Multi-problem Family and Problems of Service," *Social Casework,* 39:349–55 (June 1958).

3. Jerry Dincin, "Utilization of Professional Staff in Psychiatric Rehabilitation," *Social Work,* 10:51–57 (January 1965).

4. Donald L. Mosher, "On Advising Parents to Set Limits for Their Children," *Social Casework,* 46:86–89 (February 1965).

5. See, for example, Richard D. Brodie, Betty L. Singer, and Marian R. Winterbottom, "Integration of Research Findings and Casework Techniques," *Social Casework,* 48:360–68 (June 1967).

6. Nellie D. Stone and Joseph J. Parnicky, "Factors in Child Placement: Parental Response to Congenital Defect," *Social Work,* 11:-35–43 (April 1966).

7. Salvador Minuchin et al., *Families of the Slums: An Exploration of Their Structure and Treatment* (New York: Basic Books, 1967), p. 247.

8. Elizabeth C. Stevenson, "Casework Treatment of Parent-Child Conflicts," *Social Casework,* 49:583–88 (December 1968).

9. Lydia Rapoport, "Crisis-oriented Short-Term Casework," *Social Service Review,* 41:31–43 (March 1967).

10. Miriam Shames, "Use of Homemaker Service in Families that Neglect Their Children," *Social Work,* 9:12–18 (January 1964).

11. Otto Pollak, "Entrance of the Caseworker into Family Interaction," *Social Casework,* 45:216–20 (April 1964).

12. Minuchin et al., *Families of the Slums,* pp. 278–79.

13. Carroll M. Brodsky, Ames Fischer, and Morton R. Weinstein, "Modern Treatment of Psychosis: New Tasks for Social Therapies," *Social Work,* 9:71–78 (July 1964).

14. Thomas M. French, "Ego Analysis as a Guide to Therapy," *Psychoanalytic Quarterly,* 14:336–49 (1945).

15. Hymen Slate, "Handling the Hospital Patient's Ultimatum," *Social Casework,* 39:222–28 (April 1958).

16. Rubin Blanck, "The Case for Individual Treatment," *Social Casework,* 46:70–74 (February 1965).

17. Rapoport, "Crisis-oriented Short-term Casework."

18. Ludwig L. Geismar and Jane Krisberg, "The Family Life Improvement Project: An Experiment in Preventive Intervention: Part II," *Social Casework,* 47:663–67 (December 1966).

19. Thomas M. French, *Integration of Behavior* (Chicago: University of Chicago Press, 1952) vol. 1, chap. 11.

20. Irving Kaufman, "Maximizing the Strengths of Adults with Severe Ego Defects," *Social Casework,* 43:478–85 (November 1962).

21. Eleanor Pavenstedt, ed., *The Drifters: Children of Disorganized Lower-Class Families* (Boston: Little, Brown & Co., 1967), chaps. 10, 11.

22. Selma Fraiberg, "Counseling for the Parents of the Very Young Child," *Social Casework,* 35:47–57 (February 1954).

23. Rubin Blanck, "Marriage as a Phase of Personality Development," *Social Casework,* 48:154–60 (March 1967).

24. See, for example, Barbara Cowan et al., "Holding Unwilling Clients in Treatment," *Social Casework,* 50:146–51 (March 1969); and Hyman Grossbard, "Ego Deficiency in Delinquents," *Social Casework,* 43:171–78 (April 1962).

25. See, for example, Kaufman, "Maximizing the Strengths of Adults."

26. Robert B. Miller, "An Oblique Approach to Clients with Behavior Disorders," *Social Work,* 10:64–70 (April 1965).

27. Joshua M. Perman, "Role of Transference in Casework with Public Assistance Families," *Social Work,* 8:47–54 (October 1963).

28. Lawrence Kohlberg, "Development of Moral Character and Moral Ideology," in *Review of Child Development Research,* ed. Martin L. Hoffman and Lois W. Hoffman (New York: Russell Sage Foundation, 1964) vol. 1, pp. 383–431.

29. Jerome Kagan, "Acquisition and Significance of Sex Typing

and Sex Role Identity," in *Review of Child Development Research*, ed. Martin L. Hoffman and Lois W. Hoffman (New York: Russell Sage Foundation, 1964), vol. 1, pp. 137–67.

30. Magda Bondy, "Casework with Families and Patients Facing Cardiovascular Surgery," *Journal of Jewish Communal Services*, 36:294–306 (Spring 1960).

31. Harvey A. Abrams, "The Role of Social Work in Relocation for Employment," *Social Casework*, 49:475–80 (October 1968).

32. See, for example, Daniel Rosenblatt, "Role Therapy in a Mental Hospital," *Social Casework*, 46:263–70 (May 1965); and Brodsky, Fischer, and Weinstein, "Modern Treatment of Psychosis."

33. Brodsky, Fischer, and Weinstein, "Modern Treatment of Psychosis."

34. Ada Shew Cyrus, "Group Treatment of Ten Disadvantaged Mothers," *Social Casework*, 48:80–84 (February 1967).

35. Solomon Kobrin, "Sociological Aspects of the Development of a Street Corner Group: An Exploratory Study," *American Journal of Orthopsychiatry*, 31:685–702 (October 1961).

SEVEN

Focus on Resistance to Using Help

This chapter discusses the four matching diagnostic and treatment categories of resistance to using help. These matching treatment categories are aimed at lessening the client's discomfort and, hence, his defensiveness about the practitioner's positive or negative expectations regarding his using help by using the relationship.

IN giving consideration to the second category of resistance—resistance to carrying the client role and to using help—two corollaries of the principle of client participation come to the fore: (1) the principle of moving at the client's pace, since "demands for abrupt change" tend to mobilize anxiety;[1] and (2) the principle of moving from outer to progressively more inner aspects of the problem-situation.[2] Characteristically, practitioners define *movement* in helping as movement toward or away from the goals of change agreed upon by practitioner and client. It is also possible to have a situation in which no movement takes place and the problem-situation remains the same. The practitioner cannot assess movement or resistance except in relation to agreed-upon goals. Because change is the goal of helping, the practitioner continually uses the concept of movement to gauge the client's use of help: If he becomes a user of help, he should evidence movement toward mutually selected goals. In ego terms, the client uses help; in role terms, the client carries his role reciprocally with the practitioner. Even the most casual consideration, however, indicates that the client must learn this role that differs from life roles and that he must be ready to accept the role responsibilities expected of him by the practitioner. The practitioner expects the client to attempt to achieve changes in his situation or in his functioning. Although client and practitioner have agreed upon a problem focus and on the terms and goals of help and although the client holds predominantly positive conscious expectations of help and his unconscious expectations have been appropriately handled, he may be unready to move toward change either because the practitioner expects him to move too quickly or expects him to move toward dealing with more inner aspects that he feels he cannot handle. In such instances, the client resists using help and carrying the client role because of an imbalance between client-practitioner expectations.

DIAGNOSIS AND TREATMENT OF RESISTANCE

The second category of resistance uses the same classificatory principle of motivation as the first category. It proposes that the client's resistance to using help at the given time in the interview is motivated primarily by the threat inherent in the practitioner's expectations about the client's perceiving, feeling, or acting in relation to his problem situation—that is, by discomfort or role strain. This category of resistance provides a way of operationalizing the principles of moving at the client's pace and of moving from outer to more inner aspects of his difficulty. It provides a way for the practitioner to assess diagnostically client resistance or potential resistance, which indicates that the practitioner's expectations are not congruent with those of the client. Resistance of this type denotes the client's unreadiness to move in ways expected by the practitioner. It therefore becomes possible for the practitioner to use appropriate treatment measures either to lessen or to forestall resistance because he understands the motivations for the resisting behaviors.

The assessment of resistance to using help and the assessment of the client's capacity complement each other, and the practitioner continually draws on these two sources of understanding as well as on an understanding of limiting and supporting environmental factors. The assessment of capacity reveals customary patterning of ego functions and gives indications of the levels of personality development as these relate to problem-solving. This judgment also indicates treatment measures needed to improve capacity through lessening limiting factors, increasing strengths, and bringing about needed situational changes. With help of this nature, the client should be able to move toward change unless inner or outer limitations prove impossible to alter. The practitioner always distinguishes limitations in capacity and the effect of limiting situational factors from client resistance to using help. This view of resistance requires him to examine whether he has done everything possible to increase capacity and situational support. It also requires him to examine with the client the mutually agreed-upon goals to see whether they can be achieved or should be altered.

When the practitioner encounters resistance to using help, he observes client behavior that shows that the client is running away from utilizing the assistance that the practitioner is giving and is avoiding making the changes in functioning expected by the practitioner. He is running away from meeting the practitioner's role expectations of movement toward agreed-upon goals. This behavior arises in response to the helping situation. Theoretically, the client's discomfort may be evoked in several ways. A temporary imbalance may exist between client expectations and the problem-solving demands of the helping situation. In other instances, the client is testing what it is like to use help, and he is beginning to try to work on his problem, although it makes him anxious to do so. Other clients may become intellectually ready or be intellectually ready to work on inner and outer difficulties. When it comes actually to changing patterns of functioning or ways of operating, however, the clients resist since they have not accepted what goal achievement entails. Clients may resist in early interviews as they are asked to share, perhaps for the first time, intimate details with a helping person and to begin to face the implications of their situation. These same clients may show resistance at any stage in the contact when the practitioner moves too fast or enters areas that the client is not ready to consider. The practitioner also encounters the situation in which the client and practitioner are attempting to lessen limiting factors in the client's ego functioning. Any of the established ego patterns may serve as barriers to the client's using help. Lifetime defenses, maladaptive patterns, or poor functioning resulting from never having learned more appropriate patterns are not, in themselves, resistance. However, as the practitioner attempts to help the client to change and expects him to change, the incapacity may become evident. He may take this indication as a guide to the necessity for more patient and longer efforts to work on limiting factors in the client's functioning or in his situation, or he may use this indication as a guide to the necessity for revising the goals of helping.

Second Typology of Resistance

The four subcategories in resistance to using help include resistance evoked by: A, the threat inherent in the practitioner's expectations regarding the client's perception of the problem-situation; B, the threat inherent in the practitioner's expectations regarding the client's handling of needs and feelings; C, the threat inherent in the practitioner's expectations that the client make decisions or take steps to handle the problem-situation; and D, the client's perception that the practitioner has predominantly negative expectations of improvement. *Problem-situation* in this category is used to designate not only the problem for which the client asks help, but also the problematical area for the client concerning his attempts to change the situation or his functioning relative to the problem focus and goals. This second category of resistance reminds the practitioner to examine his expectations of the client in the light of client capacity for achieving change. The practitioner must ask himself not only what the client's present capacity is but also what the possibilities are for increasing that capacity. He must question the likelihood of change and what would be needed to bring about that change in relation to both time and help. The client's resistance gives indications of how fast and how far the practitioner may expect him to move. The second category of resistance proposes that the practitioner's expectations that are threatening because they are not congruent with the client's tend to arouse discomfort. Evidences of such threat and discomfort in defensiveness would, therefore, be expected, because ego theory postulates that the individual tends to defend himself against inner and outer dangers under the motivation of discomfort or anxiety when he feels helpless to deal with the threat.[3] The pointers that indicate resistance of this type will, therefore, tend to have the nature of defensiveness. Communication difficulties, expression of feelings, and transistory defenses constitute the kinds of pointers that may suggest resistance in any of the subtypes of this category. However, the practitioner always attempts to find out, more specifically, what has stimulated these general expressions and whether the client resists perceiving, feeling, or acting.

The client may show communication difficulties by refusal to talk about his problem-situation or his functioning in regard to it. Clients frequently refuse to talk when they feel forced to accept help by the nature of their situation, for example, when they are on probation or parole or when, because of illness or poverty, they feel helpless. The client may slow down communication, or he may literally deluge the practitioner with communication over the relevant and the irrelevant. In other cases, he may use inappropriate communication, talking about inconsequential matters or using generalizations that mask the realities. Welfare clients may discuss the grant as a way of avoiding discussion of relationship problems in the family. Patients may focus on aspects of their illness as a way of avoiding more personal details. Sometimes clients become so diffuse that the practitioner cannot follow the thread of conversation. Communication difficulties can also arise when the practitioner moves too close to the heart of the difficulty, or they may be used as a form of withdrawal when the client feels he has revealed too much in a previous interview. In addition, the client may express doubts that the practitioner can understand him or his problem and show these doubts by having trouble in talking about his situation.

Another group of pointers that may indicate resistance in the second category of resistance involves the use of feelings. Hostility in its manifold expressions serves as a distancing technique to keep the practitioner at bay and to avoid role commitment or self-revelation. It is the usual form of resistance of clients who feel forced by circumstances—legal, physical, or situational—to accept help. Clients can show hostility indirectly by defeating the practitioner's plans, suggestions, and efforts. They tend to do so when they feel pressured by the practitioner. Clients forget appointments, antagonize prospective employers, fail to fill out forms, or avoid going through with agreed-upon plans. They may show hostility quite directly in the interview or, indirectly, by ingratiation techniques. Some clients use the feeling of helplessness to avoid what they resist doing. In this manner, they attempt to invoke the practitioner's protection against having to deal with their difficulties. The practitioner distinguishes defensiveness from lifetime defenses. The client may use a variety of defenses—denial, projection, displacement, or any type of behavior—for defensive purposes and as a means of resisting. The client may be able to give up these defensive maneuvers when the practitioner deals appropriately with the resistance.

RESISTANCE EVOKED BY THE NEED TO PERCEIVE THE PROBLEM

Resistance in subcategory A occurs with clients whose resistance at the given time is evoked primarily by the threat inherent in the practitioner's expectations regarding the client's perception of the problem-situation—that is, by the practitioner's expectation of the client's carrying the client role.

Practitioners have dealt extensively with the fact that the use of help requires the client to perceive that he needs help and the kind of help that he needs. However, the practitioner alters this expectation to conform with his understanding of the nature and degree of physical or emotional illness or handicap that has affected client capacity.[4] As the client participates more fully and invests more in working toward change, the practitioner expects the client to begin to move toward a more realistic perception of how he is handling his problem-situation and toward increased ability to perceive the extent, nature, and implications of his difficulty and of his share in these difficulties. However, the client may resist the practitioner's attempt to help him to utilize or to increase perceptual abilities in problem-solving.

The practitioner judges that the client's resistance is of this nature when the client defensively uses avoidance or running-away behaviors to prevent changes in perception. Pointers indicating this type of resistance may include any or all of the following. Selective perceptions serve a defensive purpose and can be used as resistance. Clients frequently request a solution to the problem to avoid seeing the true nature of the problem. They ask for placement of a child or divorce from a spouse because they do not want to see their relationship difficulty. Requests for money, carfare, lodgings, or other help may have a similar import, as may be seen in clients who have literally been running away from some problem and come to the Travelers Aid for assistance. Frequently, clients hold to unrealistic motivations or motivations toward unrealistic goals as a defensive maneuver to avoid perceiving the effect and nature of limiting circumstances. Individuals who have recently become severely handicapped often hold to the goals of previous employment or of role functioning as a well person to avoid perceiving realistically the degree and nature of their disability.[5] The husband of a senile wife may cling to impossible plans for home care to escape facing the problem of separation. Frequently, the client cannot see the problem as a shared problem; he either assumes too much or too little responsibility for the marital difficulty, the parent-child relationship, or other conditions.

Generally clients see the less painful and more acceptable aspects of their situation. They find it especially difficult to see their share in the problem and usually only make progress in this respect with time and with help. They use transitory defensive operations along the way. The mother of a school child in difficulty tends at first to project blame onto the school and in various ways to act defensive. The man with recurrent employment failure often displaces his job loss onto such external circumstances as the nature of the work he was doing, the kind of employer, travel problems, and so forth. He may give up these self-protective maneuvers slowly. Frequently, the client's defensive use of selective perception tests the practitioner's understanding and perception and his ability to remain consistently empathic and accepting in the face of the realities of the client's difficulties and to support dependably the client's efforts to achieve changes.

The practitioner always pays close attention to what the client can and cannot perceive because inability to perceive may indicate limitations in capacity with which he needs to deal rather than a temporarily defensive stance that the client can abandon if the practitioner uses appropriate treatment measures to lessen discomfort and hence to lessen resistance. The resistance may also indicate unwillingness or unreadiness to work on changing limitations in capacity.

RESISTANCE EVOKED BY NEED TO HANDLE FEELINGS

Resistance in subcategory B occurs with clients whose resistance at the given time is evoked primarily by the threat inherent in the practitioner's expectations regarding the client's handling of needs and feelings related to the problem-situation—that is, expectations regarding the carrying of the client role.

The practitioner's expectations of the client role include expectations that the client will use help in handling needs and feelings unless a severe mental or physical illness or handicap limits his capacity.[6] Client participation in using help requires him to consider what is problematic in his needs and feelings and the way he is handling them. With forward movement, the practitioner expects to find an increase in the developmental motivational forces in the personality and a lessening of hampering, self-defeating patterns for handling needs and feelings. The client's feelings enter into all aspects of his relationships with others and with his situation. The practitioner usually expects the client in some degree to bring out his feelings and to improve his management of feelings. The practitioner differentiates between lifetime inability to operate on the reality principle (and characteristically defensive patterns for handling needs and feelings) and the defensiveness usually manifested in resistance. He judges the client's resistance to be of this subtype when the client's behavior shows that the practitioner's expectations that he handle needs and feelings are not congruent with those of the client and tax ego capacity and hence arouse discomfort and resistance. The following pointers may indicate resistance of this type.

The client indicates verbally or nonverbally that certain needs are threatening to him or unacceptable or that he fears the practitioner will not accept them. Clients tend to verbalize socially approved needs and defensively to avoid discussing very different needs that may be motivating them. The client referred for employment problems may voice the need to be independent and to find a job; the mother of an emotionally disturbed child may say that she needs to know the exact extent of his difficulty; and a husband may urgently request help in holding the marriage together. Each of these expressed needs may hide the opposing need that the client resists discussing since he fears that the practitioner will condemn him or because he cannot face the painful nature of his conflicting needs. In some instances, the client acts out needs he cannot express. A mother may resist discussing a child's needs as a way of showing that she herself greatly needs the practitioner's concern for herself as a person. Some clients whose life situation has frustrated needs may at first find them too painful to talk about and may suppress them. For example, a husband may find his wife's denial of his need for a closer relationship with his son hard to accept. The mother of a retarded child may find that her need for a well child has been defeated, and this desire may be extremely painful. Sometimes, the client experiences opposing needs that pull him in two directions. Frequently, these needs spring from conflicting role demands. What do I owe my husband versus what do I owe my children? What do I owe my position as a wage earner versus what do I owe my job as a mother? The client may deliberately avoid seeing these conflicting pulls because he wishes to carry both roles adequately.

The client frequently indicates a conflicting need that he wants to discuss by strongly affirming the opposite desire. As the present situation brings these needs into focus, the practitioner notes those that the client selects for discussion and those that he omits, and he attempts to differentiate limitations in capacity for which help is indicated from the temporarily defensive maneuvers which point toward resistance. Resistance of this nature is often a way of testing the practitioner's acceptance, empathy, and understanding as well as his ability to support the client consistently in moving toward change. Many clients defensively project, deny, or displace needs until they have tested the practitioner's acceptance and understanding or until the improved balance of forces in the personality enables them to use more adaptive patterns. The client who has suffered severe emotional loss at first may deny his need to be dependent on someone. The abandoned woman at first may displace her need to strike back at the husband through one or all of her children.

The client may also resist facing his feelings related to needs. In some instances he may block out his feelings and be unable to use them.[7] He may indicate verbally or nonverbally that certain feelings are threatening to him or unacceptable to him or that he fears that the practitioner will not accept them. These feelings may be guilt, hostility, or a sense of inadequacy or failure. The client may imply what he wants to bring out by affirming the opposite side of his ambivalent feelings or by discussing actions and circumstances that reveal feelings. The mother who is guilty about her impatience with a child points out how patient she has been or discusses situations that clearly reveal the impatience. The rejecting mother explains how much she has done for the child. Ambivalent feelings constitute the most usual pointers that are indicative of possible resistance. The client can express only one side of his ambivalance but seems uneasy and unconvinced or unsure or anxious, thus indicating that the other side of the feeling constitutes the possible source of resistance. Intelligent clients may intellectualize to avoid facing their feelings. Others become evasive when the practitioner approaches the subject of feelings. Sometimes the client's resistance to expressing feelings becomes evident when the feelings block his perception or his activity.

The client not only may resist bringing out feelings that he fears the practitioner will find unacceptable, but also may avoid discussing how he has handled the feelings when he fears condemnation. Pointers that denote resistance of this nature come from the client's evasiveness in explaining what has happened or how he has dealt with these feelings. Generalizations, changing the subject, explanations that omit salient details, or the use of defensive rationalization provide pointers to the client's discomfort aroused by the practitioner's expectations that he discuss his feelings or his handling of feelings. An article by Walter Haas deals with clients' resistance to finding the way to repressed feelings.[8]

RESISTANCE EVOKED BY NEED TO ACT APPROPRIATELY

Resistance in subcategory C occurs with clients whose resistance at the given time is evoked primarily by the threat inherent in the practitioner's expectations that the client make decisions or take steps to handle the problem-situation —that is, expectations of his using help and carrying the client role.

Unless the client is severely mentally or physically limited, client participation requires that the client make a decision and take action about his situation. As Bernece K. Simon points out, the client's problem usually "involves decision-making and acting upon such decisions."[9] The practitioner's expectations, in most instances, include expectations that, to an increasing extent, the client will show movement toward more effective activity and toward being able to decide and to carry through his plan. In some instances, decision-making becomes crucial. For example, when the client is facing an operation, he needs to decide about his own entrance into a home or other institutional facility or about the entrance or commitment of another family member. The practitioner distinguishes between manifestations of resistance and limitations in capacity. The client may require help in perceiving a situation more realistically before he can make a decision or act. He may require information basic to a decision or activity. In other instances, the client may need to deal with a related problem before he can move on to deal with this problem. Other clients have never been able to make decisions or may never have learned appropriate activity patterns; for such clients, the practitioner gives help to increase capacity before expecting movement in deciding and acting. The practitioner judges that the client is resisting deciding or acting when his behavior shows any of the following pointers.

The client's self-distrust may give evidence of his resistance to taking action for which he feels unready. He may ask for reassurances from the practitioner that he is making the right decision or is taking the right steps. In other cases, he may show distrust of the practitioner or a feeling that the practitioner is pressuring him to act. Hesistancy, reluctance, or doubts may constitute expressions of resistance to taking action. Sometimes the client repetitiously reviews the pros and cons, asks for other possibilities, and seems unconvinced or unsure of the course to pursue. Some clients tell the practitioner directly or indirectly that they will follow through on a plan to please the practitioner or out of gratitude.

The making of decisions or the taking of action assumes a readiness or a willingness to take responsibility. The client may demonstrate unreadiness to take responsibility by failure to follow through, by immobilization, or by an attempt to have the practitioner make decisions or take action, or he may attempt to have someone in his milieu do it.

RESISTANCE EVOKED BY PRACTITIONER'S NEGATIVE EXPECTATIONS

The final subcategory in the second type of resistance relates to clients whose resistance, at the given time, is evoked primarily by the practitioner's negative expectations of the client's being able to carry the client role or by the client's perception that the practitioner holds predominantly negative expections of improvement.

The practitioner's positive expectations of the client for

using help in carrying the client role have been discussed. The situation may arise in which the practitioner's conscious or unconscious negative expectations—or what the client perceives as negative expectations—can give rise to client discomfort and hence to resistance. Research indicates that the practitioner's positive expectations, expressed as encouragement, tend to be associated with client continuance with the agency, whereas the practitioner's lack of hope regarding the possibility of change in the problem-situation tends to be associated with discontinuance.[10] In line with these findings, it could be expected that the practitioner's negative expectations would tend to evoke resistance to using help and to carrying the client role. In some instances, the practitioner may not have been aware of his own negative expectations that the client has correctly intuited; in others, the client may misperceive. Pointers indicating resistance of this type include any of the following behaviors.

The client indicates, verbally or nonverbally, his belief that the practitioner has a poor opinion of his ability as a spouse, a parent, or an employee. The client shows that he does not expect the practitioner to give his ideas or his opinions much weight. The client may test the practitioner by trying to seduce the practitioner to take over for him, thus demonstrating a lack of faith in his ability. The request, "Tell me what to do," may have a testing purpose, although in other instances it may be based on realistic ignorance, confusion, or incapacity. Occasionally, the client indicates doubt as to whether the practitioner trusts his own ability to help. He asks such questions as: "Tell me, have you ever had a case like mine?" "Have you any children?" "Have you ever been in a situation like mine?" These questions may be ways of asking whether the practitioner considers the client's situation beyond his skill to change. Sometimes the client's questions about the practitioner's preparation, apparent youth, or cultural or ethnic group differences have the same purpose.

Perhaps the most usual client is the one who fears that the

practitioner may be unwilling to help. The client may indicate that he wonders whether the practitioner considers him worth helping because he is alcoholic, because he is such a failure, because he is in such a mess, or because he is delinquent. Such clients often test out the practitioner by breaking appointments or by being provocative in the interview. Sometimes the client asks the practitioner about other clients, wondering how he has time for him, or apologizes for taking so much of his time away from those who need help more than he does. A client's hopelessness and depression can reflect his perception, correct or incorrect, that the practitioner holds slight expectations of the possibilities of change in his case. Any of the foregoing behaviors may constitute the client's way of testing the practitioner's capacity for remaining consistently supporting and accepting of the client when he progresses at his own pace.

In summary, client resistance indicates lack of congruence in expectations. The practitioner has three choices. He may attempt to lessen resistance, to increase capacity, or to consider revision of goals. He usually moves to the third possibility only when the other two have failed.

Treatment Measures for Handling Resistance to Using Help

Assessment of resistance or potential resistance to using help should enable the practitioner to use appropriate treatment measures to lessen or to forestall resistance and thus to increase client participation. The treatment measures can be conceived of as lying on a continuum from a minimum to a maximum of support, encouragement, and initiative and activity by the practitioner.

The second category of treatment measures consists of measures to lessen or minimize the client's discomfort and, hence, resistance aroused by the practitioner's expectations regarding his using help and carrying the client role.

Theoretically, resistance motivated by discomfort should decrease with a lessening of the discomfort. These measures are designed to bridge the perceptual and affective and activity gap between practitioner and client; they also are designed to lessen the psychological distance between them by decreasing the client's feeling of being alone with his problem and the necessity for dealing with it. The treatment measures offer to the client empathic acceptance, strength, and support through the use of the professional relationship to increase motivation for using help, which in essence might be viewed as taking steps toward growth and development.

The second type of treatment measures include the following subcategories of treatment measures to lessen client discomfort: A, supporting the client's capacity to perceive and by sharing understanding and perception; B, supporting the client's ability to handle needs and feelings and by sharing feelings and acceptance of feelings; C, supporting the client's ability to decide and act and by sharing the burden and giving prompt help; and D, clarifying the practitioner's expectations and, when realistically possible, voicing hope and encouragement.

SUPPORTING THE CLIENT'S CAPACITY TO PERCEIVE

Subcategory A proposes to lessen client discomfort about perceiving aspects of the problem-situation by supporting the client's capacity to perceive and by sharing understanding and perception. To accomplish this goal, the practitioner uses various techniques. According to Lola G. Selby, he provides a therapeutic environment in which the client is free to talk and this leads to clarification.[11] He may actively guide explorations by demonstrating his understanding of helpful areas that both he and client should examine. He always attempts to sense correctly the conscious and unconscious meanings of the client's communication and to respond appropriately. Frequently, he structures for clarity when the client gets bogged down in detail or seems confused or repetitious. In a similar manner, he may recapitulate the client's material at the end of the interview or at appropriate points. These techniques underline for the client perceptions that he and the practitioner share regarding the person-problem-situation configuration and encourage the client to express his views and to trust that the practitioner will perceive his communications correctly. The practitioner may also empathically accept the fact that thinking about and facing some facets of his situation or of his handling of the problem-situation tend to make the client anxious and may be difficult for him.

Many clients can, with help, lessen their defensiveness about perceiving. The practitioner may test the client's readiness by adopting an active giving role and sharing his understanding and perceptions. He may reformulate the client's material, putting into clearer words what he thinks the client has been trying to say, or he may offer the client his own formulation, saying, in effect, "These are my views of the meaning of what you are saying, what do you think about them?" When the practitioner becomes aware of what the client is avoiding, he tries to find ways of making it easier for the client to discuss these aspects by offering relationship support, acceptance, empathy, and encouragement.

If empathy and acceptance do not accomplish the purpose of lessening discomfort, the practitioner may utilize increased initiative. He may suggest what the client seems to be omitting and bring to his attention significant and relevant considerations. If the client seems unready to consider these ideas at the given time in the interview, the practitioner may suggest that the client needs to think about them and work on them in the future. He may propose some homework. When the client has trouble in perceiving differences between the present and previous situations, the practitioner may help the client to do reality-testing if he feels that the client is ready for it and that the difficulties in reality-testing spring from temporary imbalance between expectations and ego strengths. When it is indicated, the practitioner may help the client to find ways of enlisting the efforts of family members or others whose perception of the problem-situation may be affecting the client's resistance to achieving more realistic perceptions.

However, the practitioner pays careful attention to cues that indicate aspects of the problem-situation that the client is not ready to perceive. Use of defensiveness tells the practitioner that the client may become more resistant if the practitioner expects him, for example, to see his share in the difficulty or to probe for some of his deeper feelings. Clues that indicate resistance of this nature include blocking, panic, and other symptoms of tension. The practitioner, in some instances, may use techniques of partializing. In other instances, he may defer approaching the aspects with which the client is unready to deal, as he recognizes that the client may need more time before he examines what makes him uncomfortable. He may express his confidence in the client's ability to do so later on with his support.

If the client's resistance does not yield in a reasonable length of time to the usual treatment measures for increasing capacity or for dealing with resistance and if the treatment goals require a lessening of resistance, the practitioner may use the technique of confrontation. He verbalizes the client's resistance, attempts to point out the effects of the resistance and the possible values in abandoning defensiveness and in utilizing help. He always, however, makes clear that the client must make the final decision about how much of his difficulty he can bear to face and the problems he wants the practitioner to help him to think about and to see more clearly. The practitioner may confront the client with the fact that he cannot achieve agreed-upon goals unless the client lessens his resistance. He recognizes the possibility that the client's resistance may indicate the advisability of changing the goals.

SUPPORTING THE CLIENT'S ABILITY TO HANDLE NEEDS

In the second type of treatment measures, subcategory B proposes to lessen discomfort about handling needs and feelings relative to the problem-situation by supporting the client's ability to handle needs and feelings and by sharing feelings and acceptance of feelings.

To the greatest possible extent, the practitioner supports the client's ability to handle needs and feelings. A variety of techniques helps to accomplish this purpose. The practitioner invites the client to express his concerns and to discuss relevant needs and feelings. He attempts to sense what the client is conveying and to respond appropriately by expressing his understanding or by recognizing what the client has said. When it is appropriate to the treatment goals, he encourages, at the client's pace, expressions of feelings of guilt, anxiety, hostility, inadequacy, or other painful emotions, and he responds acceptingly. He may use the techniques of universalizing or of externalizing to relieve guilt and discomfort. These techniques tend to bridge the emotional distance between client and practitioner and to assure the client of the practitioner's empathic understanding.

The practitioner always pays attention to cues indicative of needs and feelings that the client cannot tolerate at the given time, and he may defer bringing these into the open. When it is indicated, he may become more active by empathically sharing the client's feelings to determine whether the resistant client can, with help, lessen his defensiveness. He uses relationship support of empathy and acceptance to lessen the client's discomfort regarding the possibility of the practitioner's making judgments or his ability to empathize with and understand the client's feelings and needs. The practitioner may go even further as he verbalizes for the client the needs or the feelings he seems to be expressing by his tone of voice, by his description of events, or by his discussion of persons with whom he associates. When the client appears to have ambivalent needs and feelings, the practitioner may recognize this fact and support the client's ability to explore both sides of the ambivalence. He may attempt to clarify with the client what he wants or what he is predominantly feeling. In some instances, he may help the client do reality-testing by separating present feelings from past feelings or from the feelings of others, provided he judges that the client is ready to do so. When the feelings of other family members or other persons connected with the client affect or influence the client's resistance, the practitioner may develop with the client a plan to help him deal with this situation.

If, in a reasonable length of time, the practitioner has been unable to increase capacity or to lessen the client's resistance and if the treatment goals cannot otherwise be achieved, he may use the technique of confrontation, pointing out the effect of the resistance and what might be achieved if the client could lessen defensiveness and utilize help. The practitioner always clarifies the fact that the client himself must decide about the needs and feelings with which he wants help and with which he is ready to try to deal in a different way. He may confront the client with the fact that only by lessening resistance can he achieve mutually defined goals,[12] but he voices the idea that the client may want to change these goals.

SUPPORTING THE CLIENT'S ABILITY TO DECIDE AND ACT

In the second type of treatment measures, subcategory C proposes to lessen client discomfort about deciding or acting relative to the problem-situation by supporting the client's ability to decide and to act and by sharing the burden and giving prompt help. So far as it is realistically possible, the practitioner supports the client's right to decide and to act, provided the client does not contravene the rights of others. Unless circumstances demand an immediate decision, he also explicates the client's right to have time to decide and to ask help from family, from experts, and from others in making the decision. He also encourages the client to take any or all steps that the client considers essential preliminaries to planning. The practitioner clearly refuses to make decisions that the client is capable of making or, similarly, to accept the decisions of other persons for the client. For example, grown children often want to decide for the elderly parent or parents. He also supports the client in taking tentative steps, in trying out solutions and plans, and in recognizing that he has the right to fail. He attempts to make certain that the client's decision is not made to please him or someone else, in which case the client will resist following through on the decision. He forestalls this eventuality by withholding personal expressions of pleasure and approval when the client seems to be making the "right" decisions or taking the "right" steps. Instead, he may remind the client of possible difficulties or of other factors requiring consideration, or he may counsel him to try things out before deciding. When it is realistically possible, the practitioner may postpone decision-making and the taking of action when cues denote the client's unreadiness to do so or indicate that the client is acting or deciding under pressure. In some instances, he attempts to help the client decide to permit someone else to act for him.

With some clients, the practitioner may take an active giving and doing role as a way of using relationship support. He offers to share the burden and to help actively. He may make resources and services available to demonstrate his helpfulness and active doing for and with the client. The practitioner makes sure that he has provided, to the fullest extent possible, the necessary situational support and opportunities which make it possible for the client to decide and to act. In some cases, the client may be unable to act or to decide until he has had help in separating the present situation from a previous one. For example, the client's previous traumatic experience over the death of a relative in a hospital may keep him from deciding about a necessary operation for his child. Frequently, clients who experience extreme situational pressures resist the practitioner's expectations that they do more or do differently. The practitioner may close this expectation gap by freely doing for and with the client, giving his own strength and resources. These techniques may serve to diminish the discomfort of such clients as the mother in a single-parent family or the overburdened husband of an ill wife.

If, in a reasonable length of time, the practitioner cannot increase capacity or minimize the client's resistance and if treatment goals cannot otherwise be achieved, he may use the technique of confrontation by facing the client with his resistance to deciding or acting and by clarifying what the client could accomplish if he could lessen his defensiveness and use help. He also makes clear that only the client can make this decision or take this step. He may confront the client with the fact that, unless the client can lessen his resistance, he cannot achieve the goals that have been mutually defined, but he verbalizes the possibility that the client may want to change these goals.

CLARIFYING PRACTITIONER EXPECTATIONS

Subcategory D proposes to lessen client discomfort about the practitioner's possible negative expectations of change by clarifying practitioner expectations and, when realistically possible, by voicing hope and encouragement. When the client has misperceived the practitioner's expectations, the practitioner attempts to elicit the client's views and to find out the basis for them. In some instances, the client needs help in separating the present from previous encounters in taking help with other social agencies. He may remain unconvinced unless he experiences the practitioner's consistent offering of services despite resistance and his consistently positive expression of feelings.

The practitioner attempts to forestall or to minimize client discomfort by reaching out warmly and empathically to the client and by attempting to bridge social and emotional distance. He voices concern for the client and his welfare. He expresses his value of the client as a person and maintains the amount of warmth in feeling that meets the client's need and ability to tolerate warmth. He clearly expresses the hope of being able to better matters and a belief that the client's situation can be improved. Continuously throughout the giving of service, he helps the client to recognize progress. The practitioner expresses.his satisfaction and approval over the client's gains. He demonstrates confidence in the client's ability to change by allowing the client as much initiative as he is capable of using. He reviews his offering of services to determine whether he has failed to carry through promptly on his promises and whether the frequency and duration of interviews represent consistent and sustained giving of help.

When, in spite of relationship support and demonstrated willingness to help, the client continues to misperceive the practitioner's expectations as negative, the practitioner may confront the client with this fact. He clarifies the possibilities of improved problem-solving if the client could decide to lessen his defensiveness and to trust him. He points out the impossibility of achieving change unless the client can diminish resistance. If the client has correctly intuited the practitioner's negative expectations, the practitioner will have to deal with his unconscious feelings and countertransference.

Notes

1. Paul Widem, "Some Dimensions of Ego Continuity in Social Casework," *Social Work,* 11: 50–55 (October 1966).

2. Bernard Bandler, "Ego-Centered Teaching," in *Ego-Oriented Casework: Problems and Perspectives; Papers from the Smith College School for Social Work,* ed. Howard J. Parad and Roger R. Miller (New York: Family Service Association of America, 1963), pp. 223–35.

3. Herman Nunberg, *Principles of Psychoanalysis: Their Application to the Neuroses* (New York: International Universities Press, 1955), chap. 7.

4. Bernece K. Simon, *Relationship Between Theory and Practice in Social Casework, 1. Ego Assessment; 2. Ego-Supportive Casework Treatment,* Monograph 4 in the series "Social Work Practice in Medical Care and Rehabilitation Settings" (New York: National Association of Social Workers, 1960), pp. 33–34.

5. Robert J. Savard, "Casework and Resistance to Vocational Rehabilitation," *Social Casework,* 39: 564–70 (December 1958).

6. Simon, *Relationship Between Theory and Practice,* pp. 34–36.

7. See, for example, Walter Haas, "The Intergenerational Encounter: A Method of Treatment," *Social Work,* 13: 91–101 (July 1968).

8. Ibid.

9. Simon, *Relationship Between Theory and Practice,* p. 33.

10. Lilian Ripple, with Ernestina Alexander and Bernice W. Polemis, *Motivation, Capacity and Opportunity: Studies in Casework Theory and Practice,* Social Service Monographs Second Series,

School of Social Service Administration (Chicago: University of Chicago Press, 1964), pp. 123, 137–40.

11. Lola G. Selby, "Supportive Treatment: The Development of a Concept and a Helping Method," *Social Service Review,* 30: 400–14 (December 1956).

12. See, for example, Haas, "Intergenerational Encounter."

EIGHT

Goals and Goal Achievement

Relief from inner and outer stress and loosening of anxiety-free energy to deal with the tasks at hand make it possible to take as a long-term goal an increase in the client's conscious control of behavior. Improving coping patterns in each ego function partialize ego tasks and furnish short-term goals.

In the view advanced in this book, the functions of the ego and the patterns of these functions make possible the conscious control of behavior to the extent that the patterns can be consciously modified to meet the demands of reality. The method of ego analysis, based on assessment of patterning in the given individual, suggests the possibility that practitioner and client can take as a long-term goal of their work together an increase in the client's ability consciously to control behavior. The practitioner assists the client to work toward replacing feelings of helplessness or hopelessness with feelings of greater competence and mastery and of not knowing what to do with knowing better how to do. He helps the client to realize that he can achieve this goal through finding more effective ways (patterns) of functioning in given life roles or through lessening of limiting factors in his environment. The client and practitioner consider both avenues to goal achievement.

What the ego most fears is helplessness in the face of inner or outer danger—that is, of forces from within or from without that it cannot handle. Anxiety is the signal to the ego of ego insufficiency or of possible insufficiency in relation to demands made upon the ego to handle self or environment. The sources of stress experienced by the client as he comes for help derive from various combinations of inner and outer factors to which he reacts with varying degrees of anxiety. The client's anxiety denotes a lack of control over his own affairs; otherwise the anxiety signal would have effectively motivated the ego to find a new solution or to develop and use a new coping pattern. After the anxiety served its motivational purpose, feelings of relief and of comfort would have replaced the discomfort.

Masterable frustration and the accompanying anxiety arise all through life in response to usual stress that constitutes a push toward new learning and the development of new ways to cope. The learning tasks of each developmental period from birth to death give rise to usual stress as do short-term illness, various changes in life situations, or the assumption of a new role or the abandonment of an old one. Threats of death to self or loved one, long-term illness, loss of significant body parts, or such traumatic external events as fire, flood, war, or depression provide examples of unusual stress as do sustained, recurrent, and cumulative stress. Often unusual stress may be the last straw that makes the load unmanageable. However, the difficulty in distinguishing the usual from the unusual stress lies in the fact that each person's perception of what constitutes stress is unique and depends on the nature of the event, on the individual's potential for dealing with it, and on the life situation. The path, therefore, that practitioner and client take to achieve improved mastery will be based on assessment of changes that are needed and possible in the client's coping patterns. It will also be based on assessment of changes that are needed and possible in order to effect an environment in which the client can function better.

The practitioner must utilize his understanding of the client's capacity to analyze the ways in which the environment limits the use or the development of capacity, or he will fail to supply sufficient support to help the client to manage the burdens he faces. The client's functioning is limited when the functioning of role partners is not congruent with that of the client, when the environment fails to provide opportunities for the exercise or development of abilities, and when the burdens imposed exceed the client's ability to deal with them. The practitioner relates his analysis of the client's ego functioning to his analysis of psychological and social factors that need to be changed in order to make the environment less limiting and more supporting.

The practitioner has open to him four avenues of situational change.[1] He can increase support for the client from those with whom he carries reciprocal roles in the family and in other social systems. As the client functions more responsively with those around him, his anxiety tends to diminish. The practitioner can also provide supportive instrumental means and measures that offer a better opportunity for carrying role responsibilities, thus diminishing the nagging anxieties of inadequate housing, income, or social services. The practitioner can support and supplement the client's functioning through services that, in effect, shoulder some of the client's role responsibilities. However, when the client's burdens are too great and the possibilities of increasing capacity and support in the time available are nonexistent, the practitioner may need to use such substitutes for the client as placement or commitment of family members.

Increasing Support from Reciprocal Role Partners

The practitioner considers that the persons with whom the client interacts in carrying reciprocal life roles constitute the most significant part of his psychological environment. He always works to lessen the limiting effect of each role partner's functioning on others. In the case of marital partners or parents, the marital or parent-child problem is always a shared one. The practitioner clearly conveys to the client the idea that the behavior of each person affects that of the other or others and that each has had a share in the development of the problem. Each must, therefore, share in dealing with it. Sometimes one partner admits that he has contributed to the difficulty but that he has taken or can take the necessary steps toward change. He does not need help and, in support of this assertion, he marshals many indications of his ability to manage independently. He may, on the other hand, indicate that his partner is very much in need of assistance. Realizing that the idea of taking help threatens this individual's sense of adequacy, the practitioner may be more successful if he aligns himself with the client's goals. He enlists the client's help in making the marriage work better or in helping his wife. The practitioner may point out that any changes made by the wife in her handling of marital affairs will affect the partner and that, therefore, the partner may prefer to have a share in deciding about these changes. In other instances, one partner may deny that he is contributing in any way to the problem. The practitioner will probably find that a joint interview offers the most effective way to help this partner realize his share in the difficulty. In a joint interview, the practitioner confronts each partner with the perception of the other partner about how the marriage is going and with the ideas of the other partner as to what the marriage should be like. Frequently, one of the partners has failed to express to the other his perception of what is wrong with the marriage and his ideas of what he hopes from the relationship.

The practitioner tries to enable each partner, marital or parental, to realize that feelings of helplessness and of inability to manage stem from the inability to develop patterns of interaction that are both receptive and responsive. He attempts to help both partners become aware of patterns that work and those that do not. He takes with them the goal of achieving mutual regulation in the relationship—that is, with each partner accepting influence from the other and exerting influence. The practitioner points out that when each partner can rely on the other to work cooperatively in developing harmonious patterns of relating the sense of helplessness will diminish, since each will feel able to handle his share in the relationship and will have confidence in the partner's ability to do so. The practitioner and clients strive for such immediate goals as achieving shared understanding about the problem, about the difficulties, and about the possibilities of change. The practitioner helps the partners to achieve patterns of receptivity and of responsiveness to each other's ideas. The patterns of perception used by each partner should also come under consideration. He attempts to increase each partner's sensitivity to the other partner's feelings and attitudes because partners are frequently not perceptive about each other or, if they are perceptive, they do not respond appropriately. He attempts to help them to pick up cues from each other and to deal with them in ways that can lead to working out a harmonious way of looking at things. The needs of each partner should not conflict but should be complementary. Each should develop patterns of mutual sharing, of giving, and of receiving. The practitioner reviews with the clients their patterns of interacting with each other, encouraging them to try out those that are mutually more satisfying and less frustrating. He may help one partner to find need satisfactions outside the marriage if the other partner cannot provide them. He assists the partners in consciously developing trust and in achieving both closeness and separateness in the relationship in degrees comfortable for both.

Not only do the practitioner and clients aim toward increased congruence in the handling of family roles—a congruence that contributes to the better functioning of each person in the role network—but practitioner and client also look at interaction in regard to other life role situations. The role interaction of the parents and child with the teacher, of the patient and family members with physicians and other team members, and of the client with agency practitioners may be limiting to the client.

In the case of interaction between doctor and patient, the practitioner always asks the patient what he understands about his medical condition and the recommendations for treatment. He helps the doctor to give the patient the information he requires to carry his role. If, for example, the patient signs consent for an arthrodesis operation without understanding that the operation will entail his never being able to bend the joint again, this lack of understanding may seriously affect his ability to carry his role as a patient. He may become hostile, claim that he would rather have died than have had the operation had he realized its outcome, and consider himself completely disabled because of his perception of the operation as injury and mutilation at the hands of the doctor. The practitioner always uses his own assessment of the patient to convey to the doctor or to help the patient to convey a request for specific kinds of information. If, for example, the doctor does not want to tell the patient his diagnosis of carcinoma and his possible fatal prognosis, the practitioner, realizing the patient must make plans for his dependent children, lets the physician know that family responsibilities require that the patient be fully aware of his condition. Not only must the understanding of patient and doctor be similar, but their relevant perceptions also must be harmonious. The practitioner conveys to the doctor his assessment of the patient in terms that clearly individualize the patient and help the physician to perceive him in a frame of reference relevant to their mutual interaction.

Frequently, practitioners express their diagnostic thinking in terms that could apply to almost anyone. As one practitioner phrased it, "This patient has many strengths; his family is supporting and he depends heavily on the hospital to carry him through his illness." This brief psychosocial description should be rephrased in terms that more clearly identify the cognitive, perceptual, relational, and activity patterning used by the patient to handle his diagnosis:

> In the past six years Mr. X has found a way of viewing his diagnosis of leukemia that has enabled him to function well in his masculine roles. He has used the periods of remission to find work and to carry his responsibility as a breadwinner and as a father. When he loses these jobs because of a recurrence of the illness, he sustains himself emotionally and works through his depression with the hope and belief that the slump is temporary and that he will again be able to manage independently. His wife and children and father all perceive this patient as an exceptionally strong, masculine, and independent individual and sustain him by their feelings of confidence in and admiration for his ability to handle his illness. The patient uses the hospital to support him in his strivings to handle his illness.

The possibility of the lack of harmony between patient and doctor exists in relation to the management of needs and feelings. If the doctor needs to have a passive dependent patient or a successful medical outcome regardless of the psychosocial outcome, his needs may conflict with those of the patient. The practitioners in well-baby and pediatrics clinics should help physicians to accept the fact that mothers need guidance, not only in preparing formulas and giving physical care, but also in meeting the psychosocial needs of their children. In maternity departments, the practitioner should help the doctor to accept the need of parents to prepare for carrying their parental roles. Moreover, the practitioner can help the physician to identify populations at risk. Immature parents, socially and emotionally deprived parents, and emotionally conflicted parents have needs that will interfere with their being able to carry their parental roles unless the clinic recognizes these needs and gives appropriate preventive services. Physicians need to be convinced that these parents need not only medical care but skilled counseling. The physicians must see that the clinic gives what these mothers require. In regard to relationships, the practitioner attempts always to strengthen mutual confidence between doctor and patient and to help the doctor to provide the support and encouragement that enables the patient to believe in the doctor's concern for him as an individual. In this way, the practitioner helps to bridge the social and emotional distance between the two. The practitioner can frequently smooth out misunderstandings and help to develop better communication. He also strives to improve the patient's coping patterns vis-à-vis the physician. He helps him to ask for information, to perceive the doctor as a helping person, to perceive his illness realistically, to view medical care in constructive ways, to use this care to achieve a more healthy functioning, and to act effectively as a patient. Effective action includes making the necessary decisions regarding medical care and carrying through on decisions.

In the foregoing ways, the practitioner assesses and deals with interaction between the parents, the child, and the teacher and between the client and practitioners in other social agencies. When each person in the reciprocal role, either in the family or outside the family, can develop patterns that are receptive to ideas, perceptions, feelings, and relationship qualities in the other person and that are responsive to input from the other person, each role partner has a way of managing their interaction through mutual regulation and through give and take. In this event, the role functioning becomes mutually more supportive and more satisfying. The patient's capacity to carry his role makes it possible for the physician to operate more effectively in his role; in turn, the physician's capacity to carry his role helps the patient to operate more effectively in his role. The goal in helping role partners is to assist them in achieving patterning that is harmonious rather than patterning that conflicts or fails to achieve mutual satisfaction and support. The practitioner tries to lessen the distance between persons in the bureaucratic structure and the client. He helps them individualize the client rather than assign him the anonymity of a "case."

Increasing Social Supports

The practitioner always evaluates whether it would be possible for the client to carry his role adequately without changed social provisions, and he attempts to furnish increased environmental support as needed. The practitioner uses his understanding of complex systems to act as advocate for the client in order to change restrictive policies or restrictive administration of policies and to improve service delivery and resources to meet needs. Housing is probably the most basic requirement for adequate living. Ludwig L. Geismar and Jane Krisberg found that they almost always had to begin by improving the housing before the clients could move toward other changes.[2] The clients and the practitioner must first decide whether it is possible to make adequate the plumbing, heating, and general sanitary conditions of the present housing. Does the client know the proper city agency to call in case the landlord is violating city codes? If a move is indicated, will the client seek public or private housing? Improvement in capacity and increasing social supports for capacity go hand in hand. The practitioner should inquire about previous patterns. How have the clients located a house in the past? Do they know how to secure real estate listings or how to apply for public housing? Will both spouses see the new house before deciding to rent, and how would they list their requirements? The practitioner should help the clients to plan their move and support them in carrying it through because an impulsive move can leave them no better off than before. He assists clients in securing adequate clothing and household equipment, using secondhand resources where available. Because no parent can care adequately for children on a below-minimum budget, he aids the clients in using available resources for job counseling, selective placement, and job training. He may need to spend considerable time in developing capacity before the client can utilize these opportunities. For example, a mother separated from her husband was unready to enroll in the Work Incentive Program until she developed, with the practitioner's help, new patterns for managing her relationship with her husband who had been harassing her and new ways of handling the children who were reacting to the loss of their father. Relocation may be the only answer when no local job opportunities can be found. The practitioner uses group experiences and, when needed, develops client groups to furnish group support and social experiences. In every possible way, the practitioner attempts to connect the client with new opportunities that will increase his skills and capacities, such as cooking and sewing classes and groups that provide social experiences. In some cases, the new opportunity that the individual requires is separation from family. When the conjugal family and the family of origin have a merged structure, the young people may become able to function as parents only when they move to a home of their own. Adolescents may need to find separate living quarters to free them from embroilment in family difficulties. The schizophrenic client may do better in a boarding home when the family has contributed to his pathology and will continue to aggravate it.

A client who has lived under chronically inadequate conditions for long periods of time may become chronically anxious and hopeless. He may show his anxiety by aggressive demands, hostility, or apathy. Only when he is relieved of sustained pressure does the client's anxiety diminish sufficiently for him to begin to invest energy in acquiring changed ways of functioning.

Role Supplementation to Improve Functioning

Clients differ in their ability to carry specific kinds of burdens. Demands made by situational difficulties almost always require particular kinds of capacities and often exact the kind of response that the client is least fitted to make because of inner vulnerability to the given stress. The lack of appropriate adaptive patterns arouses a greater than usual sense of anxiety and helplessness. The practitioner always assesses the possibilities of increasing capacity and role support in the time available for dealing with the problem. For example, children move so quickly from one developmental period to the next that it may be impossible to increase the parent's capacity before the children have sustained serious and irreparable damage. When the practitioner judges that the discrepancies between burdens and capacities and role support are alterable in a feasible length of time or when capacity is adequate if supplemented, he may use the technique of role supplementation. He uses a child development center or day care facility to relieve an overburdened mother, a volunteer tutor to help with a learning difficulty, a home aide or visiting nurse to assist in the care of an aged or ill family member, or a Big Brother or Sister to furnish a role model. Some localities have Friendly Visitors and Meals on Wheels for the shut-ins. At the same time the practitioner may, when it is indicated, attempt to improve parenting or homemaking skills or to strengthen reciprocal role functioning.

ROLE SUBSTITUTES

When the practitioner's assessment shows that the nature of the client's burdens or lack of support overtax his capacity and that changes in the burdens, capacity, and support cannot be achieved in the time available, he may use the technique of providing a role substitute for the client. He may recommend placement of the children, commitment of the retarded child, or placement of an aged, ill, or emotionally disturbed family member. In such cases, he tries to develop the client's ability to see his burdens realistically and to participate in making choices that consider the well-being of all concerned. Frequently, such a decision can relieve long-standing anxiety and hopeless frustration caused by the inability to manage adequately. In the following case, the problem of carrying the mothering role with six children under eleven years of age without any role support from the father imposed impossible burdens on the socially deprived, mentally retarded woman.

> The court had awarded custody of the children to the agency following a child neglect charge. The children attended school irregularly, ran wild in the neighborhood, were unkempt and uncontrolled. The divorced father called on the family occasionally to make drunken disturbances and to fight with the mother. The eldest girl carried many of the parenting responsibilities, but housing was inadequate for decent family living. Examination showed the mother to be mentally retarded and physically run down, but she showed warmth to the children. She had never learned how to mother because she had been brought up in an institution from which she escaped to make a runaway marriage. Because the mother could not grasp or deal with the needs of six children already showing damage, the practitioner did not consider it feasible to try to help her shoulder this burden. He, therefore, attempted to enable her to perceive realistically her own limitations, such as poor health and nervous exhaustion, the needs of six growing children, the difficulties of managing without the husband, and the requirement for the children to attend school and be disciplined. The mother consented to placement of the four oldest children, and she was assisted in moving into more adequate housing and in getting medical attention. As a result of court action, the father began to contribute financially and, through the practitioner's help, to take the mother regularly to visit the children in their foster homes and to take interest in them. The use of role substitutes to function in lieu of parents with the oldest children, the use of supporting social provisions, and the increased role support from the father lessened the mother's anxiety so that she could use the practitioner's teaching about child care and management of the youngest children.

Deciding with the Client Where to Begin

At the time the practitioner makes initial contact, the client usually indicates where he places the need for change—in self, in the environment, or in both. When the client sees the limiting factors as lying outside himself, he usually asks help for his spouse or child or requests provision of resources, of opportunities, or of ways to lessen his burdens. The practitioner usually begins where the client seems ready to take help, but he may later go on to deal with other areas as the client becomes ready to do so. For example, following her husband's second desertion, a client applied for public assistance for herself and her four small children. Her first requests were for financial support, household equipment, clothing, and school lunches. She was, at first, self-involved, feeling overwhelmed, overburdened, and angry at being abandoned. With relief from anxiety caused by outer pressures, the mother asked for and was given help in understanding the needs of each child. She became more receptive to their communications and could perceive matters of discipline realistically, whereas previously she had seen any misbehavior as defiance. Above all, she recognized the value of trusting her children and found that her trust in her own ability to carry her role had been restored.

Sometimes a father who has recently lost his wife can see only the situational stress and asks for homemaker services for the family. Another father may believe that he has sufficient family resources to care for house and children but wants help in perceiving correctly and responding appropriately to the different reactions of each child to the loss of the mother. He may also want to talk about ways of handling his own grief and anger. Only later does this father see the need for a homemaker and for assistance in planning school, work, and housing changes. Similarly, the first client later comes to realize his need for help in the way he deals with his loss.

The client makes clear that he places the need for change within self when, for example, his story of difficulties with a teenage son reveals that his own way of handling the boy causes him concern. Sometimes, the very force with which the client places responsibility on his role partner betrays the fact that he questions the way he has been handling the relationship. When the client comes in a crisis situation, the practitioner is always aware of the possibility that the crisis has reactivated an old problem and that the client may now be ready to examine his previously ineffective adaptive patterns. A young man referred for help in arranging admission to a tuberculosis hospital provides a relevant illustration.

> The client told the practitioner that his only concern was the fact that he would not graduate from college in June and so would not be able to support his mother as he had planned. Knowing that the prospect of long hospitalization can stir up dependency and authority conflicts, the practitioner inquired at the next interview about the parents. They were both living, but the client said he hated his father for continually reproaching the mother with the fact that the patient's oldest sister was illegitimate. She was being brought up in the family, but the mother always worked in the mills to help financially. The client abreacted his anger against the father. At the next interview, he said that he had thought things over and could see that his father was not so bad; he had tried to give all the children an education. Perhaps the parents got along reasonably well. He could recognize that things might seem worse to a youngster than to an adult. By the third interview, the client introduced the idea that his brothers and sisters could help support the parents if necessary. He said he had to decide what he owed himself and what he owed his parents. He now realized it was not necessary for him to give up his hopes for marriage and a home of his own. The practitioner supported his ability to make a realistic choice and his goal of getting well and resuming his career.

When the client is first seen, he may castigate himself as an unfit parent, a failure at his job, or inadequate in some way. The client is really talking about a feeling of ego inadequacy to deal with his problem. He may become less anxious when the practitioner clarifies the fact that the client is feeling helpless but that when he can discover more effective ways of coping or when the situational stress is more manageable, he will feel less anxious. When the client asks help both with his patterns of management and with environmental pressures, the practitioner may suggest that they attempt together to sort out what in self and what outside self cause him concern. In this way, the practitioner develops a cognitive map of the way they will proceed together. In other cases, the practitioner may recognize that the client's feeling of helplessness comes partly from within or from without, whichever the client can recognize, but he suggests that other factors, inner or situational, probably contribute to his anxiety. He tries to make the client conscious of the fact that, when he has achieved some situational changes, he will be able to manage better and with less anxiety. Similarly, as the client achieves adaptive changes in self or environment, the practitioner helps him to become aware of his increased sense of mastery and competence. The client is now on top of his troubles. He knows where he is going, or how to deal with his problem. The practitioner tries at each step to help the client see that doing something about his difficulty lessens anxiety and that being aware of each new inner or outer change brings him nearer to the more final goal.

In helping the client move toward the goal of improved functioning, the practitioner often needs to be aware of the opposing tendencies in the personality toward progression and regression. In one mental hygiene clinic, a client who had been given help with his immediate difficulty refused additional treatment. He talked about plans for finding work, although he had never been able to hold a steady job. The therapist pointed out that he had been hearing two opposing messages from the client. One was the story of all his difficulties, and one was the assertion he could always get a job and make out. The practitioner thought the client was talking about two pulls—the pull toward illness and getting into trouble and the pull toward health. If the client seriously wanted to consider finding a better way to manage, he would have to decide on the first steps he could take and what he would need to do differently. The practitioner allied himself with the small impetus to health, offering a return appointment so that the client could discuss how his plan had worked out.

The method of ego analysis proposed in this book offers a beginning step away from what Herman Piven refers to as overgeneralized practice theory.[3] It provides a method for analyzing ego functioning in ways that better individualize each client because the practitioner bases his assessment of capacity on the client's unique patterning of each function. Practitioner and client can examine discrete aspects of his behavior and ask whether they work well. If not, the client can attempt to discover and try out some small change in the way he operates. This approach partializes the task for client and practitioner and sets practical, achievable goals. Treatment is thus logically related to diagnostic assessment of what needs to be changed. Similarly, the changes indicated in the client's situation to make it less limiting and more supporting can be related logically to an assessment of capacity and limitations in capacity. The practitioner helps the client to assume as his goal the lessening of helplessness and the achieving of increased ability to manage self and situation with greater satisfaction and less pain, that is, the goal of increased conscious control.

Notes

1. Frances Upham, "The Changing Roles of Welfare Employee and Client," *Public Welfare*, 27:318–27 (October 1969).

2. Ludwig L. Geismar and Jane Krisberg, "The Family Life Improvement Project: An Experiment in Preventive Intervention: Part II," *Social Casework*, 47:663–67 (December 1966).

3. Herman Piven, "The Fragmentation of Social Work," *Social Casework*, 50: 88–94 (February 1969).

Appendix

Assessment of motivation of resistance to taking help at the given time	***Treatment measures for forestalling or lessening resistance to taking help at the given time***
Subcategory A	*Subcategory A*
Client does not know what to expect: cognitive or perceptual ambiguities	Clarify what client wants and expects in taking help
Does not know what he wants from the agency Does not know about the agency or services available Does not understand application, intake, and/or helping process Has biases or misperceptions about agency or practitioner	Explain agency services available, intake and application process, terms of service, client-practitioner roles Demonstrate the helping process Clarify problem focus and goal(s) of help Develop communication between practitioner-client Use confrontation
Subcategory B	*Subcategory B*
Client's conscious positive expectations differ from practitioner's or not understood by practitioner	Support client's conscious motivation and reconcile discordant expectations (worker-client)
Expects a definite kind of help	Relate supportingly to client's request

Expects help to be offered in a particular way Has rigid or unrealistic expectations of help	Meet usual client expectations Attempt to enlarge and develop client's view of possibilities Connect client expectations with agency services Use confrontation
Subcategory C	*Subcategory C*
Client has conscious negative expectations: distrusts or fears help	Supply temporary external motivation for taking help
Doubts helping can result in positive changes Distrusts social agencies on bases of previous experiences Distrusts practitioner's ability to help and/or distrusts practitioner's motivations for helping	Use practitioner's own desire to help and hope Use the authority of skill and social authority Use more than usual initiative and persistence in active giving of help Use confrontation
Subcategory D	*Subcategory D*
Client's unconscious positive and negative expectations of help	Utilize positive unconscious expectations and prevent blocking from unconscious negative expectations
Transference Manifestations in the relationship Reactivated desires, concerns, needs, and anticipations Unconscious wishes or fears derived from client's pathology Casts practitioner in the negative parental or authority role Unconsciously desires parental protection and care	Attempt to meet some of client's unconscious emotional needs Develop the relationship before asking client to work on his problems Avoid being cast in the negative transference role Discuss the negative transference Use confrontation

Assessment of motivation of resistance to using help at the given time	*Treatment measures for forestalling or lessening resistance to using help at the given time*
Subcategory A	*Subcategory A*
Discomfort over the practitioner's expectations that the client perceive realistically self-problem-situation	Support the client's capacity to perceive and share understanding and perception
Client uses selective perception Client unable to perceive problem and/or its effect Client cannot change perceptual patterns to meet new situation	Provide therapeutic environment in which client is free to talk Help client communicate Use empathy and acceptance to support ability to perceive Share understanding and/or perceptions Partialize Use confrontation Change goals if necessary
Subcategory B	*Subcategory B*
Discomfort over practitioner's expectations regarding client's handling of needs and feelings	Support the client's ability to handle needs and feelings; accept feelings and share feelings
Client indicates that certain needs are threatening Client has opposing needs he cannot reconcile Client unable to face feelings related to needs Client finds feelings or certain kinds of feelings threatening Client unable to face how he is handling needs and/or feelings	Encourage appropriate expression of feelings Universalize and externalize Use empathy and acceptance Help client do reality-testing re feelings self-others and/or past-present Use confrontation Change goals if necessary

Subcategory C

Discomfort over practitioner's expectations that the client decide or act relative to his problem

Client distrusts his ability to decide and procrastinates or avoids deciding

Client fails to carry through on plans he has decided upon

Client threatened by responsibility involved in acting or deciding

Client appears immobilized by anxiety over problem-situation

Subcategory C

Support client's ability to decide and act; share the burden and give prompt help

Support the client's right to decide

Help him learn how to decide and/or to secure help in deciding

Postpone decisions when indicated

Make resources and services available to help client decide and act

Use confrontation

Change goals if necessary

Subcategory D

Discomfort over practitioner's negative expectations of client's ability to change or over client's perception that these expectations are negative

Client shows he believes practitioner has poor opinion of his ability or little hope of change

Client distrusts practitioner's willingness and/or ability to help

Client shows he believes practitioner considers him unworthy of help

Subcategory D

Clarify practitioner's expectations and voice realistic hope and encouragement

Help client to correct misperceptions

Reach out warmly and empathically

Express realistic hope

Encourage client realistically

Demonstrate confidence in client's ability to change

Deal with own unconscious negative expectations

Use confrontation

Ego-analysis model: *What needs to be changed and what can be changed to improve problem-solving*

PROBLEM

Clustering of problems	*Multiple causes*	*Multiple effects*	*Extent*	*Duration*	*Significance*	*Selection of beginning problem*	*Selection of other problems*
1, 2, 3, 4, etc.						a. Most pressing b. External c. Can be dealt with	

PERSON

Maladaptive limiting patterns	⟵	Thinking, understanding, knowing	⟶	Effective, adaptive patterns
	⟵	Perception of problem and what is standing in way of problem-solving; of self and of others	⟶	
	⟵	Handling needs and feelings	⟶	
	⟵	Handling relationships	⟶	
	⟵	Acting: patterns of role behavior	⟶	
	⟵	Integration of new learning	⟶	

SITUATION

	⟵	Family, friends	Community	⟶	
Limiting factors					Supporting factors
	⟵	Living conditions, finances, work	Agency	⟶	

Plan: To use capacities and environmental support and lessen limiting factors in both.

Assessment of capacity and limitations in capacity in relation to problem focus

Integrative function: integrating new patterns	**Patterning of perception: assigning culturally learned meaning to all sensory data, inner and outer**	**Cognition: processing and storing of perceptual data**	**Management of needs and feelings: learned needs and patterns for handling needs and feelings**	**Management of relationships: patterns of giving and receiving and of mutual regulation**	**Executive function or executant capacity**
Active patterning which shows Ability to achieve new learning in response to changing reality Ability to use new opportunities Ability to reopen old issues and to relearn Ability for healing of trauma and reconcilia-	Active patterning of outer perception Invests energy and interest in orienting self to external realities, to other persons Shows ability to learn new perceptual patterns for viewing self-situation Can passively	Active patterning of thought Uses thinking in problem-solving Uses concepts and conceptual thinking to deal with reality Anticipates and uses judgment before acting Vocabulary adequate Uses communica-	Active patterning of needs and handling needs Learned ego and social needs Invests energy in securing appropriate need satisfaction Invests pleasure in ego functioning and competence Has patterns for postponing and for secur-	Active patterning of managing relationship *Patterns for managing closeness* Has learned to trust Can invest in a relationship Can achieve intimacy *Patterns for managing distance* Can allow sepa-	Active patterning Ability to decide Ability to follow through on decisions Ability to be active in carrying roles actively and competently Ability to learn new patterns to meet changing situations Limitations in capacity

tion of conflict Limitations in capacity Limitations in ability to achieve new learning or relearning	take in other's perceptions, as appropriate Active patterning of inner perception Can look at own ideas, motivations, feelings, and actions Active patterning of reality-testing Distinguishes wishes from reality; inner from outer data Limitations in capacity Maladaptive patterns or failure to learn patterns	tion in problem-solving Passive patterning Seeks and uses information needed in problem-solving Open to ideas and understanding from others re self-problem Limitations in capacity Maladaptive patterns or has never learned foregoing patterns May use primary process thinking	ing substitute gratifications Can find new sources of gratification Has patterns for appropriate handling of feelings Defenses are flexible and realistic Limitations in capacity Has never learned ego or social needs Cannot operate on reality principle Uses maladaptive patterns for handling needs and feelings Uses crippling defenses	rateness between self-other *Patterns of passive receptivity to feelings and needs of others* Can identify with others *Patterns of responsiveness* Can give as well as receive Limitations in capacity Cannot trust Fears and/or provokes rejection Cannot invest in a relationship Holds on to partner Cannot receive Cannot respond appropriately	Mainly passive patterns of role functioning Inability to decide and to act

Treatment measures for strengthening capacity and lessening limitations in capacity

Integrative function	Functions of perception	Cognitive functions	Management of needs and feelings	Management of object relationships	Executive function
Support client's capacity to achieve new learning and/or relearning Provide opportunities and motivation for learning	Outer perception Support client's adaptive patterns and ability to perceive Help client learn new perceptual patterns for seeing self-others situation Help role partners achieve congruent patterns and/or reconcile culturally conflicting ones Help client give up distrusting,	Rational thinking Support and encourage patterns for using this in problem-solving Labeling and vocabulary Support and teach Conceptual thinking Support and strengthen reality concepts and conceptual thinking and/or teach concepts	Help client invest energy in ego and social needs and learn to achieve satisfaction from competent functioning Help client select new needs when old ones become unattainable Help client find more appropriate and effective patterns for securing need satisfaction	Support adaptive patterns which promote mutual regulation and complementarity Help client achieve closeness by strengthening trust and ability to invest in a relationship Help client see self-partner as individual Help client become passively	Support client's deciding and acting appropriately Help client use passive mode when necessary Teach patterns of deciding Teach patterns of carrying through on decisions Teach active role patterns Support adaptive patterns and/or help client to use them

negative, or maladaptive patterns Help client correct selective perceptual patterns or ones distorted by pathology Inner perception Support or teach patterns of inner perception Reality-testing Help client to do reality-testing Passive patterns Help client be receptive to others' perceptions	of choice, initiative, etc. Anticipation Support and/or teach patterns of anticipating and judging Communication Support and develop patterns of communicating Help client recognize maladaptive patterns and try new ones	Help client recognize inappropriate needs and/or patterns for gratifying the needs Help client learn to operate on the reality principle Support appropriate patterns for handling feelings Help client achieve more constructive patterns for handling feelings Strengthen helpful defenses Redirect crippling defenses	receptive to feelings, needs of others and to identify Help client respond appropriately Help client become aware of self-defeating patterns Help clients try out patterns to achieve mutual regulation and satisfactions

Index

DATE DUE

NOV. 1 6 1984			
NOV 08 '95			